SOUTHERN COASTAL
HOME LANDSCAPING

SOUTHERN COASTAL
HOME LANDSCAPING

Stephen and Kristin Pategas

CREATIVE HOMEOWNER®, Upper Saddle River, New Jersey

SOUTHERN COASTAL HOME LANDSCAPING

MANAGING EDITOR	Fran Donegan
GRAPHIC DESIGNER	Kathryn Wityk
EDITORIAL ASSISTANT	Sara Markowitz
DIGITAL IMAGING SPECIALIST	Mary Dolan
INDEXER	Erica Caridio, The Last Word
COVER DESIGN	Kathryn Wityk
ILLUSTRATORS	Jeff Grunewald, Steve Buchanan (Portfolio of Designs); Michelle Angle Farrar, Lee Hov, Robert LaPointe, Rick Daskam, Teresa Nicole Green (Guide to Installation)

CREATIVE HOMEOWNER

VICE PRESIDENT AND PUBLISHER	Timothy O. Bakke
MANAGING EDITOR	Fran J. Donegan
ART DIRECTOR	David Geer
PRODUCTION COORDINATOR	Sara M. Markowitz

Manufactured in the United States of America

Current Printing (last digit)
10 9 8 7 6 5 4 3 2 1

Southern Coastal Home Landscaping
Library of Congress Control Number: 2010924855
ISBN-10: 1-58011-510-1
ISBN-13: 978-1-58011-510-0

CREATIVE HOMEOWNER®
A Division of Federal Marketing Corp.
24 Park Way
Upper Saddle River, NJ 07458
www.creativehomeowner.com

About the Authors

Stephen and **Kristin Pategas** are co-owners of Hortus Oasis, a boutique landscape design firm in Winter Park, Florida. This award-winning team places an emphasis on sustainable gardening.

Stephen is a registered landscape architect and a member of the American Society of Landscape Architects and the Garden Writers Association. His areas of expertise include residential and specialty garden design, plant materials, garden ornamentation, and a variety of garden styles.

Kristin is a Florida Certified Landscape Designer and a member of the Association of Professional Landscape Designers and the Garden Writers Association. Kristin's specialties include wildlife, herb, and vegetable gardens; topiaries; container gardening; and garden living.

Kristin and Stephen garden in Zone 9b, and they test new plants at Hortus Oasis, their 1925 Mediterranean revival home in Winter Park. Visit: *HortusOasis.com*

Landscape Design Consultants

John Ahrens is principal at King's Creek Landscape Management in Austin. His firm has worked throughout the Texas Hill Country, Colorado, and in the Austin and San Antonio areas. The firm specializes in indigenous stone work and water features, as well as in landscapes that include mostly native and "Texas tough" naturalized plantings. Barry Landry, RLA, and Nena Scott assist John with designs.

Michael Buccino has been designing desert landscapes since 1966. A landscape architect and graduate of Cal Poly, Pomona, he and the members of his small Palm Desert firm, Michael Buccino Associates, undertake residential, commercial, and public projects.

Rosa Finsley founded King's Creek Gardens, a Cedar Hill nursery and landscape design firm, in 1970. She has designed residential, public, and commercial gardens throughout Texas, including the Historic River Link for the Riverwalk in San Antonio. She is known for her naturalistic designs. Cheryl Bryant occasionally assists Rosa.

Glenn Morris has designed southern landscapes for many years. Trained as a landscape architect at North Carolina State University, he specializes in homeowner-directed problem solving and has received an award for design excellence from the American Society of Landscape Architects. Mr. Morris has also written extensively about gardening and design.

Dan Sears is principal in the Sears Design Group of Raleigh, N.C., a firm specializing in residential land planning and landscape design. In 25 years as a landscape architect, he has won numerous regional and national design awards and has had many projects published in magazines and journals. Mr. Sears has been a member of the North Carolina Board of Landscape Architects.

Carolyn Singer owns Foothill Cottage Gardens, a nursery she developed from her own gardens in the Sierra foothills near Grass Valley. Since 1980, she has sold perennials and taught gardening classes at the nursery, as well as designed landscapes for foothill and valley residents. She lectures widely and has written about gardening for national and regional publications.

Jimmy and **Becky Stewart** are professional gardeners in Atlanta, Ga., where they design and install residential gardens. As designers, they strive to create year-round interest in their gardens. As avid plant enthusiasts, they are constantly experimenting with new and different plants to see which do best in the Atlanta area. Their designs have been featured in many publications.

Jenny Webber is a self-employed landscape architect in Oakland, CA. Also trained in horticulture and fine arts, she specializes in ecologically balanced and creative landscapes. She has won several awards for her designs and has written about gardening and design for national publications.

Contents

Safety First

Though all concepts and methods in this book have been reviewed for safety, it is not possible to overstate the importance of using the safest working methods possible. What follows are reminders—do's and don'ts for yard work and landscaping. They are not substitutes for your own common sense.

■ *Always* use caution, care, and good judgment when following the procedures described in this book.

■ *Always* determine locations of underground utility lines before you dig, and then avoid them by a safe distance. Buried lines may be for gas, electricity, communications, or water. Start research by contacting your local building officials. Also contact local utility companies; they will often send a representative free of charge to help you map their lines. In addition, there are private utility locator firms that may be listed in your Yellow Pages. Note: previous owners may have installed underground drainage, sprinkler, and lighting lines without mapping them.

■ *Always* read and heed the manufacturer's instructions for using a tool, especially the warnings.

■ *Always* ensure that the electrical setup is safe; be sure that no circuit is overloaded and that all power tools and electrical outlets are properly grounded and protected by a ground-fault circuit interrupter (GFCI). Do not use power tools in wet locations.

■ *Always* wear eye protection when using chemicals, sawing wood, pruning trees and shrubs, using power tools, and striking metal onto metal or concrete.

■ *Always* read labels on chemicals, solvents, and other products; provide ventilation; heed warnings.

■ *Always* wear heavy rubber gloves rated for chemicals, not mere household rubber gloves, when handling toxins.

■ *Always* wear appropriate gloves in situations in which your hands could be injured by rough surfaces, sharp edges, thorns, or poisonous plants.

■ *Always* wear a disposable face mask or a special filtering respirator when creating sawdust or working with toxic gardening substances.

■ *Always* keep your hands and other body parts away from the business ends of blades, cutters, and bits.

■ *Always* obtain approval from local building officials before undertaking construction of permanent structures.

■ *Never* work with power tools when you are tired or under the influence of alcohol or drugs.

■ *Never* carry sharp or pointed tools, such as knives or saws, in your pockets. If you carry such tools, use special-purpose tool scabbards.

Horticultural nomenclature

Eighteenth-century Swedish botanist Carolus Linnaeus was the first to classify plants using the two-name, or "binomial," system, which we still employ today. Linnaeus chose Latin as his language of preference because, at that time, most educated people could both speak and write Latin. In the right circles, it was a universal, international language; the Latin names of plants still provide the best way for two people to be sure they're talking about exactly the same plant.

The two scientific names identifying a plant are based on the *genus* and *species*. A genus is a group of plants marked by common characteristics. For example, plants from the yarrow genus are all named *Achillea* after the Greek hero Achilles who, according to legend, used yarrow to heal his soldiers' wounds during the Trojan war. All oaks are classified under *Quercus*, and maples as *Acer*, indicating their general commonalities.

The species is a subdivision of the genus, identified separately from the genus because of more specific qualities. If English were used for the world of animals, dog would be the genus and dalmation the species. *Achillea millefolium* is a species of yarrow with leaves divided into a thousand tiny parts. (*Mille* refers to thousands, and folium refers to leaves or foliage.) Another species, woolly yarrow, in Latin is *Achillea tomentosa*; *tomentosa* refers to its hairy leaves.

In a plant's scientific name, the word identifying the genus always comes first and is capitalized as a proper noun. The species name is a descriptive word used as an adjective to modify and further describe the noun; it is always lower case.

Occasionally there is a third Latin name denoting a variety or subdivision of a species that arises in nature spontaneously. For example, the beach or shore pine is *Pinus contorta*. The lodgepole pine, a variety of that species, is *Pinus contorta* var. *latifolia*. *Pinus* indicates both are from the pine family, *contorta* describes the twisted form in which the trees grow, and—in the case of the lodgepole pine—the variety name *latifolia* explains that the leaves (needles) are broader than those of beach pine.

Apple blossom yarrow is referred to as Achillea millefolium. *These long-blooming perennials produce showy, flat clusters of small pink flowers on stiff stalks 2 to 3 ft. tall.*

If a plant is of garden origin—that is, it doesn't exist in the wild—it will have an additional name listed after its Latin name in single quotes; this is the cultivar. The geranium cultivar 'Johnson's Blue' has become a staple in the perennials section of nurseries, as has the yarrow 'Moonshine'.

Although the scientific names may seem confusing, with too many syllables strung together, they are valuable. Common plant names are charming but can lead to confusion because they often vary from region to region and country to country. In addition, often several plants with very different characteristics share the same common name. The scientific name is precise and descriptive. With a little Latin under your belt, you can learn a lot about a plant just from its name. For example, *reptans* means creeping. You know a plant with reptans in its name will be low to the ground and spreading. If a plant has *officinalis* in its name, you can be sure it was at one time used for medicinal purposes. A *sempervirens* will stay green throughout the year in most climates; *semperflorens* is ever-flowering.

WHAT'S IN A NAME? ────────────────────────────────────

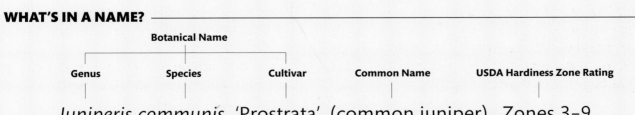

Botanical Name

| Genus | Species | Cultivar | Common Name | USDA Hardiness Zone Rating |

Juniperis communis 'Prostrata' (common juniper), Zones 3–9

About This Book

Of all the home improvement projects homeowners tackle, few offer greater rewards than landscaping. Paths, patios, fences, arbors, and most of all, plantings can enhance home life in countless ways, large and small, functional and pleasurable, every day of the year. At the main entrance, an attractive brick walkway flanked by eye-catching shrubs and perennials provides a cheerful send-off in the morning and welcomes you home from work in the evening. A carefully placed grouping of small trees, shrubs, and fence panels creates privacy on the patio or screens a nearby eyesore from view. An island bed showcases your favorite plants while dividing the backyard into several areas for several different activities.

Unlike some home improvements, the rewards of landscaping can lie as much in the activity as in the result. Planting and caring for lovely shrubs, perennials, and other plants can afford years of enjoyment. And for those who like to build things, outdoor construction projects can be a special treat.

While the installation and maintenance of plants and outdoor structures are within the means and abilities of most people, few of us are as comfortable determining exactly which plants or structures to use and how best to combine them. It's one thing to decide to dress up the front entrance or patio and another to come up with a design for doing so.

That's where this book comes in. In the Portfolio of Designs, you'll find 19 designs, plus a variation for each based on common home landscaping situations. Drawing on years of experience, we balance functional requirements and aesthetic possibilities, choosing the right plant or structure for the task—confident of its proven performance in similar situations. We cover areas that are right on the seashore to inland areas where the effects of salt are not an issue.

Complementing the Portfolio of Designs is the Plant Profiles section, which provides information on all of the plants used in the book. The Guide to Installation, the book's third section, will help you install and maintain the plants and structures called for in the designs.

Portfolio of Designs

This section is the heart of the book, providing examples of landscaping situations and solutions that are at once inspiring and accessible. Some are simple, others more complex, but each one can be installed in a few weekends by homeowners with no special training or experience.

For each situation, we present two designs, the second a variation of the first. As the sample pages on the facing page show,
the first design is displayed on a two-page spread. A perspective illustration (called a "rendering") shows what the design will look like several years after installation, when the perennials and many of the shrubs have reached mature size. The rendering also shows the planting as it will appear at a particular time of year. A site plan shows the positions of the plants and structures on a scaled grid. Text introduces the situation and the design and describes the plants and projects used. The Concept Box summarizes in a glance whether the site is sunny or shady, what season is depicted, and what Hardiness Zones it is designed for. Additional notes are added if the plants selected are low water use or moderately to highly salt tolerant.

The second design, presented on the second two-page spread, addresses the same situation as the first but differs in one or more important aspects. It might show a planting suited for a shady rather than a sunny site, incorporate different structures or kinds of plants, or it might be for a coastal garden. As for the first design, we present a rendering, site plan, and written information, but in briefer form. The second spread also includes photographs of landscapes in situations similar to those featured in the two designs. The photos showcase variations or details that you may wish to use in the designs we show or in designs of your own.

Installed exactly as shown here, these designs will provide years of enjoyment. But individual needs and properties will differ, and we encourage you to alter the designs to suit your site and desires. Many types of alterations are easy to make. You can add or remove plants and adjust the sizes of paths, patios, and fences to suit larger or smaller sites. You can rearrange groupings and substitute favorite plants to suit your taste. Or you can integrate the design with your existing landscaping. If you are uncertain about how to solve specific problems or about the effects of changes you'd like to make, consult with staff at a local nursery or with a landscape architect or designer in your area.

PORTFOLIO OF DESIGNS

Concept Box
Tells whether the site is sunny or shady, what season is depicted in the rendering, Hardiness Zones, and design information.

FIRST DESIGN OPTION

Summary
An overview of the situation and the design.

Rendering
Shows how the design will look when plants are well established.

Site Plan
Positions all plants and structures on a scaled grid.

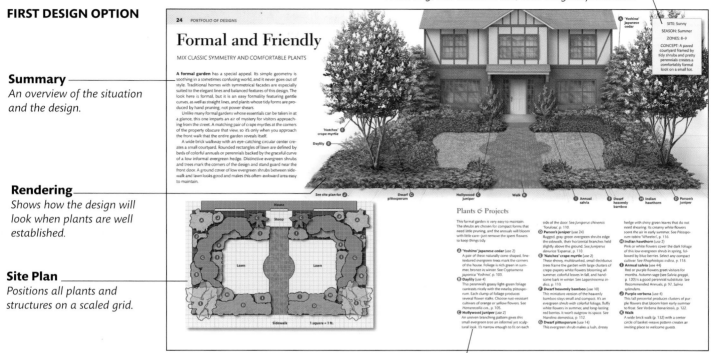

Plants & Projects
Noteworthy qualities of the plants and structures and their contributions to the design.

Rendering
Depicts the design when plants are well established.

Variations on a Theme
Photos of inspiring designs in similar situations.

SECOND DESIGN OPTION

Summary
Addressing the same situation as the first design, this variation may differ in design concept, site conditions, or plant selection.

Concept Box
Site, season, Hardiness Zones, and design summary.

Site Plan
Plants and structures on a scaled grid.

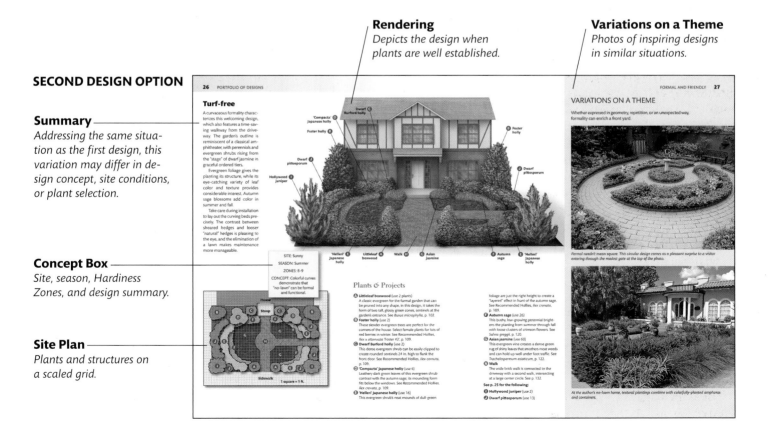

PLANT PROFILES

Choices

Selections here help you choose from the many varieties of certain popular plants.

Detailed Plant Information

Descriptions of each plant's noteworthy qualities and requirements for planting and care.

Plant Portraits

Photos of selected plants.

GUIDE TO INSTALLATION

Sidebars

Detailed information on special topics, set within ruled boxes.

Step-by-Step

Illustrations show process; steps are keyed by number to discussion in the main text.

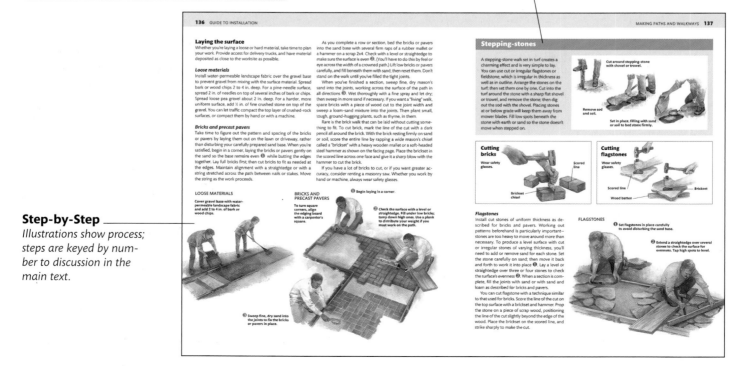

Plant Profiles

This section of the book includes a description of each of the plants featured in the Portfolio. These profiles outline the plants' basic preferences for environmental conditions, such as their Hardiness Zone(s), soil, moisture, salt tolerance, sun or shade, and they provide advice about planting and ongoing care.

We selected plants carefully, following a few simple guidelines: every plant should be a proven performer in its Zone once established, and it should thrive without pampering. All plants should be available from a major local nursery or garden center; if they're not in stock, they could be ordered, or ask the nursery staff to recommend suitable substitutes.

In the Portfolio section, you'll note that plants are referred to by their common name but are cross-referenced to the Plant Profiles section by their Latin, or scientific, name. While common names are familiar to many people, they can be confusing. Distinctly different plants can share the same common name, or one plant can have several different common names. Latin names, therefore, ensure accuracy and are more appropriate for a reference section such as this. Although you can confidently purchase most of the plants in this book from local nurseries using the common name, knowing the Latin name allows you to make sure that the plant you're ordering is actually the one that is shown in our design.

Guide to Installation

In this section you'll find detailed instructions and illustrations covering all the techniques you'll need to install any design from start to finish. Here we explain how to think your way through a landscaping project and anticipate the various steps. Then you'll learn how to do each part of the job: readying the site; laying out the design; choosing materials; building paths, trellises, or other structures; preparing the soil for planting; buying the recommended plants and putting them in place; and caring for the plants to keep them healthy and attractive year after year.

We've taken care to make installation of built elements simple and straightforward. The paths, trellises, fences, and arbors (elements called "hardscape" in the trade) all use basic materials available from local suppliers, and they can be assembled by people who have no special skills or tools beyond those commonly used for home maintenance. The designs can easily be adapted to meet specific needs or to fit in with the style of your house or other landscaping features.

Installing different designs requires different techniques. You can find what you need by following the cross-references in the Portfolio to pages in the Guide to Installation, or by skimming the Guide. If you continue to improve your landscape by adding more than one design, you'll find that many basic techniques are reused from one project to the next. You might want to start with one of the smaller, simpler designs. Gradually you'll develop the skills and confidence to do any project you choose.

Most of the designs in this book can be installed in a weekend or two; some will take a little longer. Digging planting beds, building retaining walls, and erecting fences and arbors can be strenuous work. If you lack the time or energy for the more arduous installation tasks, consider hiring a neighborhood teenager to help out; local landscaping services can provide more comprehensive help.

SOUTHERN COASTAL HARDINESS ZONES

This map is based on one developed by the U.S. Department of Agriculture. It divides the region into "Hardiness Zones" based on minimum winter temperatures. When you buy plants, most will have "hardiness" designations, which correspond to a USDA Hardiness Zone on the map below. A Zone 8 plant, for example, can be expected to survive winter temperatures as low as 10°F, and it can be used with confidence in Zone 8 and perhaps in other zones. We note the Hardiness Zone(s) for each plant. It is useful to know your zone and note the zone designation of any plants that you wish to add to those in this book.

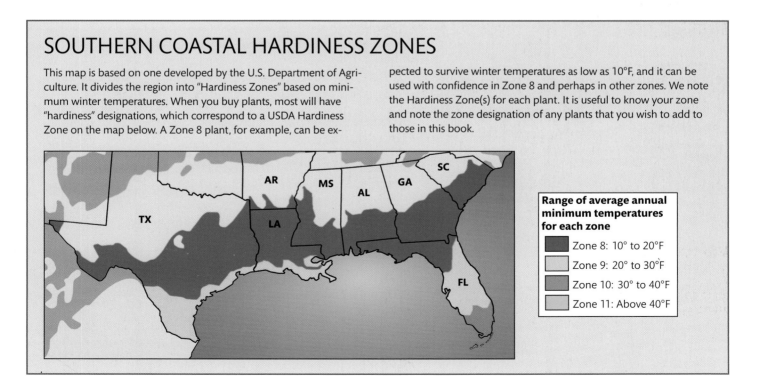

Range of average annual minimum temperatures for each zone

Zone 8: 10° to 20°F
Zone 9: 20° to 30°F
Zone 10: 30° to 40°F
Zone 11: Above 40°F

Portfolio *of* Designs

This section presents designs for 19 situations common in home landscapes in the southern coastal region. You'll find designs to enhance entrances, porches, and patios. There are gardens of colorful perennials and shrubs, as well as structures and plantings to create shady hideaways, dress up nondescript walls, and deal with slopes—all addressing the environmental challenges of the coastal landscape. Large color illustrations show what the designs will look like, and site plans delineate the layout and planting scheme. Texts explain the designs and describe the plants and projects appearing in them. Installed as shown or adapted to meet your site and personal preferences, these designs can make your property more attractive, more useful, and—most important—more enjoyable for you, your family, and your friends.

Southern Hospitality

MAKE A PLEASANT PASSAGE TO YOUR FRONT DOOR

Why wait until a visitor reaches the front door to extend a cordial greeting? An entryway landscape of well-chosen plants and a revamped walkway not only make the short journey a pleasant one, they can also enhance your home's most public face and help settle it comfortably in its surroundings.

The curved walk in this design extends a helpful "Please come this way" to visitors, while creating a roomy planting area near the house. The walk bridges a grassy "inlet" created by the free-flowing lines of the beds. The flowing masses of plants, lawn, and walkway pavement nicely com-

plement the journey to the front door.

Two handsome trees and a skirting of shrubs form a partial screen between the walkway and front door and the street. A striking collection of evergreens transforms the foundation planting near the house into a shrub border. Ground covers edge the walkway with pretty foliage and flowers. A decorative trellis near the driveway softens an empty wall and marks the entry. Bright hummingbird-attracting flowers or colorful autumn foliage covers the trellis year-round, enticing visitors to start their stroll to the front door.

River birch **B**

'Helleri' **F**
Japanese holly

Variegated **I**
pittosporum

Creeping lilyturf **G**

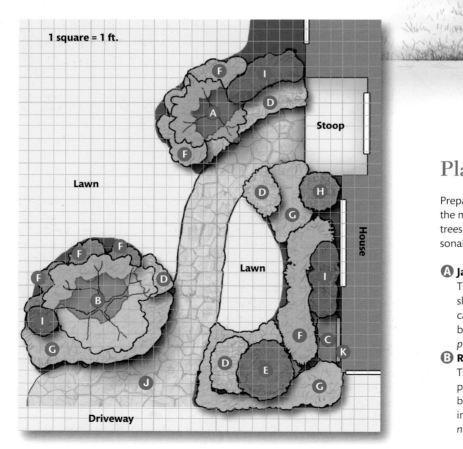

1 square = 1 ft.

Lawn

Stoop

House

Lawn

Driveway

Plants & Projects

Preparing the planting beds and laying the walk are the main tasks in this design. Comprising mostly trees and shrubs, the planting requires only seasonal cleanup and pruning once it's installed.

A **Japanese maple** (use 1 plant)
This small deciduous tree will thrive in the shade of the taller birch, providing colorful delicate leaves in the fall and a graceful tracery of branches during the winter months. See *Acer palmatum*, p. 94.

B **River birch** (use 1)
The multiple trunks of this deciduous tree display colorful biege, tan, or copper-color peeling bark. Leaves are glossy green in summer, turning tan or gold as fall approaches. See *Betula nigra*, p. 99.

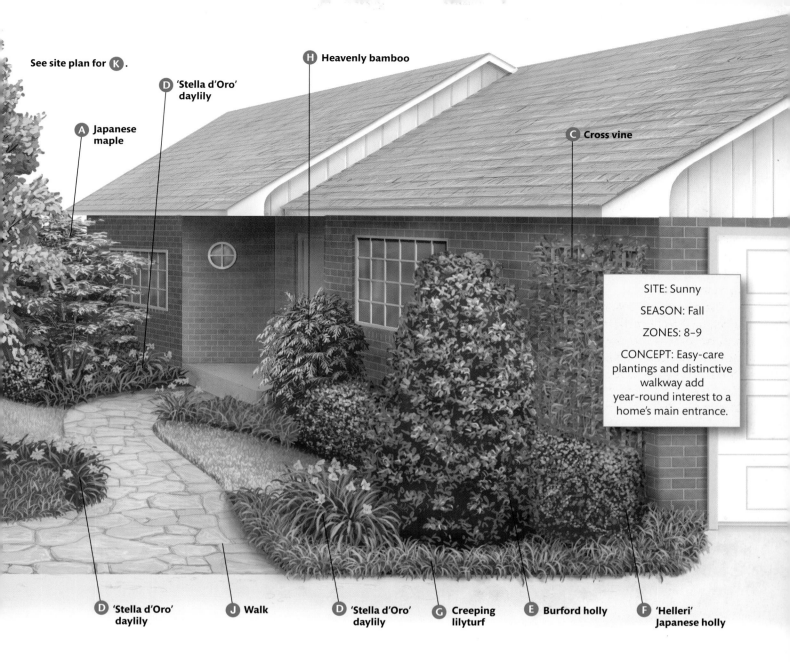

See site plan for **K**.

D 'Stella d'Oro' daylily

H Heavenly bamboo

A Japanese maple

C Cross vine

SITE: Sunny

SEASON: Fall

ZONES: 8–9

CONCEPT: Easy-care plantings and distinctive walkway add year-round interest to a home's main entrance.

D 'Stella d'Oro' daylily

J Walk

D 'Stella d'Oro' daylily

G Creeping lilyturf

E Burford holly

F 'Helleri' Japanese holly

C Cross vine (use 1)
This evergreen vine showcases trumpet-shaped flowers of yellow to red-orange in the spring. Cross vine will take the shade of house eaves. Train the young tendrils up the trellis to cover. See *Bignonia capreolata*, p. 99.

D 'Stella d'Oro' daylily (use 15)
This cultivar is one of the longest-blooming daylilies, producing golden-yellow flowers from late spring to frost. Even without the glowing flowers, this perennial's grassy light green foliage contrasts nicely

with the nearby lilyturf. See *Hemerocallis cvs.*, p. 105.

E Burford holly (use 1)
This evergreen shrub is easily maintained in a conical form. Its large leaves are a great backdrop for its red winter berries. See Recommended Hollies, *Ilex cornuta* 'Burfordii' p. 109.

F 'Helleri' Japanese holly (use 10)
This evergreen shrub fills the space under the windows with mounds of small, shiny leaves. See Recommended Hollies, *Ilex crenata*, p. 109.

G Creeping lilyturf (use 39)
This evergreen perennial makes a grasslike mat of dark-green leaves along the walk. Small spikes of violet, purple, or white flowers appear in summer. See *Liriope spicata*, p. 111.

H Heavenly bamboo (use 1)
This evergreen shrub has leaves that change color each season and provides white summer flowers and long-lasting red berries. See *Nandina domestica*, p. 112.

I Variegated pittosporum (use 7)
This evergreen shrub brings a

dressy look and year-round color to the foundation with its rounded mounds of glossy gray-green leaves mottled with white. Creamy white flowers scent the air in early summer. See *Pittosporum tobira* 'Variegata', p. 116.

J Walk
Flagstones of random size and shape are ideal for the curved walk. See p. 132.

K Trellis
This trellis can be assembled in a few hours; it is easily removed in the future to repaint or repair the wall. See p. 154.

VARIATIONS ON A THEME

While they differ in many ways, each of these entryway landscapes looks just right for its house and site.

Neat as a pin, this entry features a brick courtyard, a door-step garden, and a sweeping border lining a flawless lawn.

Lined with ornamental grasses, this design is at once natural and tastefully composed.

A curving stroll garden leads to this front door, its brick path lined with colorful annuals and perennials.

A shady welcome

If your entry is shady—receiving less than six hours of sunlight a day—try this planting scheme, which replaces the sun-loving plants from the previous design with others that prefer the shade. Overall, the emphasis is still on year-round good looks.

Shade brings out the best in many southern plants. In spring, shown here, the planting is awash with flowers. During the summer months, the dogwood and redbud make a lovely covered walkway to the front door, while shrubs, hostas, and ferns provide a cool display of attractive foliage. Much of the foliage carries on right through the winter; then the rain lily announces the summer rains, and the cycle begins anew.

Plants & Projects

Ⓐ Japanese painted fern (use 12 plants)
The loveliest of ferns, its delicately colored deciduous fronds blend green, silver, and maroon. They also add a lush, rich look beneath the dogwoods. See Recommended Ferns, *Athyrium niponicum* 'Pictum', p. 104.

Ⓑ Littleleaf boxwood (use 2)
Clipped or pruned to a more "natural" shape, this evergreen shrub joins the mahonia in framing the entry. The dark green leaves exude a distinct fragrance. See *Buxus microphylla*, p. 102.

Ⓒ Redbud (use 1)
Small pink flowers line the branches of this small deciduous tree in early spring. Heart-shaped leaves turn gold in the fall. This fast-growing tree needs little pruning; just remove lower limbs. See *Cercis canadensis*, p. 102.

See site plan for Ⓔ Ⓛ Ⓝ.

Redbud Ⓒ

Littleleaf boxwood Ⓑ

Dogwood Ⓓ

Ⓖ 'Pink Gumpo' azalea   Japanese painted fern Ⓐ   Walk Ⓜ   Leatherleaf mahonia Ⓕ   Mondo grass Ⓙ   Japanese maple Ⓚ   Rain lily Ⓘ   'Roseum Elegans' rhododendron Ⓗ

Ⓓ **Dogwood** (use 1)
This is one of the finest small trees; it has white flowers in spring and foliage that turns crimson in fall, when bright red berries ripen. See *Cornus florida*, p. 103.

Ⓔ **'Elegans' hosta** (use 11)
The large, blue-gray, textured leaves of this perennial add color to the shade from spring until frost. See *Hosta sieboldiana* 'Elegans', p. 106.

Ⓕ **Leatherleaf mahonia** (use 3)
Leathery horizontal leaflets of this upright evergreen shrub make it a standout in the landscape. In early spring, it produces fragrant golden-yellow flowers, followed by showy clusters of blue berries. See *Mahonia bealei*, p. 112.

Ⓖ **'Pink Gumpo' azalea** (use 11)
These low, spreading evergreen shrubs are eye-catching from the street or drive. Mounds of fine-textured foliage are covered by clusters of frilly pink flowers that extend the season. See Recommended Rhododendrons and Azaleas, *Rhododendron* hybrids, p. 119.

Ⓗ **'Roseum Elegans' rhododendron** (use 1)
This evergreen shrub features glossy leaves and clusters of pink flowers in late spring. See Recommended Rhododendrons and Azaleas, *Rhododendron* 'Roseum Elegans' p. 119.

Ⓘ **Rain lily** (use 3)
This deciduous lily "sleeps" in the winter, but thin dark green leaves appear in early spring. These are followed by trumpet-shaped lilies of white on stalks held above the foliage when summer rains return. See Recommended bulbs, *Zephyranthes atamasca*, p. 101.

Ⓙ **Mondo grass** (use 89 sprigs)
The thin, leathery, leaves of this perennial create an attractive edging. See *Ophiopogon japonicus*, p. 113.

See pp. 16–17 for the following:

Ⓚ **Japanese maple** (use 1)
Ⓛ **Cross vine** (use 1)
Ⓜ **Walk**
Ⓝ **Trellis**

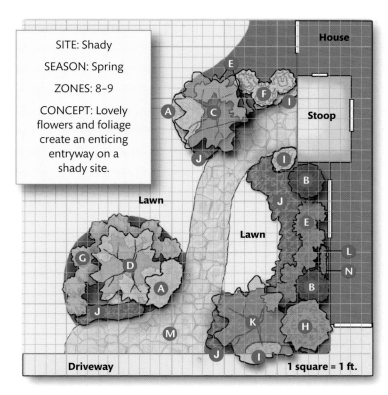

SITE: Shady

SEASON: Spring

ZONES: 8–9

CONCEPT: Lovely flowers and foliage create an enticing entryway on a shady site.

House

Stoop

Lawn

Lawn

Driveway

1 square = 1 ft.

A Foundation with Flair

FLOWERS AND FOLIAGE DRESS UP A RAISED ENTRY

A home with a raised entry invites down-to-earth foundation plants that anchor the house to its surroundings and hide unattractive concrete-block underpinnings. In the hospitable climate of the South, a durable, low-maintenance planting need not mean the usual lineup of clipped junipers. As this design shows, a foundation planting can be more varied, more colorful, and more fun.

Within the graceful arc of a low boxwood hedge is a balanced arrangement of shrubs in sizes that fit under windows and hide the foundation at the same time. Larger shrubs and a small tree punctuate the planting and contribute to the variety of foliage textures and colors.

The predominantly evergreen foliage looks good year-round, and in spring and early summer, it is a fine backdrop for a lovely floral display. White flowers sparkle on the trees and shrubs, with spiky creeping lily-turf at their feet. Twining up posts or over railings, the Confederate jasmine greets visitors with its deliciously scented creamy flowers.

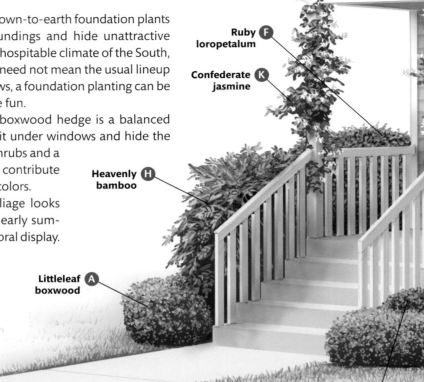

Plants & Projects

Once established, the plants in this design require little maintenance beyond seasonal cleanup and a yearly pruning. The boxwood hedge will need trimming once or twice a year. Trimming the spent crape myrtle blooms encourages more flowers.

A **Littleleaf boxwood**
(use 32 plants)
A classic sheared evergreen hedge defines the foundation garden; this compact shrub's small, glossy green leaves give it a fine texture. See *Buxus microphylla*, p. 102.

B **'Compacta' Japanese holly**
(use 1)
Fill the corner next to the stoop with this shrub. It can be shaped into a ball or cone by shearing. See Recommended Hollies, *Ilex crenata*, p. 109.

C **'Helleri' Japanese holly**
(use 3)
Smaller than 'Compacta', this evergreen shrub won't outgrow its place, making tidy mounds of small, rounded, dull-green leaves. See Recommended Hollies, *Ilex crenata*, p. 109.

D **'Acoma' crape myrtle** (use 1)
Dense clusters of white crepe-paperlike flowers light up this small tree in late spring. Dark-green deciduous leaves turn bright colors in fall, and peeling bark is attractive in winter. See *Lagerstroemia indica*, p. 110.

E **Creeping lilyturf** (use 8)
This evergreen perennial makes a grasslike mat of dark leaves along the pittosporum hedge. Small spikes of violet or white flowers appear in summer. See *Liriope spicata*, p. 111.

F **Ruby loropetalum** (use 1)
An elegant presence next to the stoop, this evergreen shrub bears lacy dark pink flowers in spring and may bloom sporadically through the summer. For a low-water-use garden, substitute with *Acca sellowiana*, p. 94. See *Loropetalum chinense*, p. 112.

G **'Little Gem' magnolia** (use 1)
This smaller cousin of the evergreen southern magnolia fits perfectly at the corner of the house. Spring's fragrant white flowers are followed by large pods of bright red seeds that songbirds love. See *Magnolia grandiflora*, p. 112.

H **Heavenly bamboo** (use 3)
This colorful evergreen shrub has layers of lacy leaves tinged gold in spring, changing to summer green and turning orange-red in winter, white flowers in summer, and months of red berries. See *Nandina domestica*, p. 112.

I **Dwarf heavenly bamboo**
(use 3)
This miniature version of the heavenly bamboo stays small and compact. This shrub has colorful foliage, fluffy white flowers in summer, and long-lasting red berries. See *Nandina domestica*, p. 112.

J **Variegated pittosporum**
(use 8)
This evergreen shrub brings year-round color to the foundation with its rounded mounds of glossy gray-green leaves mottled with white. Creamy white flowers scent the air in early summer. See *Pittosporum tobira* 'Variegata', p. 116.

K **Confederate jasmine** (use 2)
On summer evenings you can enjoy the fragrance of this evergreen vine's flowers. See *Trachelospermum jasminoides*, p. 122.

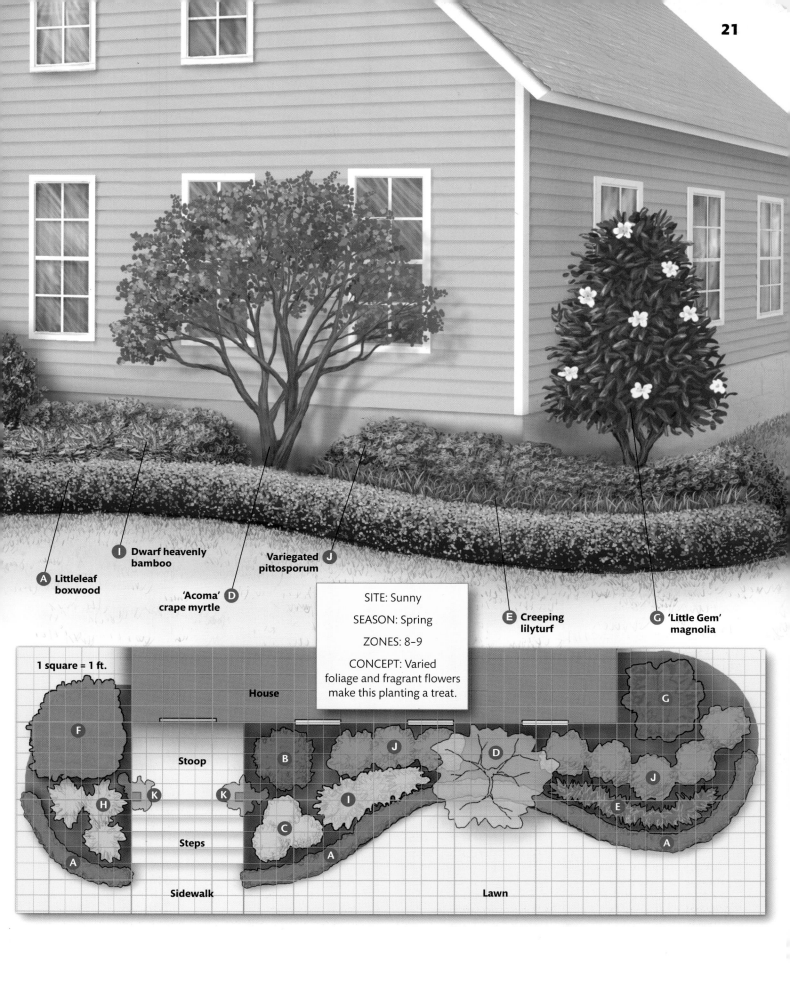

I Dwarf heavenly bamboo

A Littleleaf boxwood

'Acoma' D crape myrtle

Variegated pittosporum J

E Creeping lilyturf

G 'Little Gem' magnolia

SITE: Sunny

SEASON: Spring

ZONES: 8–9

CONCEPT: Varied foliage and fragrant flowers make this planting a treat.

1 square = 1 ft.

House

Stoop

Steps

Sidewalk

Lawn

Setting for a shady porch

Porch sitting, one of summer's favorite pastimes, can be made even more pleasurable with this planting. Like the previous design, this one combines deciduous and evergreen plants and mixes handsome foliage and pretty flowers to look good in all four seasons. All of the suggested plants will thrive in a shady location.

The central Japanese maple screens the porch from the street without obstructing the view of sitters on the porch. Informal hedges of dwarf camellia and holly skirt the porch foundation. Yellow variegated aucubas flank the stoop behind small patches of annuals, and a grassy edging outlines the beds.

Fragrant flowers perfume the porch for months, beginning in late winter with tea olive, followed in earliest spring with Carolina jasmine and late spring with confederate jasmine. Vine-covered porch posts and hanging baskets of annuals scattered around the porch complete the cozy setting.

Plants & Projects

Ⓐ Japanese maple (use 1)
This small deciduous tree screens the porch even in winter with eye-catching sculptural branches. Choose a cultivar with cool green leaves in summer; they'll turn a vivid red in fall. See *Acer palmatum*, p. 94.

Ⓑ Annuals
Impatiens, begonias, moss rose, and coleus provide color in all seasons in the beds by the steps and the hanging baskets on the porch. See Recommended Annuals, p. 96.

Ⓒ Japanese painted fern (use 8)
Lovely ferns with delicately colored deciduous fronds of green, silver, and maroon, they add a lush, rich look beneath the shade of the Japanese maple. See Recommended Ferns, *Athyrium niponicum* 'Pictum', p. 104.

Ⓓ Aucuba (use 2)
These striking evergreen shrubs with shiny, leathery green leaves flecked with bright yellow spots provide a colorful statement at the front door. See *Aucuba japonica* 'Variegata', p. 98.

Ⓔ 'Shishigashira' camellia (use 5)
Blooming fall and winter with bright rose flowers, this evergreen, low-growing shrub will tie down the corner of the porch. See *Camellia sasanqua* 'Shishigashira', p. 102.

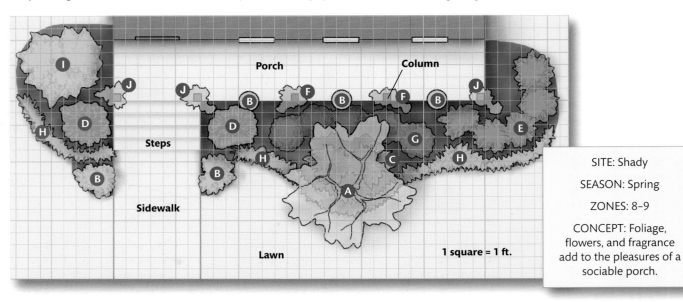

SITE: Shady

SEASON: Spring

ZONES: 8–9

CONCEPT: Foliage, flowers, and fragrance add to the pleasures of a sociable porch.

J **Confederate jasmine**

E **'Shishigashira' camellia**

F **Carolina jasmine** (use 2)
This evergreen vine offers something year-round. Fragrant yellow trumpet-shaped flowers greet visitors in early spring. Neat green leaves in summer turn maroon for the winter. See *Gelsemium sempervirens*, p. 105.

G **Dwarf yaupon holly** (use 5)
A small evergreen shrub that forms compact mounds of small gray-green leaves, it stays just the right size for the base of the porch. See Recommended Hollies, *Ilex vomitoria* 'Nana' p. 109.

H **Lilyturf** (use 28)
Grasslike clumps of evergreen leaves make an attractive year-round edging, featuring white or purple flowers in summer. See *Liriope muscari*, p. 111.

I **Tea olive** (use 1)
This large, upright shrub of stiff, holly-like leaves blooms from autumn to spring with tiny, cream-colored blossoms that are powerfully fragrant. See *Osmanthus fragrans*, p. 113.

J **See p. 20 for the following:**
Confederate jasmine (use 3)

VARIATIONS ON A THEME

Anything but boring, these designs illustrate some of the imaginative possibilities for foundation plantings.

This dramatic planting plays on the contrasts between foliage and flowers. Spiky agaves rise above the colorful flowers of low-growing verbena.

Pink azaleas light up this shady site. Additional evergreen shrubs and a carpet of mondo grass add year-round contrasting color and texture.

Simple and striking, in this planting a neat boxwood hedge corrals large, loose hydrangeas.

Formal and Friendly

MIX CLASSIC SYMMETRY AND COMFORTABLE PLANTS

A formal garden has a special appeal. Its simple geometry is soothing in a sometimes confusing world, and it never goes out of style. Traditional homes with symmetrical facades are especially suited to the elegant lines and balanced features of this design. The look here is formal, but it is an easy formality featuring gentle curves, as well as straight lines, and plants whose tidy forms are produced by hand pruning, not power shears.

Unlike many formal gardens whose essentials can be taken in at a glance, this one imparts an air of mystery for visitors approaching from the street. A matching pair of crape myrtles at the corners of the property obscure that view, so it's only when you approach the front walk that the entire garden reveals itself.

A wide brick walkway with an eye-catching circular center creates a small courtyard. Rounded rectangles of lawn are defined by beds of colorful annuals or perennials backed by the graceful curve of a low informal evergreen hedge. Distinctive evergreen shrubs and trees mark the corners of the design and stand guard near the front door. A ground cover of low evergreen shrubs between sidewalk and lawn looks good and makes this often-awkward area easy to maintain.

'Natchez' crape myrtle **E**

Daylily **B**

See site plan for **J** .

Dwarf **G** pittosporum

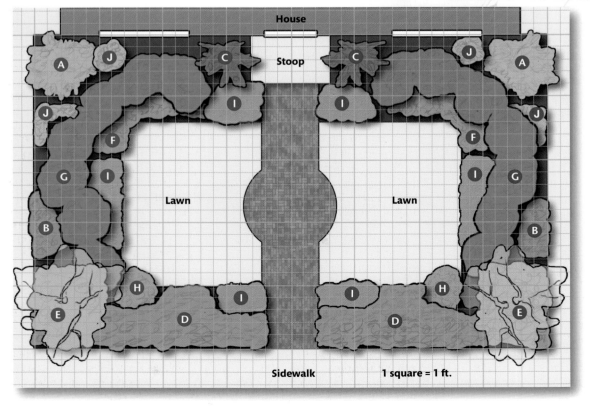

House

Stoop

Lawn

Lawn

Sidewalk

1 square = 1 ft.

A 'Yoshino' Japanese cedar

SITE: Sunny

SEASON: Summer

ZONES: 8–9

CONCEPT: A paved courtyard framed by tidy shrubs and pretty perennials creates a comfortably formal look on a small lot.

Hollywood **C** juniper

Walk **K**

I Annual salvia

F Dwarf heavenly bamboo

H Indian hawthorn

D Parson's juniper

Plants & Projects

This formal garden is very easy to maintain. The shrubs are chosen for compact forms that need little pruning, and the annuals will bloom with little care—just remove the spent flowers to keep things tidy.

A **'Yoshino' Japanese cedar** (use 2)
A pair of these naturally cone-shaped, fine-textured evergreen trees mark the corners of the house. Foliage is rich green in summer, bronze in winter. See *Cryptomeria japonica* 'Yoshino', p. 103.

B **Daylily** (use 4)
This perennial's grassy light-green foliage contrasts nicely with the nearby pittosporum. Each clump of foliage produces several flower stalks. Choose rust-resistant cultivars of orange or yellow flowers. See *Hemerocallis cvs.*, p. 105.

C **Hollywood juniper** (use 2)
An uneven branching pattern gives this small evergreen tree an informal yet sculptural look. It's narrow enough to fit on each

side of the door. See *Juniperus chinensis* 'Torulosa', p. 110.

D **Parson's juniper** (use 24)
Rugged, gray-green evergreen shrubs edge the sidewalk, their horizontal branches held slightly above the ground. See *Juniperus davurica* 'Expansa', p. 110.

E **'Natchez' crape myrtle** (use 2)
These showy, multitrunked, small deciduous trees frame the garden with large clusters of crepe-papery white flowers blooming all summer, colorful leaves in fall, and handsome bark in winter. See *Lagerstroemia indica*, p. 110.

F **Dwarf heavenly bamboo** (use 10)
This miniature version of the heavenly bamboo stays small and compact. It's an evergreen shrub with colorful foliage, fluffy white flowers in summer, and long-lasting red berries. It won't outgrow its space. See *Nandina domestica*, p. 112.

G **Dwarf pittosporum** (use 14)
This evergreen shrub makes a lush, dressy

hedge with shiny green leaves that do not need shearing. Its creamy white flowers scent the air in early summer. See *Pittosporum tobira* 'Wheeleri', p. 116.

H **Indian hawthorn** (use 2)
Pink or white flowers cover the dark foliage of this low evergreen shrub in spring, followed by blue berries. Select any compact cultivar. See *Rhaphiolepis indica*, p. 118.

I **Annual salvia** (use 44)
Red or purple flowers greet visitors for months. Autumn sage (see *Salvia greggii*, p. 120) is a good perennial substitute. See Recommended Annuals, p. 97, *Salvia splendens*.

J **Purple verbena** (use 4)
This tall perennial produces clusters of purple flowers that bloom from early summer to frost. See *Verbena bonariensis*, p. 122.

K **Walk**
A wide brick walk (p. 132) with a center circle of basket-weave pattern creates an inviting place to welcome guests.

Turf-free

A curvaceous formality characterizes this welcoming design, which also features a time-saving walkway from the driveway. The garden's outline is reminiscent of a classical amphitheater, with perennials and evergreen shrubs rising from the "stage" of dwarf jasmine in graceful ordered tiers.

Evergreen foliage gives the planting its structure, while its eye-catching variety of leaf color and texture provides considerable interest. Autumn sage blossoms add color in summer and fall.

Take care during installation to lay out the curving beds precisely. The contrast between sheared hedges and looser "natural" hedges is pleasing to the eye, and the elimination of a lawn makes maintenance more manageable.

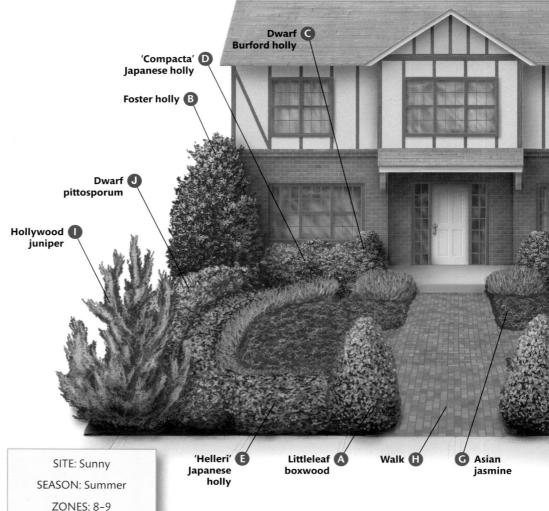

Dwarf Burford holly **C**

'Compacta' Japanese holly **D**

Foster holly **B**

Dwarf pittosporum **J**

Hollywood juniper **I**

'Helleri' Japanese holly **E**

Littleleaf boxwood **A**

Walk **H**

Asian jasmine **G**

SITE: Sunny

SEASON: Summer

ZONES: 8–9

CONCEPT: Colorful curves demonstrate that "no-lawn" can be formal and functional.

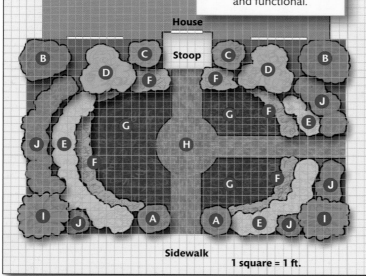

House

Stoop

Sidewalk

1 square = 1 ft.

Plants & Projects

A Littleleaf boxwood (use 2 plants)
A classic evergreen for the formal garden that can be pruned into any shape, in this design, it takes the form of two tall, glossy green cones, sentinels at the garden's entrance. See *Buxus microphylla*, p. 102.

B Foster holly (use 2)
These slender evergreen trees are perfect for the corners of the house. Select female plants for lots of red berries in winter. See Recommended Hollies, *Ilex x attenuata* 'Foster #2', p. 109.

C Dwarf Burford holly (use 2)
This dense evergreen shrub can be easily clipped to create rounded sentinels 24 in. high to flank the front door. See Recommended Hollies, *Ilex cornuta*, p. 109.

D 'Compacta' Japanese holly (use 6)
Leathery dark green leaves of this evergreen shrub contrast with the autumn sage; its mounding form fits below the windows. See Recommended Hollies, *Ilex crenata*, p. 109.

E 'Helleri' Japanese holly (use 16)
This evergreen shrub's neat mounds of dull-green

B Foster holly

J Dwarf pittosporum

F Autumn sage

E 'Helleri' Japanese holly

VARIATIONS ON A THEME

Whether expressed in geometry, repetition, or an unexpected way, formality can enrich a front yard.

Formal needn't mean square. This circular design comes as a pleasant surprise to a visitor entering through the modest gate at the top of the photo.

foliage are just the right height to create a "layered" effect in front of the autumn sage. See Recommended Hollies, *Ilex crenata*, p. 109.

F **Autumn sage** (use 26)
This bushy, low-growing perennial brightens the planting from summer through fall with loose clusters of crimson flowers. See *Salvia greggii*, p. 120.

G **Asian jasmine** (use 60)
This evergreen vine creates a dense green rug of shiny leaves that smothers most weeds and can hold up well under foot traffic. See *Trachelospermum asiaticum*, p. 122.

H **Walk**
The wide brick walk is connected to the driveway with a second walk, intersecting at a large center circle. See p. 132.

See p. 25 for the following:

I **Hollywood juniper** (use 2)

J **Dwarf pittosporum** (use 13)

At the author's no-lawn home, textural plantings combine with colorfully-planted amphoras and containers.

Streetwise and Stylish

GIVE YOUR CURBSIDE STRIP A NEW LOOK

Homeowners seldom think much about the area that runs between the sidewalk and street. At best this is a tidy patch of lawn; at worst, a weed-choked eyesore. Yet this is one of the most public parts of many properties. Planting this strip with attractive perennials, shrubs, and trees can give pleasure to passersby and visitors who park next to the curb, as well as enhance the streetscape you view from the house. (This strip is usually city-owned, so check local ordinances for restrictions before you start a remake.)

It might help to think of this curbside strip as an island bed between two defined boundaries: the street and the sidewalk. These beds are divided further by a wide pedestrian walkway, providing ample room for visitors to get in and out of front and rear car doors. A pair of handsome evergreen trees form a gate-

way. The diagonal skew of this design keeps the symmetry of the plantings on each side from appearing staid. You can expand the beds to fill a longer strip or plant lawn next to the beds.

This can be a difficult site. Summer drought and heat, pedestrian and car traffic, and the "attention" of errant dogs are the usual conditions found along the street. Plants have to be tough to perform well here, but they need not look tough. These combine colorful foliage and flowers for a dramatic impact from spring until fall. Evergreen foliage looks good through the winter. The plantings beneath the trees won't grow tall enough to block your view of the street as you pull out of the driveway.

Japanese ligustrum **B**

Dwarf heavenly bamboo **D**

Indian hawthorne **E**

Mexican bush sage **F**

'Stella d'Oro' daylily **A**

Parson's juniper **C**

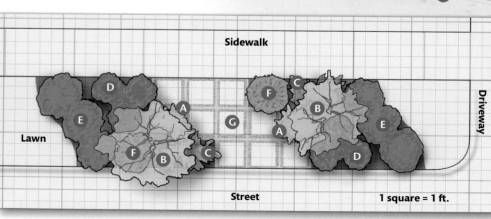

Sidewalk

Lawn

Driveway

Street   1 square = 1 ft.

SITE: Sunny

SEASON: Summer

ZONES: 8–9

CONCEPT: Small but varied low-water-use planting transforms an often neglected area and treats visitors and passersby to a colorful display.

Plants & Projects

Tough as they are, these plants will benefit from a generous bark mulch, which conserves moisture and helps control weeds in this highly visible location. You'll need to prune the shrubs occasionally to keep them tidy and healthy. Divide the clumps of daylilies when they get crowded.

A 'Stella d'Oro' daylily (use 8)
This very popular perennial produces golden-yellow flowers from late spring until frost; quite a feat considering that each flower lasts only a day. The grassy foliage is attractive, too. See *Hemerocallis cvs.*, p. 105.

B Japanese ligustrum (use 2)
The dark green, waxy leaves of this small broad-leaved evergreen tree are a perfect background for the fragrant white flowers it bears in early summer. Dark-blue berries follow in fall and winter. It grows quickly; prune lower branches as necessary to accommodate visitors using the walk. See *Ligustrum japonicum*, p. 111.

C Parson's juniper (use 2)
Rugged, gray-green evergreen shrubs edge the sidewalk and curb, their horizontal branches held slightly above the ground.

See *Juniperus davurica* 'Expansa', p. 110.

D Dwarf heavenly bamboo (use 11)
This miniature version of the heavenly bamboo stays small and compact. An evergreen shrub with colorful foliage, fluffy white flowers in summer, and long-lasting red berries, it won't outgrow its space. See *Nandina domestica*, p. 112.

E Indian hawthorn (use 6)
Pink or white flowers cover the dark foliage of this low, spreading evergreen shrub in spring, followed by blue berries. Select any compact cultivar. See *Rhaphiolepis indica*, p. 118.

F Mexican bush sage (use 3)
This beautiful evergreen perennial adds soft texture and blue flower color to this landscape. This velvety plant will bloom in autumn and spring. See *Salvia leucantha*, p. 120.

G Walk
This design provides interest underfoot. Set the framework of pressure-treated 2x4s on a sand-and-gravel base (see p. 132); position the square precast concrete pavers in the center of each cell; and fill between paver and frame with crushed rock, tamped firm.

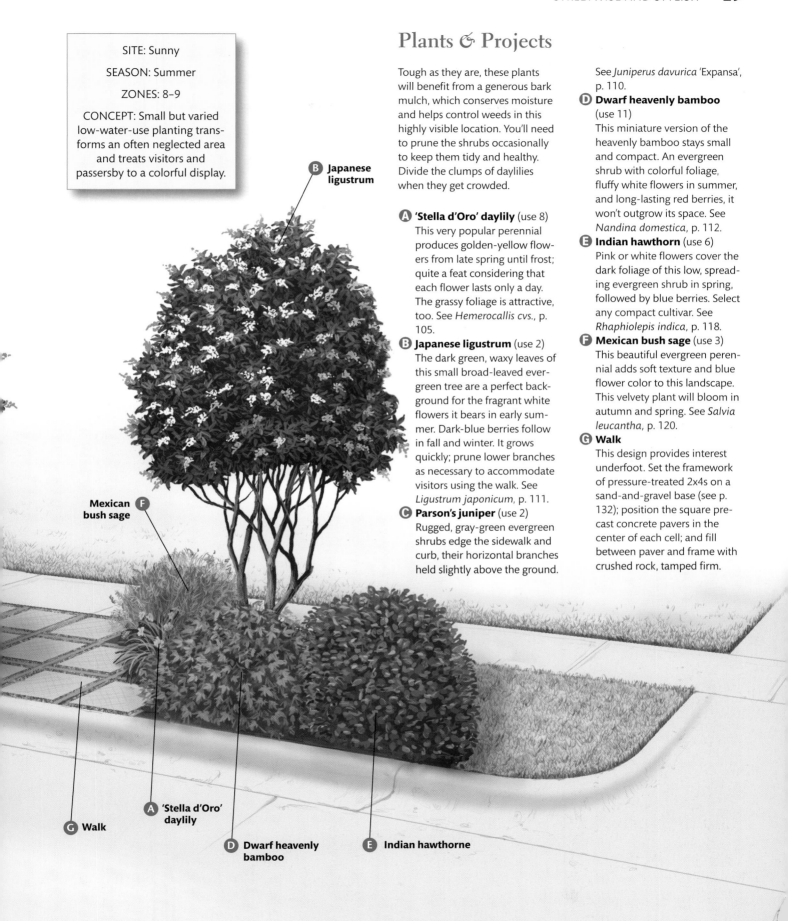

B Japanese ligustrum

F Mexican bush sage

G Walk

A 'Stella d'Oro' daylily

D Dwarf heavenly bamboo

E Indian hawthorne

VARIATIONS ON A THEME

Streetside gardening can be a challenge, but a thoughtful selection of tough plants can turn an awkward spot into a showpiece.

A colorful streetside planting includes flowers and ornamental grasses that flow from the house right across the sidewalk.

These brightly colored perennials and shrubs are a cheerful sight to drivers and sidewalk passersby alike.

A curbside planting can make a big, bold impression that greets visitors long before they arrive at your curb. This narrow bed consists of a row of rounded boxwoods punctuated by the slender trunks of crape myrtles.

Leafy pass-through

This design features shade-loving plants for those who live on the cool shady streets that make many neighborhoods so pleasant. Emphasizing foliage more than flowers, the effect is more subdued than the previous design but still cheerful.

A pair of small trees once again anchor the design. They flower in early spring, followed by the azaleas flanking the walk. A mix of rich green foliage, accented by the large blue leaves of the hostas, carries the planting through the summer and fall. The azaleas, lilyturf, and redbuds look good through the winter.

Plants & Projects

A Redbud (use 2 plants)
Small pink flowers line the branches of this petite deciduous tree in early spring. Heart-shaped leaves turn gold in the fall. This fast-growing tree needs little pruning; just remove lower limbs. See *Cercis canadensis*, p. 102.

B 'Elegans' hosta (use 14)
The huge, blue-gray, textured leaves of this perennial add cool color to the shade from spring until frost, contrasting with the finer-leaved azaleas. In late summer, white flowers peek just above the foliage. For the warmer parts of Zone 9, use 'Harbour Dwarf' Nandina.

See *Hosta sieboldiana* 'Elegans', p. 106.

C Creeping lilyturf (use 43)
This evergreen perennial makes a tough grasslike mat of dark-green leaves along the sidewalk and curb. Small spikes of violet, purple, or white flowers appear in summer. See *Liriope spicata*, p. 111.

D 'Gumpo' azalea (use 14)
These low, spreading evergreen shrubs form mounds of fine-textured foliage; an ideal background for the lovely display of frilly flowers that brighten the shade in late spring. Use pink or white cultivars, or both. Foliage looks fresh all year. See Recommended Rhododendrons and Azaleas, *Rhododendron hybrid*, p. 119.

See p. 29 for the following:
E Walk

> SITE: Shady
>
> SEASON: Late spring
>
> ZONES: 8–9
>
> CONCEPT: Enhance the looks of a shady curb with lovely foliage and a spring flush of flowers.

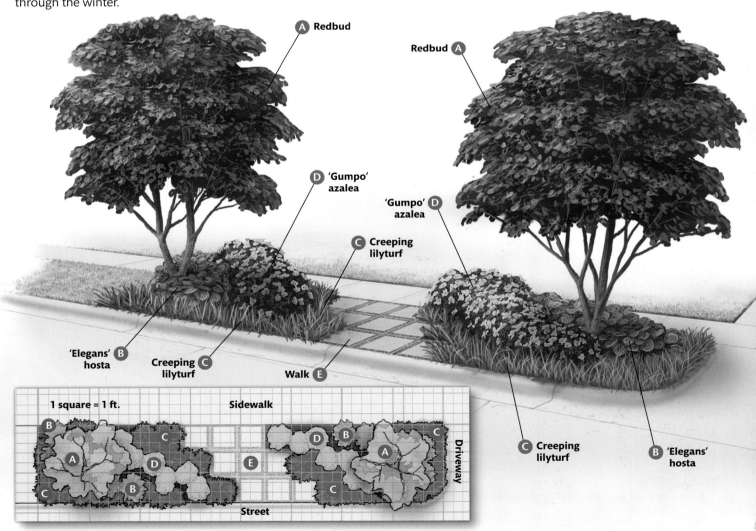

A Redbud

Redbud A

D 'Gumpo' azalea

'Gumpo' D azalea

C Creeping lilyturf

'Elegans' B hosta

Creeping C lilyturf

Walk E

C Creeping lilyturf

B 'Elegans' hosta

1 square = 1 ft.   Sidewalk

Driveway

Street

Key West

DRESS UP THE FAMILY'S DAY-TO-DAY ENTRANCE

When people think of landscaping the entrance to their home, the public entry at the front of the house comes immediately to mind. It's easy to forget that the back door often gets more use. If you make the journey between back door and driveway or stand-alone garage many times each day, why not make it as pleasant a trip as possible? For many properties, a simple planting such as the one shown here can transform the space bounded by the house, garage, and driveway, making it at once more inviting and more functional.

In a high-traffic area frequented by ball-bouncing, bicycle-riding children as well as busy adults, delicate, fussy plants have no place. This design employs durable plants, all of which look good year-round. The shrubs and ornamental grass link the house and the garage and separate the more private backyard from the busy driveway. A Japanese ligustrum anchors the backyard planting, a composition of shrubs and annuals that is equally pleasing whether viewed on your way to and from the back door or while relaxing on a backyard deck or patio. The evergreen paspalum grass will sway in the breeze. With moderate salt tolerance and low-water-use plantings, this garden will thrive just a block or so from the beach.

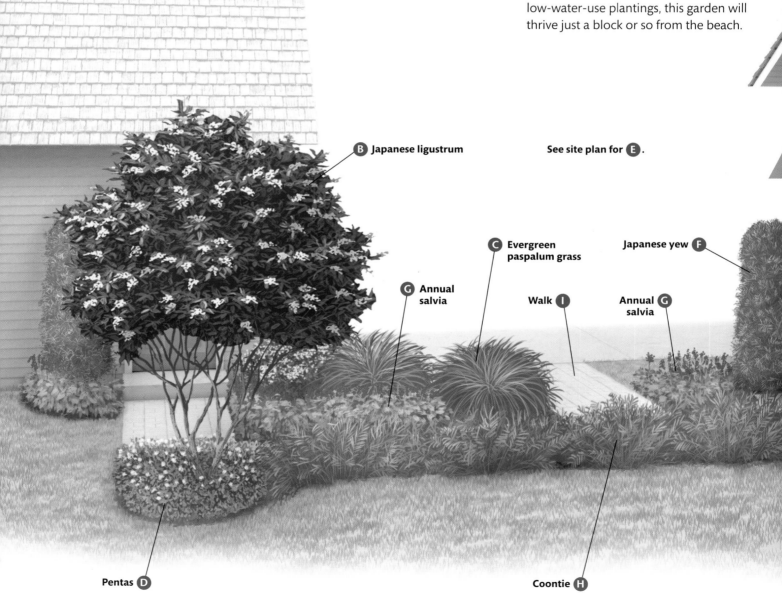

B Japanese ligustrum

See site plan for E .

C Evergreen paspalum grass

Japanese yew F

G Annual salvia

Walk I

Annual salvia G

Pentas D

Coontie H

Plants & Projects

If you don't need the path to the garage door as shown here, move the ligustrum near the garage, and plant additional coonties. Maintenance is not demanding—just seasonal pruning and cleanup to keep the shrubs and perennials healthy and periodic hand pruning to keep the hedges tidy.

Ⓐ Dwarf Burford holly (use 7)
This dense evergreen shrub can be easily clipped to create an informal, rounded hedge 30 in. high. For Zone 10, substitute with *Carrisa macrocarpa*, p. 102. See Recommended Hollies, *Ilex cornuta*, p. 109.

Ⓑ Japanese ligustrum (use 1)
The dark-green, waxy leaves of this small, broad-leaved evergreen tree are a perfect background for the fragrant white flowers it bears in early summer. Dark-blue berries follow in fall and winter. It grows quickly; prune lower branches as necessary to accommodate visitors using the walk. See *Ligustrum japonicum*, p. 111.

Ⓒ Evergreen paspalum grass (use 2)
This fine-textured ornamental grass forms an attractive dense mound that sways easily in the breeze. Tall spikes of small flowers appear in spring. See *Paspalum quadrifarium*, p. 113.

Ⓓ Pentas (use 4)
This perennial is a favorite of butterfly lovers. Its nectar-rich flowers bloom almost year-round. See Recommended Perennials, *Pentas lanceolata*, p. 115.

Ⓔ Plumbago (use 1)
The slender stems and small green leaves of this shrub are hidden for months under a cover of sky-blue flowers. The heavy bloom is even more eye-catching with the bright red salvia. See *Plumbago auriculata*, p. 117.

Ⓕ Japanese yew (use 2)
These evergreen sentinels anchor the house and garage to the path. Trim into a 3-ft.-wide-by-7-ft.-high column. See *Podocarpus macrophyllus*, p. 117.

Ⓖ Annual salvia (use 13)
These red flowering annuals greet visitors for months, even in harsh coastal conditions. See Recommended Annuals, *Salvia splendens*, p. 97.

Ⓗ Coontie (use 4)
A sculptural accent hedge that separates the walk from the lawn area, this plant adapts well to changing light conditions and will handle the increased shade as the ligustrum grows. See *Zamia pumila*, p. 123.

Ⓘ Walk
A concrete paver walk of 4 x 8- and 8 x 8-in. pavers suit this semiformal planting well. Concrete pavers come in a variety of colors and are an economical choice over traditional clay brick. See p. 132.

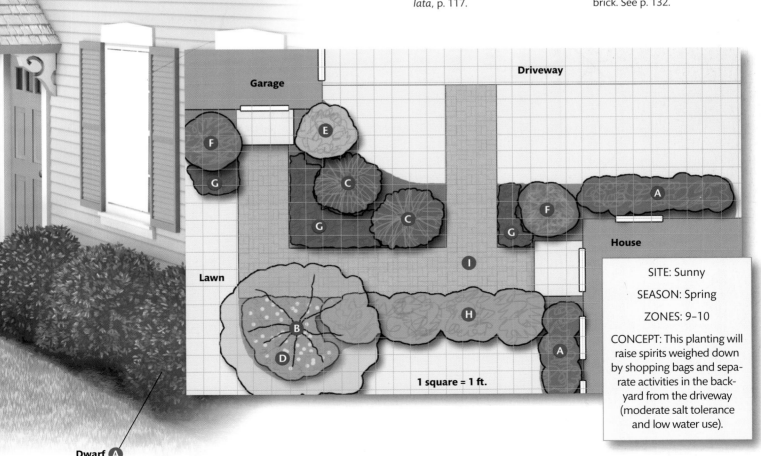

1 square = 1 ft.

SITE: Sunny

SEASON: Spring

ZONES: 9–10

CONCEPT: This planting will raise spirits weighed down by shopping bags and separate activities in the backyard from the driveway (moderate salt tolerance and low water use).

Dwarf Ⓐ Burford holly

Plantings and an attractive mix of paving materials make an informal transition from parking to the back door.

VARIATIONS ON A THEME

Plantings like these can make any journey to the back door a pleasure.

A back entry can be as elegant as the front. The flagstone patio, columnar evergreens, and fragrant mounded lavender bring to mind landscapes of southern France.

A magnolia tree surrounded by hostas and other shade-loving ground covers is a simple way to enhance a walkway. The magnolia will be in bloom in springtime, when the hostas are just emerging.

Covered connection

This design features a simple vine-covered pergola that makes something special of the journey to and from the back door. (You can extend the pergola and the foundation planting of silver buttonwood to suit your site.) A layered grouping of plantings reduces the lawn area and cuts maintenance.

The pindo, sabal, and saw palmetto palms offer a tropical look year-round. The sandpaper vine splashes lovely purple spring color overhead on the pergola. The palms and pergola provide light shade along the walkways.

Plants & Projects

Ⓐ **Orange bulbine** (use 14 plants)
The low grasslike mounds of bulbine will soon fill in to create a low mat with tall spikes covered in clusters of orange-yellow flowers from spring to fall. See *Bulbine frutescens* 'Hallmark', p. 100.

Ⓑ **Pindo palm** (use 1)
This sturdy palm will mature into a canopy of gray-green fronds, up to 5 ft. long each. Its stout trunk is decorated with the bases of old fronds and can reach 10 to 20 ft. growing slowly. In Zone 11 use the bottle palm (*Hyophorbe lagenicaulis*, p. 108). See *Butia capitata*, p. 102.

Ⓒ **Silver buttonwood** (use 8)
The silvery foliage of this shrub brings contrast to the garden. Hand-prune to just below the height of the window sills, keeping the top of the hedge narrower than the bottom. See *Conocarpus erectus* var. *sericeus*, p. 103.

Ⓓ **'New gold' lantana** (use 10)
Clusters of orange-yellow flowers top this evergreen perennial almost year-round. Their nectar attracts butterflies and night moths. See *Lantana* 'New Gold', p. 111.

Ⓔ **Queen's wreath** (use 2)
This twining evergreen vine will quickly cover the pergola. Heavy

Sabal palm **F**

See site plan for **J**.

Queen's wreath **E**

B Pindo palm

H Pergola

I Plumbago **A** Orange bulbine New gold **D** lantana Saw **G** palmeto Silver **C** buttonwood

clusters of showy purple flowers bloom in the spring. See *Petrea volubilis*, p. 116.

F **Sabal palm** (use 2)
This Southeast native palm provides a stately presence. Large flower clusters appear in the summer. See *Sabal palmetto*, p. 120.

G **Saw palmetto** (use 6)
This hardy, low clumping palm forms a dense ground cover. Ideal for coastal gardens, the silver form (*S. repens* 'Cinerea') is unique to Florida's coast. See *Serenoa repens*, p. 121.

H **Pergola**
This wooden pergola defines where the two walkways meet and creates a shady haven before entering the house. Consider enlarging the pergola to tuck a bench in the adjoining landscape bed. See p. 159.

See p. 37 for the following:

I **Plumbago** (use 2)

J **Walk**

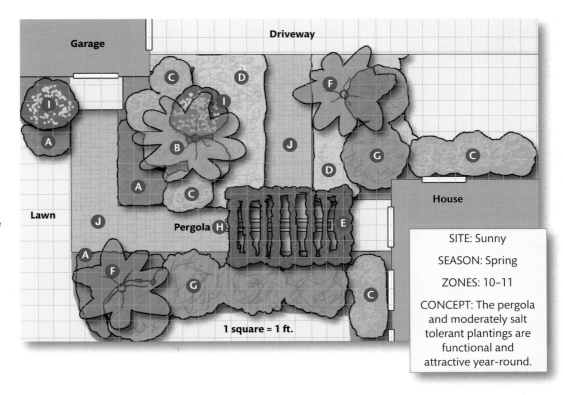

Garage

Driveway

Lawn

Pergola **H**

House

1 square = 1 ft.

SITE: Sunny

SEASON: Spring

ZONES: 10–11

CONCEPT: The pergola and moderately salt tolerant plantings are functional and attractive year-round.

Make a No-Mow Slope

A TERRACED OCEAN-SIDE PLANTING TRANSFORMS A STEEP SITE

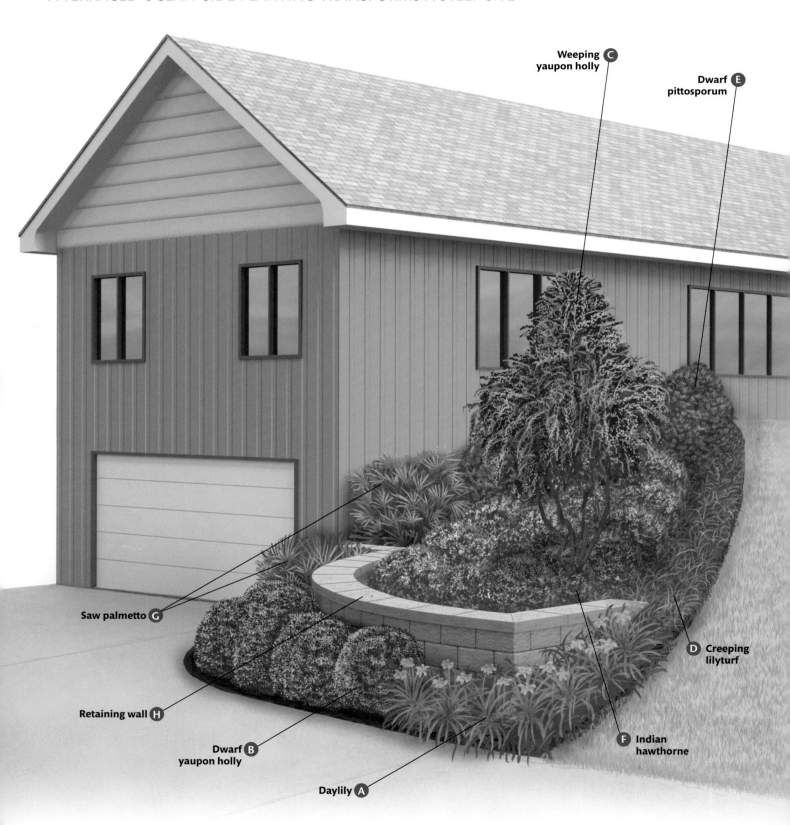

Weeping **C** yaupon holly

Dwarf **E** pittosporum

D Creeping lilyturf

F Indian hawthorne

Saw palmetto **G**

Retaining wall **H**

Dwarf **B** yaupon holly

Daylily **A**

Steep slopes can be a landscape nightmare and are a common feature of some houses directly on the ocean. They are also typically found around houses with walk-out basements or lower-level garages. They're a chore to mow, and they can present erosion and maintenance issues if you try to establish ground covers or plantings. One solution to this problem is shown here—tame the slope by building a low retaining wall and planting the area with interesting low-care trees, shrubs, and perennials. If you are on the ocean, these highly salt-tolerant plantings are just the ticket.

Here, the low wall creates two terraces that mirror the curve of the driveway. On the lower level, shapely woody evergreens rise above a carpet of colorful daylilies. On the top level, massed ranks of evergreen shrubs define the gentle curve of the remaining slope. Farther from the house, an attractive

tree with cascading foliage punctuates the end of the wall. Low-growing shrubs spill down the hill, uniting the upper and lower planting terraces and marking the transition to the front lawn. The planting is attractive whether viewed from above or below. Seen from the street, it frames the house and directs attention to the front entrance. It also screens the semi-private area of drive and garage from the more public entrance.

As the large shrubs grow, they overlap, creating horizontal layers that further reduce the visual impact of the once-dominant slope. The planting can easily be altered to accommodate existing foundation plants along the facade of the house. Or you can extend it to create a new foundation planting by adding more pittosporum and dwarf Indian hawthornes, with perhaps a saw palmetto or two where you need some height.

SITE: Sunny

SEASON: Summer

ZONES: 8–9

CONCEPT:
A retaining wall with low-water-use and high-salt-tolerance plants make a lovely hillside.

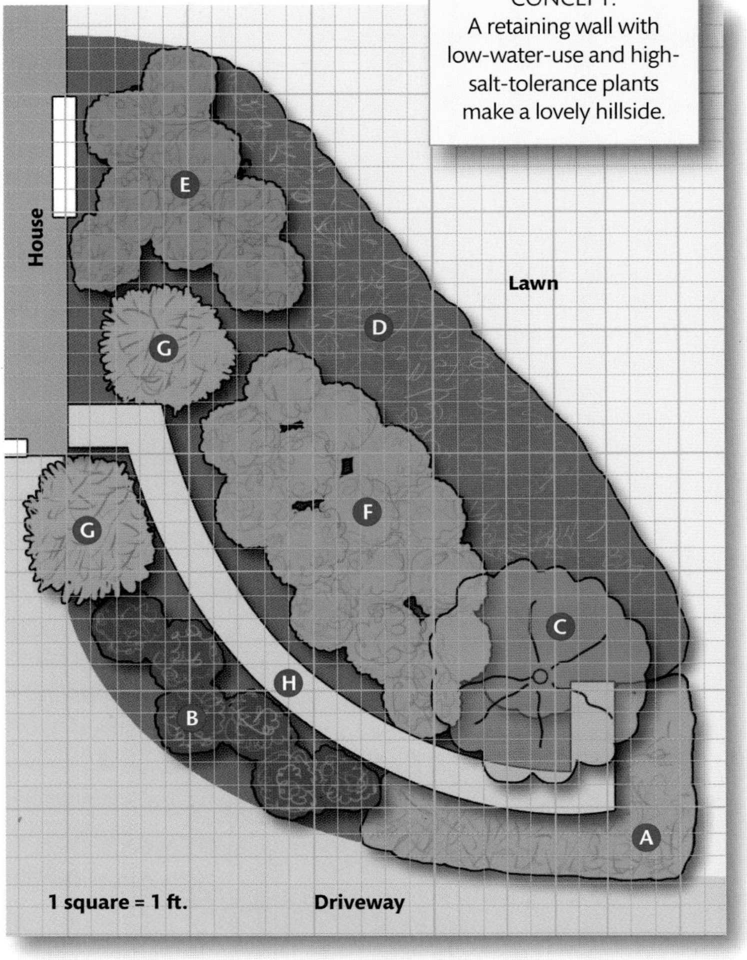

Plants & Projects

Building the retaining wall, reshaping the slope, and preparing the planting beds is a big job—you might want to hire someone with a small earthmover. Once the plants are established, this design will provide years of enjoyment with a minimum of maintenance.

Ⓐ Daylily (use 10 plants)
For an extended show of lovely lilylike flowers, combine early- and late-blooming cultivars of this useful perennial in your favorite colors. Its grassy foliage and cheerful blooms make a bright informal edging for the drive. For Zone 10 substitute with 'New Gold' lantana (p. 111). See *Hemerocallis cvs.*, p. 105.

Ⓑ Dwarf yaupon holly (use 6)
This small evergreen shrub forms compact mounds of small gray-green leaves and stays just the right size for a narrow planting bed. See Recommended Hollies, *Ilex vomitoria* 'Nana', p. 109.

Ⓒ Weeping yaupon holly (use 1)
The drooping branches of this small evergreen tree are clothed in small oval gray-green foliage. Female hollies bear loads of red berries during the winter months. Choose multitrunk specimens. See Recommended Hollies, *Ilex vomitoria* 'Pendula', p. 109.

Ⓓ Creeping lilyturf (use 80)
This evergreen perennial makes a grasslike mat of dark-green leaves up and down the slope. Small spikes of violet, purple, or white flowers appear in summer. See *Liriope spicata*, p. 111.

Ⓔ Dwarf pittosporum (use 8)
This evergreen shrub makes a lush, dressy hedge with shiny green leaves that does not need shearing. Its creamy white flowers scent the air in early summer. See *Pittosporum tobira* 'Wheeleri', p. 116.

Ⓕ Indian hawthorn (use 15)
Pink or white flowers cover the dark foliage of this low, spreading evergreen shrub in spring, followed by blue berries. Select any compact cultivar, and maintain at 24 to 30 in. height. See *Rhaphiolepis indica*, p. 118.

Ⓖ Saw palmetto (use 2)
This hardy, low clumping palm forms a dense ground cover that needs no maintenance. Ideal for coastal gardens, the silver form (*S. repens* 'Cinerea') is unique to Florida's coast. See *Serenoa repens*, p. 121.

Ⓗ Retaining wall
Using a precast concrete wall system. See p. 144.

House

Lawn

1 square = 1 ft.   Driveway

Design for a shady slope

If your slope is shaded by the house or a large tree nearby, here's a design similar to that on the previous pages but with a selection of shade-tolerant trees, shrubs, and perennials that have a low to moderate salt tolerance.

Evergreen and deciduous foliage gives the planting a year-round presence. But spring (shown here) is the prettiest season, beginning with dogwood blossoms and later the bulbs. At the base of the wall, the delicate fiddle-heads of the ferns emerge. Then all the shrubs chime in—papery white hydrangea blossoms and striking trusses of pink rhododendrons. When autumn arrives, the citrusy apricot scent of the tea olive will permeate the area and encourage visitors to find the small scented blossoms.

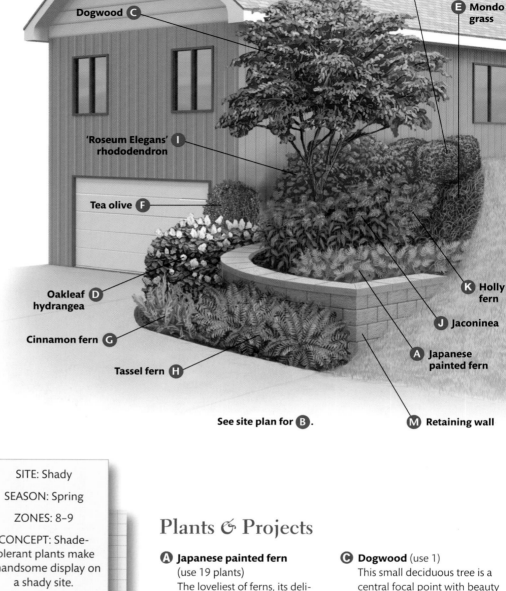

Dwarf **L** yaupon holly

Dogwood **C**

E Mondo grass

'Roseum Elegans' **I** rhododendron

Tea olive **F**

Oakleaf **D** hydrangea

Cinnamon fern **G**

Tassel fern **H**

K Holly fern

J Jaconinea

A Japanese painted fern

See site plan for **B**.

M Retaining wall

SITE: Shady

SEASON: Spring

ZONES: 8–9

CONCEPT: Shade-tolerant plants make a handsome display on a shady site.

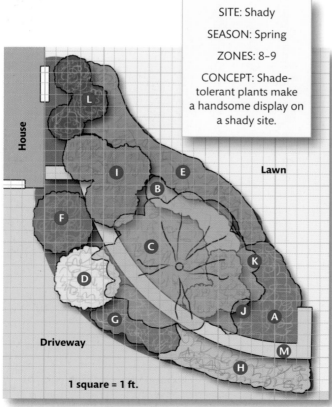

House

Lawn

Driveway

1 square = 1 ft.

Plants & Projects

A Japanese painted fern (use 19 plants)
The loveliest of ferns, its delicately colored deciduous fronds blend green, silver, and maroon. They also add a lush, rich look beneath the dogwoods. See Recommended Ferns *Athyrium niponicum* 'Pictum' p. 104.

B Bulbs
Under the dogwood and tucked between the holly fern and mondo grass is a spot for flowering bulbs, including caladiums, lily of the Nile, or rain lilies. If the bulbs go dormant in winter, consider enlarging the bed of mondo grass and interplanting with the bulbs of your choice. See Recommended Bulbs, p. 100.

C Dogwood (use 1)
This small deciduous tree is a central focal point with beauty in every season: white flower-like bracts in spring, lovely light-green foliage that turns crimson in fall, and bright-red winter berries. Remove the lower limbs to accommodate nearby shrubs. See *Cornus florida*, p. 103.

D Oakleaf hydrangea (use 1)
Oakleaf-shaped leaves and attractive reddish bark distinguish this deciduous shrub. It forms a handsome thicket at the base of the slope, with white flowers in spring and purple to red fall foliage. See *Hydrangea quercifolia*, p. 108.

E Mondo grass (use 25)
The thin, leathery, grassy leaves

of this evergreen perennial create an attractive deep-green mass up and down the slope. See *Ophiopogon japonicus*, p. 113.

F **Tea olive** (use 1)
This large, upright shrub of stiff, hollylike leaves blooms from winter until early spring with tiny, cream-colored blossoms that are powerfully fragrant. See *Osmanthus fragrans*, p. 113.

G **Cinnamon fern** (use 2)
The interesting fiddleheads of this hardy fern unfurl into broad, pale green, plumelike fronds that create a woodland feel at the base of the wall. Fronds turn gold, then brown in autumn. See Recommended Ferns, *Osmunda cinnamomea*, p. 104.

H **Tassel fern** (use 4)
This evergreen fern of stiff, finely divided fronds will soften the hard line of the retaining wall and provide a contrast to the neighboring cinnamon fern. See Recommended Ferns, *Polystichum polyblepharum*, p. 104.

I **'Roseum Elegans' rhododendron** (use 3)
This fast-growing evergreen shrub graces the top of the slope with its glossy leaves and rosy pink May flowers. See Recommended Rhododendrons and Azaleas, *Rhododendron* 'Roseum Elegans', p. 119.

J **Jacobinea** (use 3)
In summer, this shrub's large, coarse leaves are topped with showy pink flowers that look like feather dusters. See *Justicia carnea*, p. 110.

K **Holly fern** (use 8)
Glossy, coarse-textured leaves distinguish this dark-green fern. It makes a handsome companion to the finely textured Japanese painted fern. See Recommended Ferns, *Cyrtomium falcatum*, p. 104.

See p. 37 for the following:

L **Dwarf yaupon holly** (use 3)

M **Retaining wall**

VARIATIONS ON A THEME

How you tame a slope depends on your purpose as well as your ingenuity.

A terraced vegetable garden puts the produce at a handy height for care and harvesting.

This splendid border makes superb use of its sloping site. Walking along its edge, a visitor is rewarded with something of interest on every sight line, from foot-height to treetop.

Under the Old Shade Tree

CREATE A COZY GARDEN IN A COOL SPOT

This planting is designed to help homeowners blessed with a large shade tree make the most of their good fortune. A bench swing is provided, of course. What better spot to rest on a hot summer day and generate your own cooling breeze? But why stop there? The tree's high, wide canopy affords an ideal setting for a planting of understory shrubs and perennials. The result is a woodland garden that warrants a visit any day of the year.

The planting roughly coincides with the pool of shade cast by the tree. Enlarge or reduce the bed to match your shade situation. Keep the deep-shade lovers closer to the trunk. Evergreen shrubs and masses of mostly evergreen perennials extend around the perimeter. You can position the large mahonias to provide privacy, screen a view from the bench swing, or block early-morning or late-afternoon sun. Smaller plants with colorful foliage are placed nearer to the path and bench swing, where they can be appreciated at close range. The tea olive blooms in fall and releases its powerful citrusy apricot fragrance. The exotic pink blossoms of the jacobinea also shine.

Pretty as these flowers are, the real attraction here is the foliage. It's a little woodland oasis of leaves in a range of textures and colors that brighten the shade. Because almost all of the plants are evergreen, the display continues throughout the year—the variegated foliage of aucuba and Japanese painted fern provides a display against the backdrop of the tea olive, cast-iron plant, and mondo grass.

Plants & Projects

For best results, thin the tree canopy to produce dappled rather than deep shade. Also remove limbs up to a height of 8 ft. to provide headroom. The tree's roots compete for moisture with anything planted nearby. The plants here normally do well in these conditions but need watering during prolonged dry spells. Mulch generously, and add fresh mulch every year or two. (See planting under a shade tree, p. 162.)

A Cast-iron plant (use 21 plants)
This tough evergreen perennial thrives with little light or water. It will spread to form a mass of stiff green leaves at the base of the tree trunk. See *Aspidistra elatior*, p. 98.

B Japanese painted fern (use 15)
This lovely, deciduous fern is delicately colored in green, silver, and maroon. It adds a lush, rich look and a bright spot of color near the bench swing. See Recommended ferns, *Athyrium niponicum* 'Pictum', p. 104.

C Gold-dust aucuba (use 3)
These striking evergreen shrubs with shiny, leathery green leaves flecked with bright yellow provide a colorful backdrop for the bench swing. See *Aucuba japonica* 'Variegata', p. 98.

D Prostrate Japanese plum yew (use 8)
A low-growing evergreen shrub that spreads to form a wide cushion of dark-green needles that contrasts handsomely with the mahonia. See *Cephalotaxus harringtonia* 'Prostrata', p. 102.

E Holly fern (use 21)
Glossy, coarse-textured leaves distinguish this dark-green fern. It makes a handsome companion to the other ferns. See Recommended ferns, *Cyrtomium falcatum*, p. 104.

F Autumn fern (use 15)
The newly emerging fronds of this fern are a copper color, but they soon turn dark green as they mature. This clumping fern may freeze back to the ground in harsh winters. See Recommended ferns, *Dryopteris erythrosora*, p. 104.

G Jacobinea (use 3)
In summer, this shrub's large, coarse leaves are topped with showy pink flowers. See *Justicia carnea*, p. 110.

H Leatherleaf mahonia (use 9)
This large evergreen shrub forms an erect clump of stout stems and leathery dark-green foliage. Fragrant yellow spring flowers produce showy blue fruit clusters that attract birds. See *Mahonia bealei*, p. 112.

I Mondo grass (use 38)
The thin, leathery, grassy leaves of this evergreen perennial create an attractive deep-green carpet. See *Ophiopogon japonicus*, p. 113.

J Tea olive (use 1)
A slow-growing evergreen shrub with an open form in shade. The glossy dark-green leaves resemble those of holly. Bears sweet-scented flowers in late autumn and winter. See *Osmanthus fragrans*, p. 113.

K Bench swing
This adult version of a swing set is simple and elegant, but the grandkids will love to use it, too. See p. 158.

L Path
Natural fieldstone that's 1½ to 2 in. thick and at least 12 to 16 in. overall will create sure footing for this winding path. Fill in between the stones with wood chips. See p. 132.

SITE: Shady

SEASON: Fall

ZONES: 8–9

CONCEPT: A shade garden beneath a venerable old tree makes a lovely spot for sitting or strolling.

Prostrate Japanese D plum yew

Autumn fern F

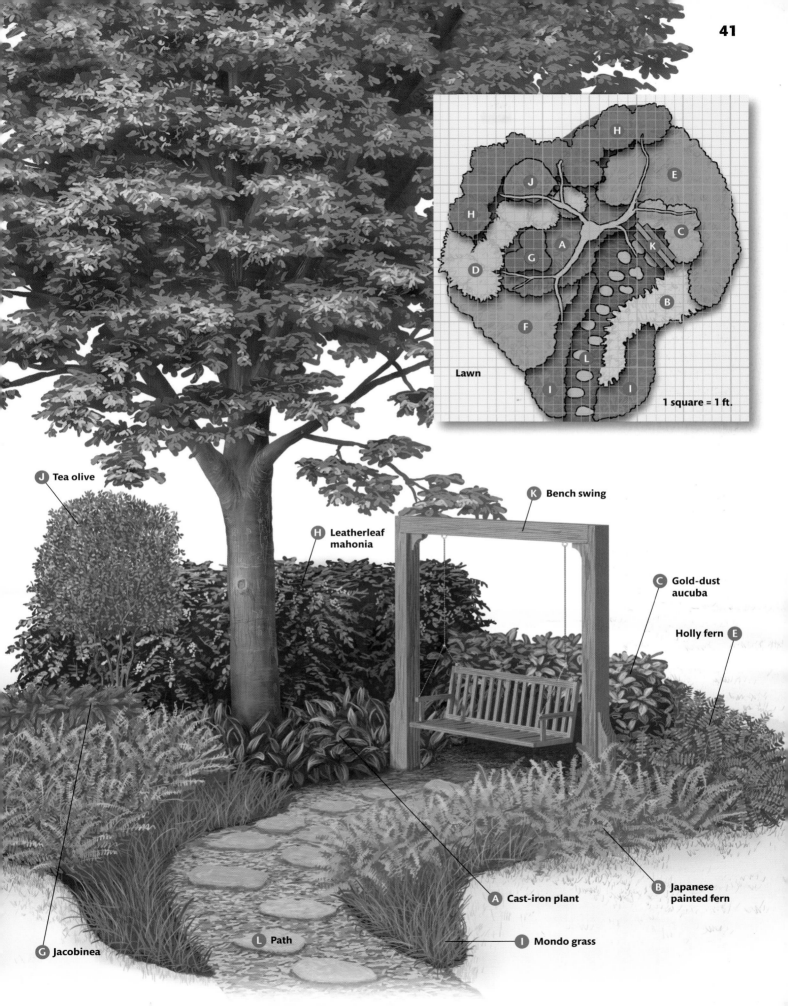

1 square = 1 ft.

Lawn

J Tea olive

H Leatherleaf mahonia

K Bench swing

C Gold-dust aucuba

Holly fern E

A Cast-iron plant

B Japanese painted fern

G Jacobinea

L Path

I Mondo grass

VARIATIONS ON A THEME

Take advantage of a venerable specimen to create a special garden spot and don't forget the seating.

Colorful accents in cushions, glazed pots, and flowers enhance this private garden.

A collection of shade trees and large screening shrubs is an ideal spot for a simple gravel patio.

Under the dappled light of this river birch, rose bushes receive enough sun to bloom abundantly.

Color and texture in dry shade

A mature pine tree—its lower limbs either shed naturally or trimmed off, its upper branches forming a graceful spreading crown—can shelter a shade garden. Casting lighter shade and with less-competitive roots than those of many shade trees, it allows a wider range of understory plants.

This planting replaces several tall shrubs in the previous design with ferns to produce the feel of an open woodland. If you prefer more screening than provided here, work in a clump of mahonias or gold-dust aucuba.

Containers with annuals set into the masses of mondo grass provide colorful focal points that change through the seasons. They are visible from the bench or from outside of the garden.

Plants & Projects

Ⓐ **Annuals** (as needed)
Growing annuals in containers eliminates the problem of nutrient and moisture competition from the roots of the shade tree. Change these plantings often for seasonal interest. In summer (the season shown here), try begonias, impatiens, or moss rose. The terra-cotta containers are a nice color contrast to the dark greens of the mondo grass. See Recommended Annuals, p. 96.

Ⓑ **'Elegans' hosta** (use 3)
The huge, blue-gray, textured leaves of this perennial are a marvelous centerpiece among the ferns. White summer flowers are a bonus. In Zone 9 use 'Shishigashira' *camellia*, p. 102, instead. See *Hosta sieboldiana* 'Elegans', p. 106.

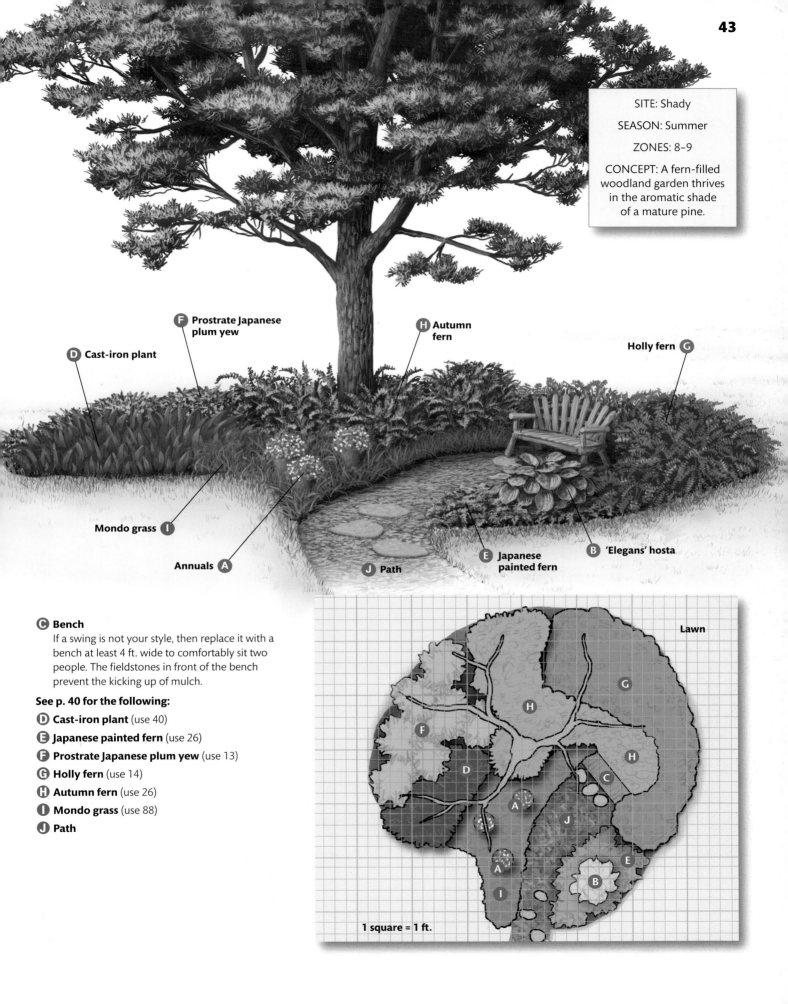

SITE: Shady

SEASON: Summer

ZONES: 8–9

CONCEPT: A fern-filled woodland garden thrives in the aromatic shade of a mature pine.

F Prostrate Japanese plum yew

D Cast-iron plant

H Autumn fern

Holly fern G

Mondo grass I

Annuals A

J Path

E Japanese painted fern

B 'Elegans' hosta

C Bench

If a swing is not your style, then replace it with a bench at least 4 ft. wide to comfortably sit two people. The fieldstones in front of the bench prevent the kicking up of mulch.

See p. 40 for the following:

D Cast-iron plant (use 40)

E Japanese painted fern (use 26)

F Prostrate Japanese plum yew (use 13)

G Holly fern (use 14)

H Autumn fern (use 26)

I Mondo grass (use 88)

J Path

Lawn

1 square = 1 ft.

A Pleasant Passage

RECLAIM A NARROW SIDE YARD FOR A SHADE GARDEN

Many residential lots include a slim strip of land between the house and a property line. Usually overlooked by everyone except children and dogs racing between the front yard and the back, this often shady corridor can become a valued addition to the landscape.

The wall of the house and a tall, opaque fence on the property line shade the space most of the day and give it a closed-in feeling, like that of a long empty hallway or a narrow room. In the design shown here, a flagstone path curves gently under an arbor and through a selection of trees, shrubs, and perennials to make a garden that invites adults, and even children, to linger as they stroll from one part of the property to another. The curved path makes the corridor seem wider, and the plants clustered at the bends create cozy "garden rooms." The arbor entry is marked by broad-leaved evergreens with flowers that entice visitors in spring. The handsome foliage and flowers of azaleas form the "walls" of the garden rooms. An edging of painted ferns, holly ferns, and mondo grass adds color, while a magnolia about halfway along the path provides a light roof of fragrant flowers and glossy green leaves.

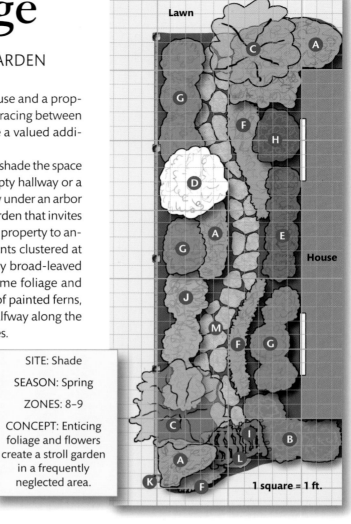

SITE: Shade

SEASON: Spring

ZONES: 8–9

CONCEPT: Enticing foliage and flowers create a stroll garden in a frequently neglected area.

1 square = 1 ft.

Plants & Projects

Lay the flagstone path first, taking time to make graceful curves—they're instrumental in making the space seem larger than it is. Upkeep is minimal: just spring and fall cleanup, pruning shrubs, and renewing the mulch every year.

Ⓐ Japanese painted fern (use 16) Lovely deciduous ferns add a lush, rich touch beneath the ligustrums, their delicately painted fronds blending together green, silver, and maroon. See Recommended Ferns, *Athyrium niponicum* 'Pictum', p. 104.

Ⓑ 'Shishigashira' camellia (use 2) Blooming in fall and winter, this evergreen shrub is the last to provide seasonal bloom color, with the azaleas appearing first in the spring. See *Camellia sasanqua* 'Shishigashira', p. 102.

Ⓒ Japanese ligustrum (use 2) These small trees mark the entrances to the garden with glossy evergreen leaves that showcase fragrant white flowers in early summer and dark blue-black berries in fall and winter. Grows umbrella-like, with multiple trunks. Remove the lower limbs so you can walk underneath. See *Ligustrum japonicum*, p. 111.

Ⓓ 'Little Gem' magnolia (use 1) This smaller cousin of the evergreen southern magnolia fits perfectly in this narrow side yard. Spring's fragrant white flowers are followed by large pods of bright-red seeds that songbirds love. See *Magnolia grandiflora* 'Little Gem', p. 112.

Ⓔ Leatherleaf mahonia (use 4) This upright, straight-stemmed evergreen shrub is ideal for tight, shady spaces. Dark blue-green leaves set off the fragrant yellow flowers in late winter and early spring. Soon, sky blue berries ripen and last through fall. See *Mahonia bealei*, p. 112.

Ⓕ Mondo grass (use 26) The thin, leathery, grassy leaves of this evergreen perennial create an attractive ground cover edging the path. See *Ophiopogon japonicus*, p. 113.

Ⓖ 'George Lindley Taber' azalea (use 7) Noted for its large, light-pink spring flowers, this evergreen azalea also offers a loose, soft form that is pleasing beside the path. See Recommended Rhododendrons and Azaleas, *Rhododendron* 'George Lindley Taber' p. 119.

Ⓗ Plumleaf azalea (use 1) This deciduous shrub adds as much as a month of midsummer color to the garden with its large clusters of orange-red flowers. Delicately textured foliage shows well against the fence, too. See Recommended Rhododendrons and Azaleas *Rhododendron prunifolium*, p. 119.

Ⓘ Confederate jasmine (use 2) On early summer evenings you can sit nearby and enjoy the fragrance of this evergreen vine's white flowers. Twining stems of glossy dark-green leaves will climb and cover the arbor. See *Trachelospermum jasminoides*, p. 122.

Ⓙ Holly fern (use 8) Glossy, coarse-textured leaves distinguish this dark-green fern. It makes a handsome companion to the surrounding ferns. See *Cyrtomium falcatum*, p. 104.

Ⓚ Fence This simple privacy fence has a stylish touch—a simple arc cut into the top of each panel. See p. 157. As an alternative, build a straight-top privacy screen that allows air circulation. See p. 156.

Ⓛ Arbor This vine-covered arbor marks the entrance to the side garden. See p. 155.

Ⓜ Path Providing just the right touch of informality, flagstones in random sizes trace a gracefully curving route through the planting. See p. 132.

C Japanese ligustrum

D 'Little Gem' magnolia

C Japanese ligustrum

H Plumleaf azalea

E Leatherleaf mahonia

G 'George Lindley Taber' azalea

M Path

I Confederate jasmine

B 'Shishigashira' camellia

A Japanese painted fern

J Holly fern

F Mondo grass

I Arbor

K Fence

A handsome brick-lined gravel walk, an attractive gate, window boxes, and vines create a passage of formal simplicity.

VARIATIONS ON A THEME

A narrow passage is a design challenge. These examples succeed in creating spaces you want to, rather than have to, walk through.

Shade-loving plants and crushed stone propel feet along this stone-edged walkway.

Stroll for herbs

Let the sunshine in to grow herbs and fragrant plants. Get privacy from a hedge that won't block sunlight. The evergreen anise with scented foliage encloses an equally appealing stroll garden with a culinary purpose. Other additions include Burford hollies at the entrances, multiple containers of herbs, a kumquat set amongst perennials, and an evergreen ground cover. Additional stepping-stones provide easy access to the bounty of herbs. Don't attempt this stroll without a harvest basket.

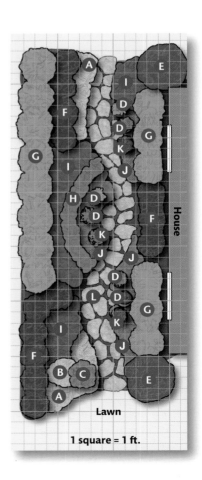

1 square = 1 ft.

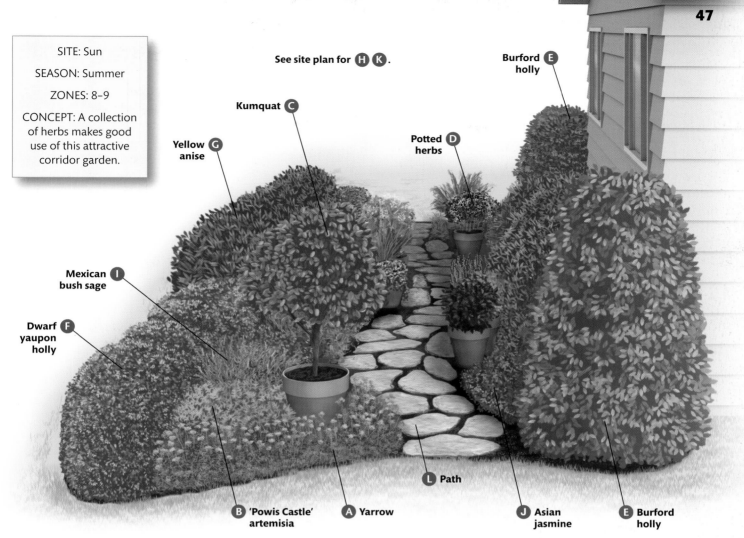

SITE: Sun

SEASON: Summer

ZONES: 8–9

CONCEPT: A collection of herbs makes good use of this attractive corridor garden.

See site plan for **H** **K**.

Burford holly **E**

Kumquat **C**

Potted herbs **D**

Yellow anise **G**

Mexican bush sage **I**

Dwarf yaupon holly **F**

B 'Powis Castle' artemisia

A Yarrow

L Path

J Asian jasmine

E Burford holly

Plants & Projects

A **Yarrow** (use 7 plants)
Brush against the fine gray-green foliage of this plant as you stroll to release a pungent aroma. The clusters of flowers are held on tall stalks and available in a variety of colors. See *Achillea* spp., p. 94.

B **'Powis Castle' artemisia** (use 1)
This mounding perennial has aromatic lacy silver foliage adding to the silvery foliage of the yarrow and Mexican bush sage. See *Artemisia* 'Powis Castle', p. 96.

C **Kumquat** (use 1)
This miniature citrus is grown in a terra-cotta container that can be brought inside if the temperatures are going to drop below 20°F. The showy orange fruits are attractive and delicious. See *Fortunella* spp., p. 105.

D **Herbs** (as needed)
Herbs grow best in the South when in containers. The improved drainage and cooling effect of terra-cotta allow herbs to handle the heat and rains. Choose a variety of herbs, and harvest often. See Recommended Herbs, p. 106.

E **Burford holly** (use 2)
This evergreen shrub is easily maintained in a conical form by shearing. Its large leaves are a great backdrop for a fine show of red winter berries. See Recommended Hollies, *Ilex cornuta* 'Burfordii', p. 109.

F **Dwarf yaupon holly** (use 13)
This small evergreen shrub forms compact mounds of small gray-green leaves and stays just the right size for this narrow side yard. See Recommended Hollies, *Ilex vomitoria* 'Nana', p. 109.

G **Yellow anise** (use 14)
This adaptable evergreen shrub should be on everyone's wish list of hedges. It wears a thick coat of yellow-green elliptical leaves reaching all the way to the ground. When the leaves are cut or crushed, they release a pleasing licorice scent. See *Illicium parviflorum*, p. 108.

H **Rosemary** (use 6)
This well-known kitchen herb is also a handsome evergreen shrub. Its gray-green, needle-like leaves are fragrant and tasty. Plant and trim into a solid hedge, 18 in. high. See Recommended Herbs, *Rosmarinus officinalis*, p. 107.

I **Mexican bush sage** (use 8)
This beautiful evergreen perennial adds soft texture and blue flower color that invites you to touch and stroke. This velvety plant is spotted along the path to draw your eye and feet along. See *Salvia leucantha*, p. 120.

J **Asian jasmine** (use 12)
This evergreen vine creates a dense mat of shiny leaves that smothers most weeds and holds up well under foot traffic. A perfect backdrop to the containers. See *Trachelospermum asiaticum*, p. 122.

K **Containers** (use 10)
Terra-cotta containers are recommended here for their excellent drainage and cooling effect on roots in the hot summer months of the coastal South. Place each pot on a level stepping-stone on compacted soil that is free of organic debris.

See p. 44 for the following:

L Path

Colorful Collection

MAKE YOUR DAILY MAIL RUN A PERENNIAL PLEASURE

For some, the lowly mailbox may seem a surprising candidate for landscaping. But posted like a sentry by the driveway entrance, the mailbox is highly visible to visitors and passersby. And it is one of the few places on your property that you visit nearly every day. A handsome planting, such as the one shown here, pleases the passing public and rewards your daily journey, as well as that of your mail carrier.

Plantings around mailboxes too often suffer from timidity—too few plants in too little space. This design makes a bold display, covering a good-size area with color for many months of the year. The long-blooming perennials here are all well suited to the hot, sunny, and often dry conditions that prevail by most street-side mailboxes.

Mail arrives year-round, and no season is overlooked in this planting. Summer is the most colorful, with cheery flowers in blue, pink, red, and gold, highlighted by the yucca's eye-catching spires of creamy white blossoms. Then the evergreen foliage of many of the plants comes into its own, making the planting look fresh. A simple stone edging contains the bed and separates the lawn from the colorful low-water-use plantings.

'Golden Sword' H yucca

Stone edging I

Plants & Projects

These are all tough, heat-tolerant plants, but they do best if you add a bark mulch to help conserve moisture. Maintenance is minimal. In early spring, cut back the old stems and renew the mulch. Then enjoy your trips to the mailbox.

A **'Apple Blossom' yarrow** (use 6 plants)
A tough perennial with aromatic, delicate-looking gray-green foliage, it bears flat clusters of tiny clear pink flowers through the summer months. It's a fine companion for the neighboring sedum and autumn sage. See *Achillea* spp., p. 94.

B **'Powis Castle' artemisia** (use 1)
A perennial that forms a large mound of lacy gray-green aromatic foliage, artemisia can be evergreen in areas with mild winters. See *Artemisia* 'Powis Castle', p. 96.

C **Blue daze** (use 5)
This low-growing perennial is a great performer. The gray-green leaves are covered nearly year-round with clear, bright blue flowers. See Recommended Perennials, *Evolvulus glomeratus*, p. 114.

D **'New Gold' lantana** (use 2)
Clusters of rich orange-yellow flowers top this evergreen perennial almost year-round. Their nectar attracts butterflies and night moths. See *Lantana* 'New Gold', p. 111.

E **'Goldsturm' coneflower** (use 3)
This perennial makes a late-summer show of large, golden-yellow daisylike flowers with black centers above a mound of dark-green foliage. See Recommended Perennials, *Rudbeckia fulgida* 'Goldsturm', p. 115.

F **'Cherry Chief' autumn sage** (use 1)
Loose clusters of cherry-red flowers cover this bushy perennial from summer through fall. Evergreen in mild winters. See *Salvia greggii*, p. 120.

G **Stoke's aster** (use 3)
From June to frost, this perennial produces pretty blue flowers atop evergreen foliage. See *Stokesia laevis*, p. 121.

H **'Golden Sword' yucca** (use 1)
This shrubby perennial offers sword-shaped evergreen leaves striped with yellow and gold. It bears showy clusters of creamy flowers on tall stems in summer that attract butterflies. See *Yucca filamentosa*, p. 123.

I **Stone edging**
Keep the lawn and bed separate with an edging of small fieldstones, installed using the method described for installing a brick edging on p. 134.

SITE: Sunny

SEASON: Spring

ZONES: 8–9

CONCEPT: Low-water-use perennials enhance your trips to the mailbox.

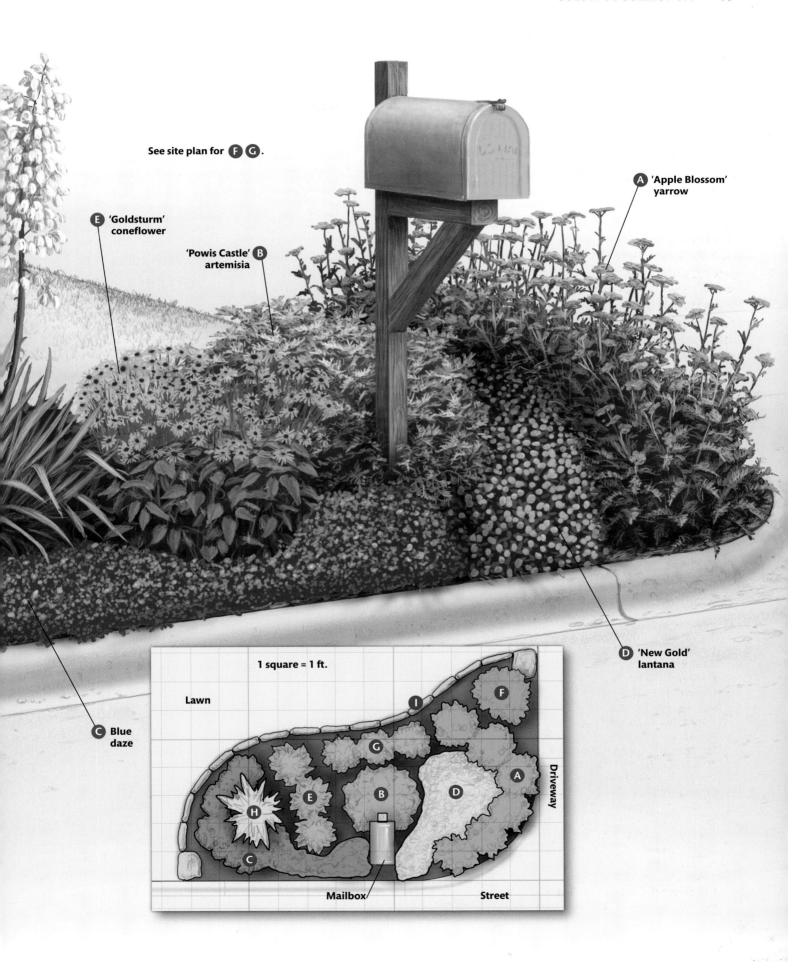

See site plan for **F** **G**.

E 'Goldsturm' coneflower

A 'Apple Blossom' yarrow

'Powis Castle' **B** artemisia

D 'New Gold' lantana

C Blue daze

1 square = 1 ft.

Lawn

I

F

G

H

E

B

D

A

Driveway

C

Mailbox

Street

Foliage selection

Foliage can create as much fanfare as flowers, with even less fuss. Here, a dark-green carpet of dwarf Asian jasmine replaces the flowering ground covers in the previous design. Dwarf heavenly bamboos provide colorful foliage year-round and add to the variety of leaf textures offered by the yucca and artemisia, which repeat from the previous design. The spiky foliage of the tall spring-blooming African irises alongside the mailbox looks good long after the elegant flowers have passed. Once established, these tough plants require only seasonal care and cleanup.

SITE: Sunny

SEASON: Fall

ZONES: 8–9

CONCEPT: Foliage rivals flowers for eye-catching interest in this low water-use planting.

See site plan for **E**.

D 'Powis Castle' artemisia

F 'Golden Sword' yucca

'Harbour Dwarf' **B** heavenly bamboo

White **A** African iris

Asian **C** jasmine

'Harbour Dwarf' **B** heavenly bamboo

Stone edging **G**

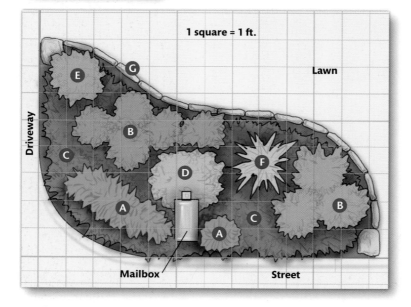

1 square = 1 ft.

Lawn

Driveway

Mailbox

Street

Plants & Projects

A **White African iris** (use 3 plants)
This iris for the South reaches 24 to 30 in. high sporting white flowers with violet and yellow throats in the spring. The foliage is handsome when the flowers fade. See *Dietes vegeta*, p. 103.

B **'Harbour Dwarf' heavenly bamboo** (use 8)
A dwarf cultivar, this evergreen shrub has a low, spreading growth habit with striking foliage. See *Nandina domestica*, p. 112.

C **Asian jasmine** (use 13)
This evergreen vine creates a dense mat of shiny leaves that smothers most weeds and holds up well under foot traffic. See *Trachelospermum asiaticum*, p. 122.

See p. 48 for the following:

D **'Powis Castle' artemisia** (use 1)

E **'Cherry Chief' autumn sage** (use 1)

F **'Golden Sword' yucca** (use 1)

G **Stone edging**

VARIATIONS ON A THEME

On the accompanying pages, we've featured designs that will enhance any mailbox. But the box itself can also be an attraction.

This streaky blue box is an excellent foil for the red-orange flowers of the honeysuckle twined around the post.

The colors of this box and post work nicely with the surrounding floral display.

Surrounded by white blooming hibiscus and seashells at its base, this box is well grounded.

Elegant Symmetry

MAKE A FORMAL GARDEN FOR THE BACKYARD

Formal landscaping often lends dignity to the public areas around a home. (See "Formal and Friendly," p. 24.) Formality can also be rewarding in a more private setting. There, the groomed plants, geometric lines, and symmetrical layout of a formal garden can help to organize the surrounding landscape, provide an elegant area for entertaining, or simply be enjoyed for their own sake.

A series of hedges and edgings define this small garden, punctuated by tidy evergreen trees and shrubs at the corners. Flowers contribute color to the garden for many months from spring right through the autumn months. The foliage looks good year-round.

Formal gardens like this one look self-contained on paper. But even more than other types of landscaping, actual formal gardens work well only when carefully correlated with other elements in the landscape, such as the house, garage, patio, and major plantings. Transitions between formal and more-casual areas are particularly important. Separating areas with expanses of lawn, changes of level, or plantings that screen sight lines helps formal and informal elements co-exist pleasingly.

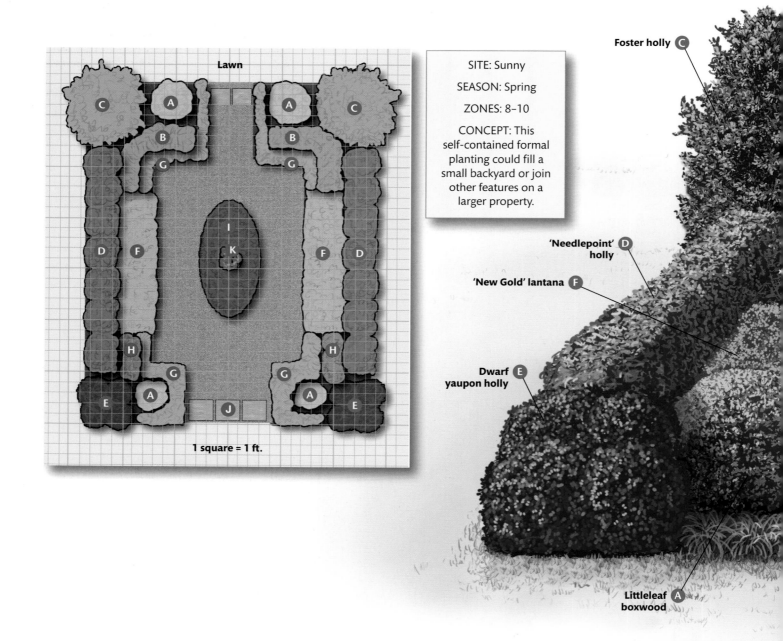

Lawn

SITE: Sunny

SEASON: Spring

ZONES: 8–10

CONCEPT: This self-contained formal planting could fill a small backyard or join other features on a larger property.

1 square = 1 ft.

Foster holly **C**

'Needlepoint' **D** holly

'New Gold' lantana **F**

Dwarf **E** yaupon holly

Littleleaf **A** boxwood

Plants & Projects

Shaping plants for a formal garden takes patience and persistence. The holly hedge will need a few years to become full, and the little-leaf boxwoods will require regular shearing to look their best. The other trees and shrubs can have loosely formal shapes as shown here or be sheared to a more rigid geometry.

Ⓐ Littleleaf boxwood (use 4)
This evergreen shrub naturally forms a compact globe. Small, bright-green glossy leaves give it a fine texture. See *Buxus microphylla*, p. 102.

Ⓑ White African iris (use 10)
This iris for the South reaches 24 to 30 in. high, sporting white flowers with violet and yellow throats in the spring. See *Dietes vegeta*, p. 103.

Ⓒ Foster holly (use 2)
The pyramidal form and deep green leaves of this broad-leaved evergreen tree add visual weight to the design. It needs little pruning and bears lots of rich red winter berries. See Recommended Hollies, *Ilex x attenuata* 'Foster #2', p. 109.

Ⓓ 'Needlepoint' holly (use 14)
A dense evergreen shrub ideal for a hedge, with shiny leaves and a magnificent show of red winter berries. In Zone 10 use natal plum, *Carrisa macrocarpa*, instead (p. 102). See Recommended Hollies, *Ilex cornuta*p. 109.

Ⓔ Dwarf yaupon holly (use 14)
This small evergreen shrub forms compact mounds of small gray-green leaves and stays just the right size for this formal garden. See Recommended Hollies, *Ilex vomitoria* 'Nana', p. 109.

Ⓕ 'New Gold' lantana (use 12)
Clusters of rich orange-yellow flowers top this evergreen perennial almost year-round. Trim in spring and fall to shape and promote flowering. See *Lantana* 'New Gold', p. 111.

Ⓖ Lilyturf (use 44)
Spiky grasslike clumps of evergreen leaves make this perennial an ideal edging. It bears small purple flowers in late summer. Space 1 ft. apart. See *Liriope muscari*, p. 111.

Ⓗ Scarlet sage (use 4)
A bushy perennial often grown as an annual. Bright-red flowers heat up the garden's corners for months in the summer and fall. See *Salvia coccinea*, p. 120.

Ⓘ Asian jasmine (use 10)
This evergreen vine creates a dense mat of shiny leaves that smothers most weeds and holds up well under foot traffic. A perfect rug for a decorative container. See *Trachelospermum asiaticum*, p. 122.

Ⓙ Path
Crushed stone looks just right here. Flagstones across the entries help keep stones out of the lawn. See p. 134.

Ⓚ Container
Choose a tall decorative container or a bowl on a pedestal as shown here. Plant with cascading annuals, such as moss rose (p. 97), or perennials such as blue daze, moneywort, or fan flower (pp. 114–115).

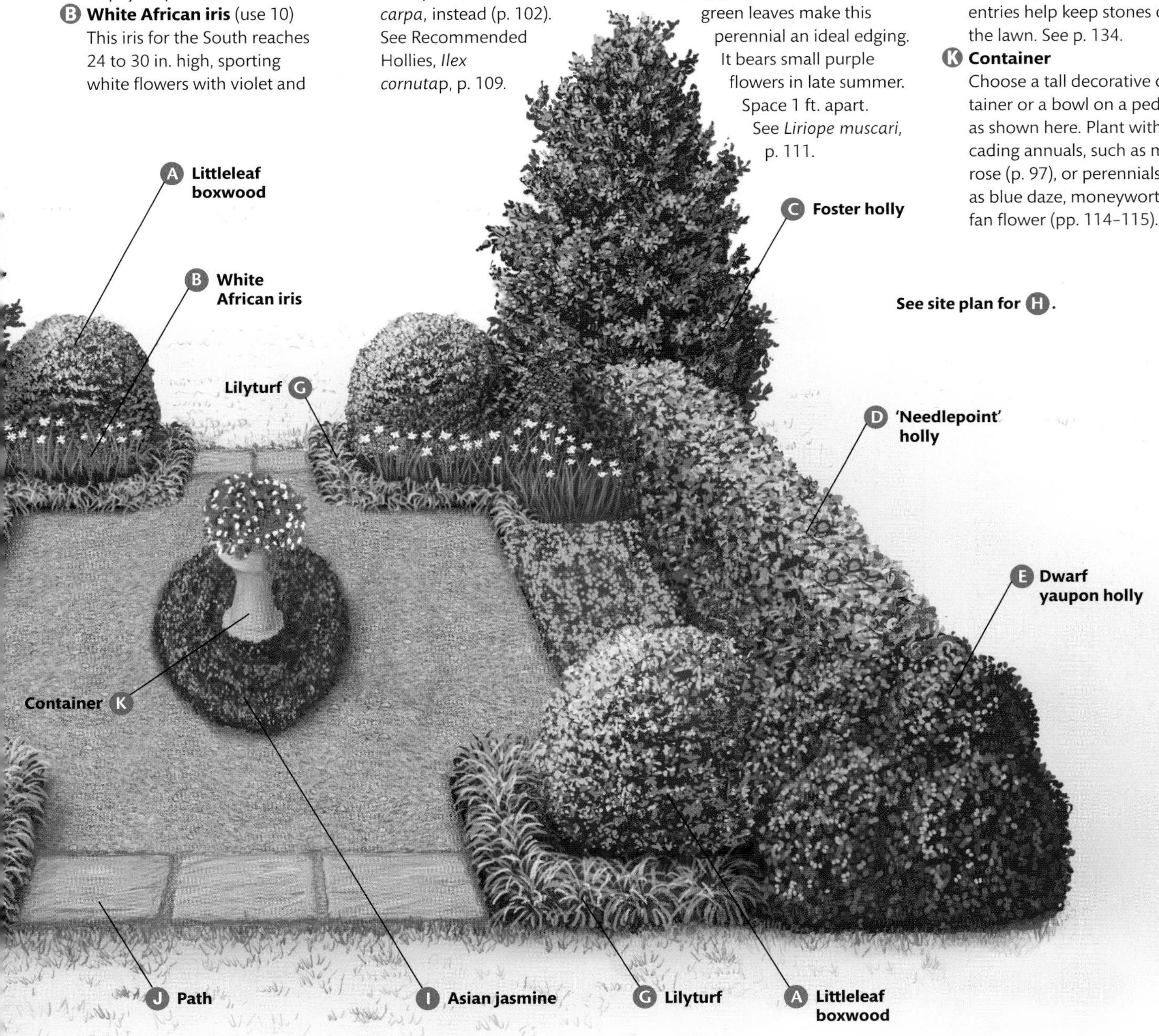

Ⓐ Littleleaf boxwood

Ⓑ White African iris

Lilyturf Ⓖ

Container Ⓚ

Ⓒ Foster holly

See site plan for Ⓗ.

Ⓓ 'Needlepoint' holly

Ⓔ Dwarf yaupon holly

Ⓙ Path   Ⓘ Asian jasmine   Ⓖ Lilyturf   Ⓐ Littleleaf boxwood

A palm terrace

In this design, which features moderate-to-high-salt-tolerant plants, a small terrace with table and chairs is given a formal setting, providing a lovely spot for an intimate lunch or an hour with a favorite book.

The geometry of this patio garden is similar to that of the previous plan, but with an allée of palms. Here, an avenue of lawn approaches the terrace. In summer, the planting abounds in flowers offering vivid colors. On the terrace, containers with lively warm-season annuals augment the sights and scents of the summer garden. Cool-season annuals make the garden an inviting spot on sunny days from fall to spring.

SITE: Sunny

SEASON: Late Spring

ZONES: 9–11

CONCEPT: This formal setting for intimate gatherings near the ocean is enhanced by palms and colorful flowers.

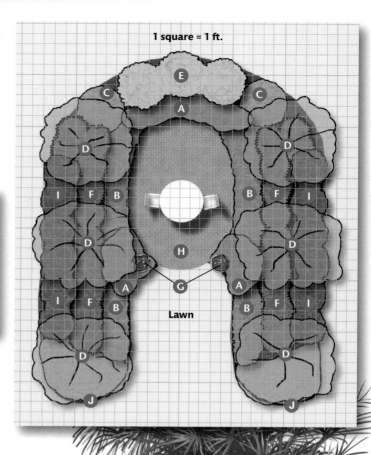

1 square = 1 ft.

Lawn

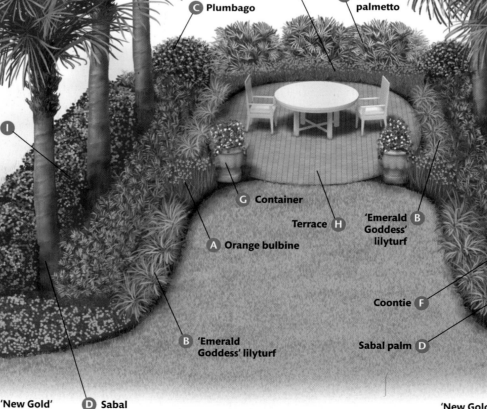

Sabal palm D

Orange A bulbine

C Plumbago

E Saw palmetto

Dwarf I yaupon holly

G Container

Terrace H

'Emerald B Goddess' lilyturf

A Orange bulbine

Coontie F

B 'Emerald Goddess' lilyturf

Sabal palm D

J 'New Gold' lantana

D Sabal palm

'New Gold' J lantana

Plants & Projects

Ⓐ Orange bulbine (use 30 plants)
The low grasslike mounds of bulbine will soon fill in to create a low mat covered with clusters of tiny orange-yellow flowers from spring to fall. See *Bulbine frutescens* 'Hallmark', p. 100.

Ⓑ 'Emerald Goddess' lilyturf (use 30)
Grasslike clumps of 2-ft.-high evergreen leaves make an attractive year-round edging. Purple flower spikes appear in summer. For Zone 11 use blue daze (p. 114). See *Liriope muscari*, p. 111.

Ⓒ Plumbago (use 2)
The slender stems and small green leaves of this shrub are hidden for months under a cover of sky blue flowers. The heavy bloom is even more eye-catching with the bright-red salvia. See *Plumbago auriculata*, p. 117.

Ⓓ Sabal palm (use 6)
This Southern native provides a stately presence as well as a bit of shade to the terrace. Large flower clusters appear in the summer. See *Sabal palmetto*, p. 120.

Ⓔ Saw palmetto (use 3)
This hardy palm forms a dense ground cover that needs no maintenance. Ideal for coastal gardens, the silver form (*S. repens* 'Cinerea') is unique to Florida's coast. See *Serenoa repens*, p. 121.

Ⓕ Coontie (use 22)
A sculptural accent plant that flanks either side of the terrace, this plant does not require any trimming and will create a handsome low hedgerow. See *Zamia pumila*, p. 123.

Ⓖ Containers
For bright accents on the terrace, fill these formal containers with long-blooming annuals. Replace the plantings in fall and spring. See Recommended Annuals, p. 96.

Ⓗ Terrace
An oval terrace accommodates a small table and chairs and can be built in a weekend or two. We've shown brick here; select paving material to complement your home. See p. 133.

See p. 53 for the following:

Ⓘ Dwarf yaupon holly (use 12),
for Zone 11 use natal plum, p. 102.

Ⓙ 'New Gold' lantana (use 8)

A green jungle with towering palms flanks the manicured turf runway.

VARIATIONS ON A THEME

Formal gardens often require more from a gardener—more time, more planning, more effort. Results like these are ample reward for such industry.

This garden-in-the-round is a striking study in foliage textures. When in bloom, the azaleas in the central bed transform the planting's character.

Combining tightly and loosely trimmed shrubs, the pillowy, layered masses of this garden invite a restful stroll.

Garden by the Pool

ENHANCE YOUR POOLSIDE PLEASURES

The cool, blue water of a backyard swimming pool can be like a little slice of heaven in summer's heat and humidity. But too often the pool is surrounded by a slab of concrete and a chain-link fence—hardly an oasis. Because your pool is likely to be at the center of your home's outdoor activities, its setting should be a welcoming gathering place.

It doesn't take an enormous budget or a complete overhaul of the landscape to create a poolside oasis. The design shown here demonstrates that a relatively small project can work magic. The plantings, patio, and arbor help blend the pool more naturally with its surroundings while creating opportunities for entertaining and relaxing. If you're ambitious, you can easily extend the elements of the design around the pool. Or add to the setting over the years.

While creating an intimate setting near the pool, the design's height and depth look good from a distance, too. All of the plants here are low-maintenance, broad-leaved evergreens with smooth rather than bristly or prickly leaves. They hold on to their foliage throughout the year, producing little litter. You won't be fishing leaves out of the water as you would with deciduous trees and shrubs. The plants that shed flowers after they bloom (loropetalum and cross vine) are positioned farthest from the pool.

> SITE: Sunny
>
> SEASON: Spring
>
> ZONES: 8–10
>
> CONCEPT: A poolside patio and low-water-use plantings offer a welcome retreat from the sun.

A Pindo palm

Ruby loropetalum **C**

'Bronze Beauty' cleyera **B**

Coontie **G**

'Harbour Dwarf' heavenly bamboo **D**

1 square = 1 ft.

Lawn

B

C

G

D

E

I

A

H

G

F

Plants & Projects

Building the arbor, installing the patio, and preparing the planting beds are slightly strenuous tasks and may require occasional dips in the pool to complete. Once the plants are established, you'll have very little to do beyond seasonal pruning and cleanup.

Ⓐ Pindo palm (use 1 plant)
This sturdy palm will mature into a canopy of gray-green foliage 10 to 20 ft. high, held up by a stout trunk decorated with the bases of old leaf stalks. Flower stalks appear in the spring. Remove them before they set fruit to minimize cleanup, or keep them around to eat. See *Butia capitata*, p. 102.

Ⓑ 'Bronze Beauty' cleyera (use 12)
Growing 8 ft. tall, this glossy evergreen shrub doubles as a handsome privacy hedge and a striking backdrop for the pink flowers and burgundy foliage of the loropetalum. See *Ternstroemia gymnanthera* 'Bronze Beauty', p. 121.

Ⓒ Ruby loropetalum (use 16)
This evergreen shrub has arching branches bearing layers of small, rounded, burgundy leaves. Expect a burst of hot pink flowers in spring, and more bloom on and off from the summer through the fall. See *Loropetalum chinense* var. *rubrum'*, p. 112.

Ⓓ 'Harbour Dwarf' heavenly bamboo (use 12)
Tiers of colorful evergreen foliage make this well-behaved shrub an excellent choice under the palm. In Zone 10 substitute with Liriope muscari (p. 111). See *Nandina domestica* 'Harbour Dwarf', p. 112.

Ⓔ Cross vine (use 2)
This twining vine will cover the arbor in lustrous dark-green leaves most years. Older leaves may turn purple and red in the fall. In spring, hundreds of yellow and orange trumpet flowers open, providing a colorful focal point and a draw for migrating hummingbirds. Scattered bloom continues from summer to autumn. See *Bignonia capreolata*, p. 99.

Ⓕ Asian jasmine (use 15)
This creeping evergreen vine that makes a thick, dark-green carpet of fine, glossy, ivylike leaves. It does not produce flowers. See *Trachelospermum asiaticum*, p. 122.

Ⓖ Coontie (use 15)
A sculptural accent behind the bench and by the pool, this small cycad forms a clump of stiff evergreen leaves that resemble feathers. It bears interesting flower cones in summer. See *Zamia pumila*, p. 123.

Ⓗ Patio
Shown here made of precast concrete pavers, the patio could be flagstones or a poured concrete extension of the pool surround. See p. 138.

Ⓘ Arbor
Simple to build, this sturdy wooden arbor supports flowering vines and shades a wooden bench. See p. 155.

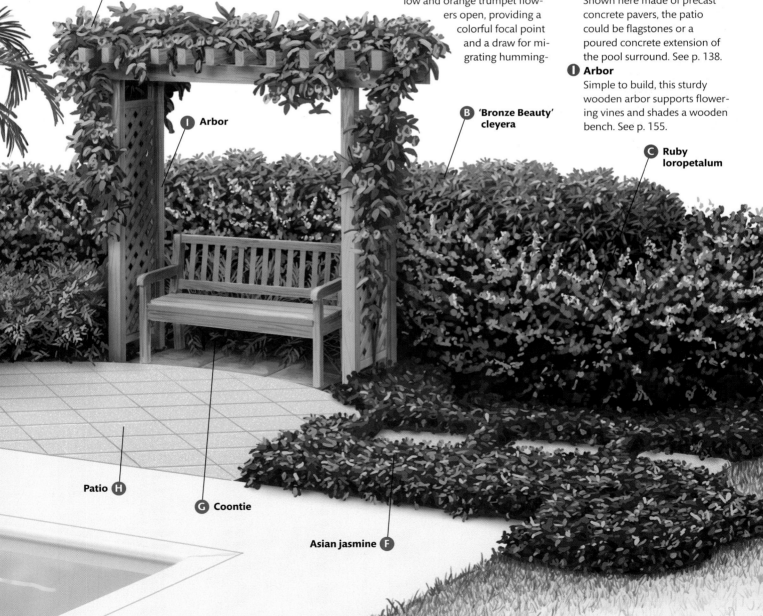

Ⓔ Cross vine

Ⓘ Arbor

Ⓑ 'Bronze Beauty' cleyera

Ⓒ Ruby loropetalum

Patio Ⓗ

Ⓖ Coontie

Asian jasmine Ⓕ

Palms by the pool

Palm trees are a natural next to water. This design makes spectacular use of native palms and other tropical plants that grow well in Zones 9 and 10. A bench swing and flagstone path scale down the cost and labor of the previous design without reducing its attractions. An old porch swing hanging from a simple post-and-beam structure provides a comfortable perch for relaxing with a book or enjoying the action in the pool.

The palms will provide a canopy of shade as they grow, and the evergreen grasses and shrubs will quickly add a sense of privacy. In spring and early summer, African irises bloom next to the bench. Their white petals open to reveal fine brush strokes of yellow and purple.

Plantings enclose the pool while grass surrounding the patio creates extra entertaining space.

VARIATIONS ON A THEME

These poolside landscapes feature imaginative plantings and structures that complement the pools they surround.

This raised deck echoes the curve of the pool's sunning ledge and provides a perfect perch.

Plants & Projects

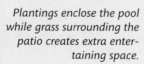

Ⓐ **Sabal palm** (use 3 plants)
This Southeast native plant provides a stately presence as well as a bit of shade. Large flower clusters appear in summer. See *Sabal palmetto*, p. 120.

Ⓑ **Hedge bamboo** (use 1)
An evergreen clumping bamboo, it has slender slightly weeping culms and small pointed leaves. See *Bambusa multiplex*, p. 98.

Ⓒ **Firebush** (use 3)
Abundant red flowers bloom all season above this evergreen shrub's dark-green leaves. See *Hamelia patens*, p. 105.

Ⓓ **Cardboard plant** (use 1)
Dramatic as a single specimen, this evergreen cycad forms a large mound of leathery prehistoric-looking foliage. See *Zamia maritima*, p. 123.

E Evergreen paspalum grass (use 13)
This tropical grass forms a graceful waist-high mound of fine-textured yellow-green foliage. See *Paspalum quadrifarium*, p. 113.

F White African iris (use 11)
White flowers rise above fans of gray-green leaves when this perennial blooms in summer. Foliage stays crisp and fresh all year. See *Dietes vegeta*, p. 103.

G 'New Gold' lantana (use 10)
Clusters of rich orange-yellow flowers top this evergreen perennial almost year-round. Their nectar attracts butterflies and night moths. See *Lantana* 'New Gold', p. 111.

H 'Emerald Goddess' lilyturf (use 12)
This ground cover features attractive grassy dark-green leaves. See *Liriope muscari* 'Emerald Goddess', p. 111.

I Bench swing
You can make a swing support using the techniques shown on p. 158, but consult a builder to ensure stability. Ready-made bench swings are also available at garden centers or home stores.

J Stepping-stones
Irregular flagstone pavers provide an attractive no-slip path to the swing. See p. 133.

SITE: Sunny
SEASON: Spring
ZONES: 9–10
CONCEPT: Tropical plants look at home beside a pool.

1 square = 1 ft. Lawn

Sabal palm A
'Emerald Goddess' lilyturf H
Cardboard plant D
Firebush C
Bench swing I
'New Gold' lantana G
White African iris F
Hedge bamboo B
'New Gold' lantana G
Steppingstones J
Evergreen paspalum grass E

A Tropical Corner

SHOWCASE EXOTIC FOLIAGE AND FLOWERS

A Sabal palm

E Confederate jasmine

B 'Acoma' crapemyrtle

Firebush **C**

G 'New Gold' lantana

I Purple verbena

F White African iris

G 'New Gold' lantana

J Decorative urn

D Plumbago

H Asian jasmine

Tropical plants lend themselves to superlatives: exquisite flowers, luxuriant foliage, profuse bloom, magnificent structure, extraordinary texture, alluring fragrance. Everything about them is out of the ordinary, with the exception of where they can grow. If you live in Florida or along the Gulf Coast, you can reliably grow many tropical plants outdoors and enjoy their extravagant display year after year.

The vibrant tropical planting shown here could be used in any sun-drenched spot on your property. We've shown it wrapping the corner of a garage; the eye-catching foliage and flowers bring interest to a usually drab area. Three palms form the backbone of this simple design, creating an instant tropical look. Under their canopies, a small tree and a handful of shrubs and perennials display interesting leaf textures and splashes of color throughout the seasons. A climbing vine trained on one of the palms completes this tropical picture.

Most tropical plants revel in the high humidity that accompanies heat in these areas. In the torrid months of summer, lush palm foliage offers a cool contrast against heat-soaked concrete or stucco walls. And when many garden plants simply give up, heat-loving firebush, plumbago, and verbena put out a bounty of flowers. In the winter months, when temperatures dip, the palms will still be luxuriant, and the plumbagos and lantanas will be covered in blossoms, reminding you that balmy days are just ahead.

Plants & Projects

These tropical plants need little care beyond regular watering and annual cleanup.

A Sabal palm (use 3 plants)
This native palm puts out a healthy crown of fanlike gray-green leaves. The richly textured trunk is handsome too, and a great support for flowering vines. See *Sabal palmetto*, p. 120.

B 'Acoma' crapemyrtle (use 1)
Dense clusters of white crepe-papery flowers light up this small tree in late spring. Dark-green deciduous leaves turn bright colors in fall, and flaking bark is attractive in winter. Use *Ligustrum japonicum* (p. 111) in Zone 10. See *Lagerstroemia indica x fauriei* 'Acoma', p. 110.

C Firebush (use 1)
This large evergreen shrub showcases brilliant scarlet flowers against bright-green foliage. Berry clusters are showy too, ripening from green to yellow to red to black. See *Hamelia patens*, p. 105.

D Plumbago (use 2)
The slender stems and small green leaves of this shrub are hidden for months under a cover of sky blue flowers. The heavy bloom is even more eye-catching when the scarlet firebush is in flower. See *Plumbago auriculata*, p. 117.

E Confederate jasmine (use 1)
This vigorous vine will clamber to the top of the palm, dressing it in small, oval leathery leaves. In late spring, masses of starry white flowers perfume the air. See *Trachelospermum jasminoides*, p. 122.

F White African iris (use 19)
This perennial ground cover forms clumps of spearlike leaves that are arranged in lovely fans. From spring to early summer, each leafy clump sends up slender branched stalks bearing white-petaled flowers with yellow and violet throats. See *Dietes vegeta*, p. 103.

G 'New Gold' lantana (use 18)
This colorful perennial forms a durable mat of dark evergreen leaves buried in clusters of tiny orange-yellow flowers. Butterflies love them. See *Lantana* 'New Gold', p. 111.

H Asian jasmine (use 8)
The small, oval leaves of this twining vine are dark green and glossy, providing a bold contrast beside gold-colored lantana. See *Trachelospermum asiaticum*, p. 122.

I Purple verbena (use 3)
From summer to fall, this upright evergreen perennial sports showy purple flowers and the colorful butterflies they attract. See *Verbena bonariensis*, p. 122.

J Decorative urns

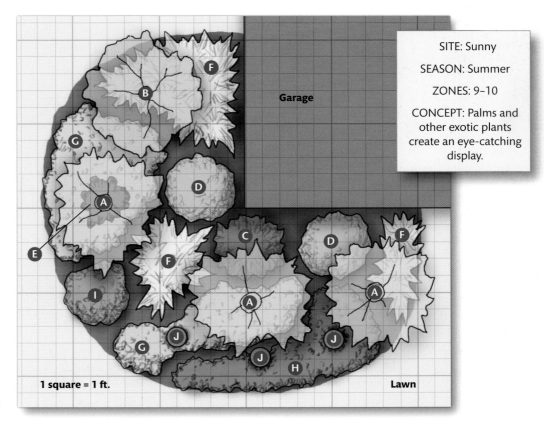

SITE: Sunny

SEASON: Summer

ZONES: 9–10

CONCEPT: Palms and other exotic plants create an eye-catching display.

1 square = 1 ft. Garage Lawn

Exotics in the shade

You can bring dazzling color to darker corners of your property, too. This design features the colorful, shimmering foliage of tropical gingers, a variety of ferns, and other exotic shade-loving specimens. Some of these plants also produce splashes of bright flowers that lighten even the deepest shade.

At the center of this planting is an elegant small palm with slender stems and sleek fronds. Adding height along the wall is a trellis supporting a fragrant flowering vine.

A collection of spectacularly sculpted and textured shrubs, perennials, ferns, and grasses vie for attention throughout the border. But few plants grab the spotlight like the zebra ginger, with its vibrantly striped foliage and its elaborate wands of white flowers in summer.

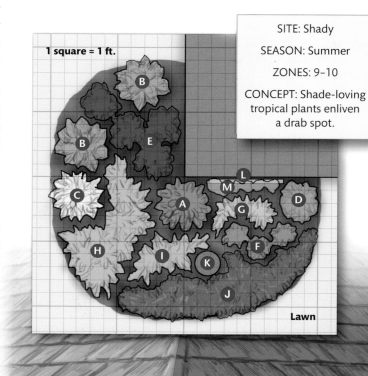

1 square = 1 ft.

SITE: Shady

SEASON: Summer

ZONES: 9–10

CONCEPT: Shade-loving tropical plants enliven a drab spot.

Lawn

Plants & Projects

Ⓐ Lady palm (use 1 plant)
Considered one of the most beautiful of all palms. Slender stems bear large fronds of lustrous, dark-green, deeply cut leaves that look like giant hands. See *Rhapis excelsa*, p. 118.

Ⓑ Blue ginger (use 2)
This jungle specimen has fleshy roots and dark-green linear leaves arranged in spirals along stems that rise 5 to 8 ft. tall. Luscious-looking clusters of deep-violet flowers bloom each autumn. See *Dichorisandra thyrsiflora*, p. 103.

Ⓒ Zebra ginger (use 1)
Named for its brilliantly striped foliage, this striking evergreen perennial contributes clusters of lightly fragrant bell-shaped

Ⓛ Trellis

Lady palm Ⓐ

Ⓜ Confederate jasmine

Ⓑ Blue ginger

'Xanadu' Ⓔ philodendron

Ⓓ Jacobinea

Zebra ginger Ⓒ

Ⓙ Mondo grass

Holly fern Ⓗ

Japanese autumn fern Ⓘ

Ⓖ Cast-iron plant

Ⓚ ZZ

'Polly' dwarf Ⓕ African mask

flowers in summer. See *Alpinia zerumbet* 'Variegata', p. 95.

D **Jacobinea** (use 1)
In summer, this shrub's large coarse leaves are topped with showy pink flowers that look like feather dusters. See *Justicia carnea*, p. 110.

E **'Xanadu' philodendron**
(use 4)
A beautiful foliage plant, this philodendron has a tidy growth habit and large, reflective, deeply lobed leaves. See *Philodendron 'Xanadu'*, p. 116.

F **'Polly' dwarf African mask**
(use 3)
This small evergreen perennial has oversize foliage colored green and purple and etched with silver veins. See *Alocasia* x *amazonica* 'Polly', p. 95.

G **Cast-iron plant** (use 9)
This perennial ground cover forms an upright clump of dark-green strappy leaves that resemble polished leather. See *Aspidistra elatior*, p. 98.

H **Holly fern** (use 8)
Glossy, coarse-textured leaves distinguish this dark-green fern. It makes a handsome companion to the finely textured autumn fern. See Recommended Ferns, *Cyrtomium falcatum*, p. 104.

I **Autumn fern**
(use 5)
The feathery fronds of this dark-green woodland fern are coppery red when new. See Recommended Ferns, *Dryopteris erythrosora*, p. 104.

J **Mondo grass** (as needed)
This perennial features neat low mounds of very fine blades. Plant small clusters 10 in. apart. Over time they spread into a soft and dense shag carpet. See *Ophiopogon japonicus*, p. 113.

K **ZZ** (use 3)
Plant this African beauty in a colorful pot for yet another eye-catching accent. It doesn't flower, but the glossy, succulent foliage is highly decorative. See *Zamioculcas zamiifolia*, p. 123.

L **Trellis**
This simple wooden structure is easy to build and attach to a wall. See p. 154.

See p. 61 for the following:

M **Confederate jasmine** (use 1)

VARIATIONS ON A THEME

If your climate isn't quite tropical, you can still have exotic flowers and lush foliage with a tropical "feel."

Container plants provide a tropical accent when the weather is warm; move them indoors when it isn't.

Combined with other colorful flower and foliage plants, red-orange cannas add a tropical note to this patio.

Greeting Place

MAKE THE MOST OF A SMALL LOT WITH AN ENTRY GARDEN

A trend in many new developments is to crowd larger houses onto smaller and smaller lots. As a consequence, homeowners need to take advantage of every opportunity for landscaping and outdoor living that their property offers.

This design makes imaginative use of the approach to the front door. Instead of a small bed of flowers by the driveway, generous beds planted with attractive trees, shrubs, and ground covers flank a spacious walkway. Made of precast pavers, the walk is really two small connected patios. Abutting the driveway, a semicircle affords ample room to get in and out of the car and to greet family and friends. Halfway to the house, a circular patio provides a place to enjoy the garden; there's even room for a bench if you'd like.

The plants are chosen for Zones 8 through 10 and will do well in many parts of the South. There is something to enjoy in every season. Pink loropetalum blossoms greet visitors in spring; white African irises continue into summer; and lantana offers flowers most of the year. The evergreen trees and shrubs need little pruning to keep their lovely shape, and they won't outgrow their spaces. As the Japanese ligustrum matures, its shady canopy and scented white flowers will keep the entry inviting on hot summer afternoons.

Japanese ligustrum A

'Harbour Dwarf' G heavenly bamboo

Asian jasmine I

Trailing lantana H   Asian jasmine I

Paving K

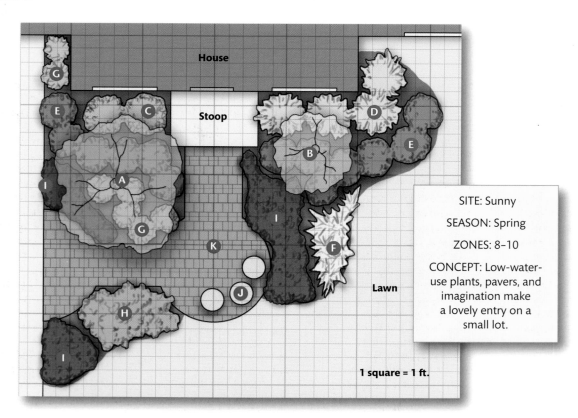

House

Stoop

Lawn

1 square = 1 ft.

SITE: Sunny

SEASON: Spring

ZONES: 8–10

CONCEPT: Low-water-use plants, pavers, and imagination make a lovely entry on a small lot.

C 'Bronze Beauty' cleyera

J Containers

E 'Nana' yaupon holly

I Asian jasmine

F White African iris

B Weeping yaupon holly

D Ruby loropetalum

E 'Nana' yaupon holly

Plants & Projects

Little pruning is needed in this planting, unless you'd like to coax more bloom from the loropetalum and lantana by deadheading or light pruning. Asian jasmine can be kept tidy by trimming it once a month from spring through fall.

A **Japanese ligustrum** (use 1) Slender trunks are topped with a crown of glossy evergreen foliage all year. In early summer, the dark foliage showcases airy clusters of white flowers, and in fall, blue berries attract birds. The tree grows quickly, keeping its attractive shape without pruning. See *Ligustrum japonicum*, p. 111.

B **Weeping yaupon holly** (use 1) The drooping branches of this small evergreen tree are clothed in small, oval gray-green foliage.

Female hollies bear red berries. See Recommended Hollies, *Ilex vomitoria* 'Pendula', p. 109.

C **'Bronze Beauty' cleyera** (use 2) This shrub is grown mainly for its smooth foliage, which looks heavily lacquered. New leaves are bronze-tinted; mature leaves are a dark green. Flowers are small and inconspicuous. See *Ternstroemia gymnanthera* 'Bronze Beauty', p. 121.

D **Ruby loropetalum** (use 4) An evergreen shrub, it produces layers of small rounded burgundy foliage and a lavish fringe of bright-pink flowers in spring. See *Loropetalum chinense* var. *rubrum*, p. 112.

E **'Nana' yaupon holly** (use 13) Popular as a small foundation plant or tall ground cover, this evergreen holly grows about 3

to 5 ft. tall and wide. It keeps a pleasing rounded shape. Leaves are small and gray-green. See Recommended Hollies, *Ilex vomitoria*, p. 109.

F **White African iris** (use 5) From spring to early summer, lovely white flowers open above this perennial's dark-green leaves. The swordlike foliage adds a dramatic vertical accent all year. See *Dietes vegeta*, p. 103.

G **'Harbour Dwarf' heavenly bamboo** (use 7) Low and compact, this evergreen shrub makes a good ground cover under the tree. Its green-gold foliage turns orange in fall and bronzy red during winter. In Zone 10, substitute with *Liriope muscari* (p. 111). See *Nandina domestica* 'Harbour Dwarf', p. 112.

H **Trailing lantana** (use 4) Masses of lavender flowers blanket this bushy perennial for much of the year. An occasional trimming encourages more bloom. See *Lantana montevidensis*, p. 110.

I **Asian jasmine** (use 15) This evergreen vine creates a dense mat of shiny leaves that smothers weeds and tolerates some foot traffic. See *Trachelospermum asiaticum*, p. 122.

J **Containers** (use 3) Grow annuals in large pots to accent the planting. Shown here are complementary bronze-leaf begonias with pink and white flowers.

K **Paving** If you don't want to trim precast pavers, consider concrete or a free-form flagstone design. See p. 133.

A lush entry in the shade

Less traditional than the previous design, and less expensive too, this entryway retains the existing walkway and uses well-adapted exotic plants, one of them a Florida native, to brighten a shady entrance.

All of these plants have naturally pleasing forms and maintain a size that won't overrun the small space. The ferns, mondo grass, and zebra ginger maintain a low profile that helps create a sense of spaciousness around the entryway. The taller lady palm and anise provide balance and structure near the house. Both are as undemanding and long-lived as they are beautiful. A garden bench provides a place for people to sit and enjoy the striking display.

Plants & Projects

Ⓐ **Lady palm** (use 1 plant)
This exceptional small palm produces many reedlike stems adorned with dark, lustrous, richly patterned foliage. Lady palm may grow up to 7 ft. tall, but it does so slowly. See *Rhapis excelsa*, p. 118.

Ⓑ **Yellow anise** (use 1)
Often sheared into hedges, this evergreen shrub also makes a nice specimen by itself. It has a pleasing conical shape and dark-green leaves that smell like licorice when crushed. See *Illicium parviflorum*, p. 108.

Ⓒ **Zebra ginger** (use 1)
This bold shrub will brighten the doorstep with its enormous yellow-striped green leaves. Its white flowers bloom on long pendant stalks in the summer. See *Alpinia zerumbet* 'Variegata', p. 95.

Ⓓ **'Xanadu' philodendron** (use 3)
With its compact mounding habit and large, shiny foliage, this evergreen shrub makes a handsome setting for the bench. See *Philodendron* 'Xanadu', p. 116.

Ⓔ **Cast-iron plant** (use 9)
This perennial is a favorite ground cover. Its evergreen leaves are stiff, have a leathery sheen, and emerge from the ground resembling pickets. See *Aspidistra elatior*, p. 98.

Ⓕ **Holly fern** (use 11)
This extraordinary fern bears stiff, erect, dark-green fronds with coarsely fringed margins.

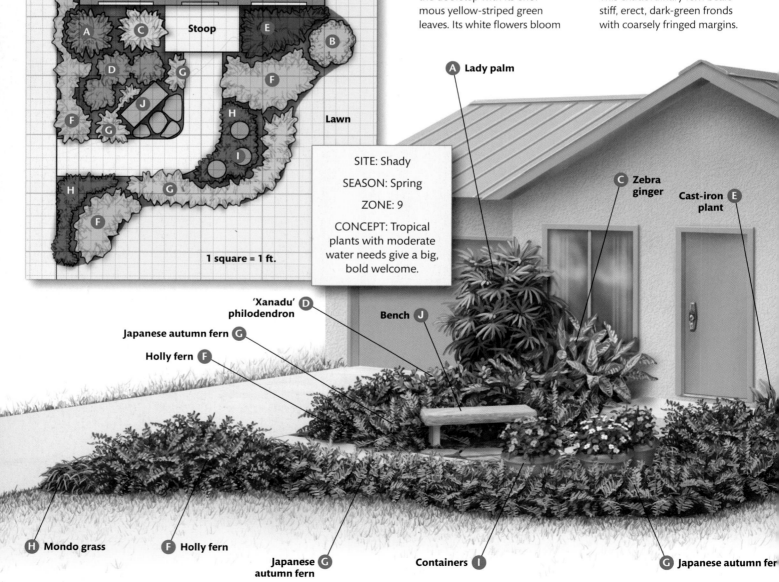

SITE: Shady

SEASON: Spring

ZONE: 9

CONCEPT: Tropical plants with moderate water needs give a big, bold welcome.

1 square = 1 ft.

See Recommended Ferns, *Cyrtomium falcatum*, p. 104.

G Japanese autumn fern (use 14)
This fern's new growth is coppery red, gradually turning green with age. See Recommended Ferns, *Dryopteris erythrosora*, p. 104.

H Mondo grass (use 19)
This evergreen perennial has narrow dark-green leaves that resemble unmowed turf. See *Ophiopogon japonicus*, p. 113.

I Containers
Impatiens in pastel colors fill terra-cotta pots in spring. Plant other annuals as the seasons change. See Annuals, p. 96.

J Pavers and bench
Pavers provide a level footing for a stone bench. See p. 132.

Colorful blooms and soft grasses surround this secluded entry garden.

B Yellow anise

F Holly fern

VARIATIONS ON A THEME

These designs offer garden settings that are interesting in their own right, not just as accompaniments to a trip to the front door.

This formal design, right, suits its architectural setting; the split path permits a leisurely garden stroll.

A sitting-height wall creates a welcoming space at the front door for greeting guests.

Patio Oasis

A FREESTANDING PATIO OFFERS OPEN-AIR ACTIVITIES

In warm climates, outdoor living can be a year-round pleasure. But many homes extend an invitation to the great outdoors only as far as a porch, deck, or patio attached to the house. The design shown here, a free-floating patio integrated with plantings, expands the possibilities for open-air gatherings to other spots on your property. Situated in an open expanse of lawn, it becomes a focal point and gathering spot. Positioned along the perimeter of the property, it defines the boundary in a neighborly way. Tucked into an out-of-the-way corner, it serves as a quiet refuge from noisier activities. Wherever you place it, the patio and plantings will provide an attractive destination and an enjoyable view for those who stay behind.

In this simple design, the patio is large enough to accommodate a gathering of eight comfortably. A small recirculating fountain is soothing to look at and to listen to. Planted close to the patio, a small tree will provide some shade as it grows, and several large shrubs at the back of the border impart a sense of privacy without closing off the views. Shrubs at the front harbor a large terra-cotta pot with a trellis supporting a flowering vine.

The plants shown are for Zones 9 and 10, but with a few substitutions this design's range can extend from Zones 8 to 11. Check with your local nursery center or consult the Plant Profiles for options. They include vibrant flowers that serve as lightning rods for butterflies, hummingbirds, and other wildlife. Gold and purple lantanas will be in bloom nearly year-round, joined throughout the season by a continuous supply of flowers in fiery reds, rich golds, and electric blues with whites.

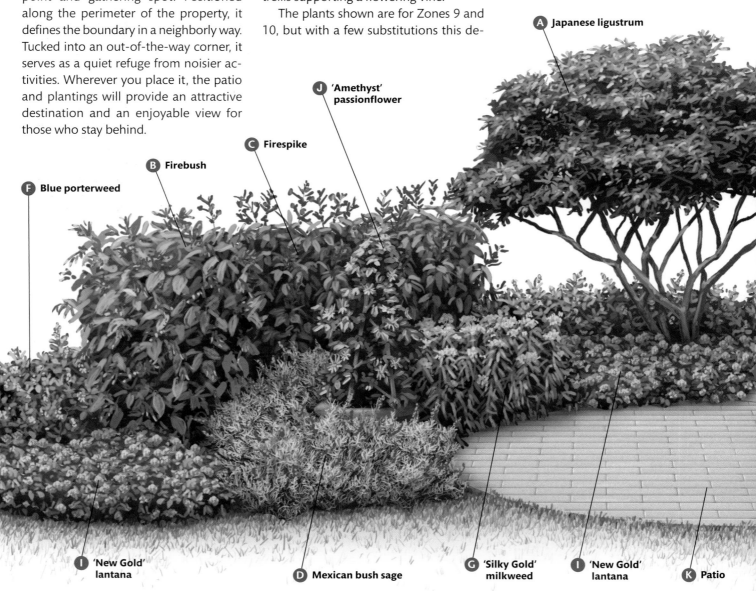

A Japanese ligustrum

J 'Amethyst' passionflower

C Firespike

B Firebush

F Blue porterweed

I 'New Gold' lantana

D Mexican bush sage

G 'Silky Gold' milkweed

I 'New Gold' lantana

K Patio

Plants & Projects

The patio and plantings can be installed in a couple of weekends. Once the plants are established, they'll need little care beyond regular watering and seasonal cleanup.

Ⓐ Japanese ligustrum (use 1)
A fast-growing evergreen tree with great structural appeal, its handsome crooked trunks are topped with smooth, pointed, polished leaves and panicles of fragrant, creamy white flowers in early summer. See *Ligustrum japonicum*, p. 111.

Ⓑ Firebush (use 2)
Masses of bright-red flowers top this showy evergreen shrub from spring to fall, maturing into shiny black berries. As autumn approaches, the large, bright-green leaves become tinged with red. See *Hamelia patens*, p. 105.

Ⓒ Firespike (use 3)
This tropical evergreen shrub has upright, rigid stems and glossy deep-green leaves with wavy margins. From winter through spring, each stem is topped with a stunning foot-long panicle of tubular crimson flowers. Hummingbirds returning south appreciate this nectar pit stop. See *Odontonema cuspidatum*, p. 113.

Ⓓ Mexican bush sage (use 7)
This beautiful plant adds soft texture and color to the border because every part of it is covered with fuzz. Velvety white flowers with purple calyces bloom in spikes above wooly stems and downy gray-green leaves. This evergreen perennial blooms best in the fall and spring. It also attracts bees, butterflies, and sometimes hummingbirds. See *Salvia leucantha*, p. 120.

Ⓔ Purple verbena (use 1)
This evergreen perennial fills a vertical space in the garden. Its thin stiff stems and narrow see-through leaves are topped for months with small pom-poms of purple flowers. See *Verbena bonariensis*, p. 122.

Ⓕ Blue porterweed (use 13)
Ideal as a low hedge around the patio, this Florida native evergreen shrub offers gray-green foliage and slender blue flower spikes that will attract butterflies. See *Stachytarpheta jamaicensis*, p. 121.

Ⓖ 'Silky Gold' milkweed (use 11)
This is a pure-gold form of everyone's favorite butterfly magnet. It blooms from spring through autumn on sturdy stalks that are lined with narrow, medium-green leaves. See *Asclepias curassavica* 'Silky Gold', p. 98.

Ⓗ Trailing lantana (use 8)
This low-spreading evergreen perennial produces rich dark-green leaves and lavish clusters of tiny lavender flowers. Each flower cluster is a landing pad for butterflies and moths. See *Lantana montevidensis*, p. 110.

Ⓘ 'New Gold' lantana (use 12)
For months—nearly year-round—rich, clear orange-yellow flowers top this shrubby perennial. It is another great nectar source for butterflies and night moths. See *Lantana 'New Gold'*, p. 111.

Ⓙ 'Amethyst' passionflower (use 1)
Grown in a pot with a small trellis for support, this evergreen twining vine bears deeply lobed dark-green leaves and knockout purple flowers. The leaves provide food for the larvae of Gulf fritillary butterflies. See *Passiflora* x 'Amethyst', p. 113.

Ⓚ Patio
Precast pavers form the patio and edge for the fountain basin. Both inexpensive and durable, pavers are also easy to install. See p. 138.

Ⓛ Water feature
Garden centers stock simple recirculating fountain kits that are easy to install. See p. 140.

SITE: Sunny

SEASON: Spring

ZONES: 9–10

CONCEPT: A small patio and garden will make an inviting destination most anywhere on your property.

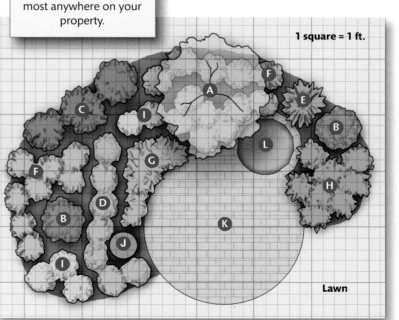

1 square = 1 ft.

Lawn

Ⓔ **Purple verbena**

Ⓑ **Firebush**

Ⓕ **Blue porterweed**

Ⓛ **Water feature**

Ⓗ **Trailing lantana**

Shady oasis

If your yard is shaded by a large tree or nearby building, you might try this design featuring palms and other tropical plants that appreciate a little shade (and regular watering).

Like the previous design, this version creates a self-contained spot for entertainment and relaxation. Instead of the bountiful flowers of sun-loving plants, these trees, shrubs, ferns, and perennials have outstanding qualities in form and foliage. The contrasting forms, textures, and colors play off one another and off the bold patterns of the irregular flagstones.

SITE: Shady

SEASON: Spring

ZONE: 9

CONCEPT: A self-contained garden is an entertainment spot for a shady site.

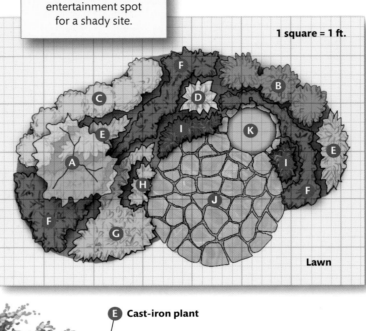

1 square = 1 ft.

Lawn

Plants & Projects

Ⓐ Yaupon holly (use 1)
This small broad-leaved evergreen tree has a vase-shaped growth habit, contoured trunks, and a dense crown of leathery leaves. Female hollies produce bright-red berries that last into winter. See Recommended Hollies, *I. vomitoria*, p. 109.

Ⓑ Lady palm (use 3 plants)
Lustrous, dark-green palm fronds on reedlike stems make this slow-growing palm an outstanding choice for a small patio. Well-established clumps can reach heights of 7 ft. See *Rhapis excelsa*, p. 118.

Ⓒ Yellow anise (use 6)
This adaptable evergreen shrub should be on everyone's wish list of hedges. It wears a thick coat of yellow-green elliptical foliage reaching all the way to the ground. When the leaves are cut or crushed, they release a licorice scent. See *Illicium parviflorum*, p. 108.

Ⓓ Zebra ginger (use 1)
This bold evergreen shrub will electrify any planting with its yellow-and-green-striped leaves and long clusters of strikingly colored bell-shaped flowers. See *Alpinia zerumbet* 'Variegata', p. 95.

Ⓔ Cast-iron plant (use 17)
Dark-green swordlike leaves of this perennial create a bold silhouette against the stripey yellow anise leaves of *Illicium parviflorum*. It is a dependable evergreen ground cover. See *Aspidistra elatior*, p. 98.

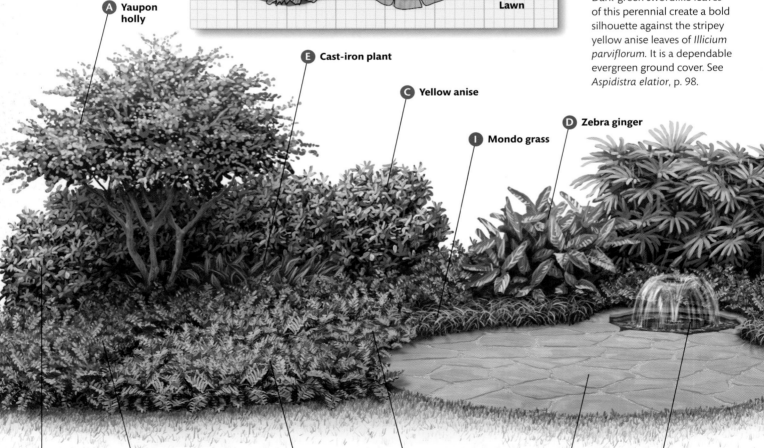

Ⓐ Yaupon holly

Ⓔ Cast-iron plant

Ⓒ Yellow anise

Ⓘ Mondo grass

Ⓓ Zebra ginger

Ⓒ Yellow anise

Ⓕ Holly fern

Ⓖ Japanese autumn fern

Ⓗ Japanese painted fern

Ⓙ Patio

Ⓚ Water feature

F Holly fern (as needed)
Prized for its coarse, shiny foliage, this unusual-looking fern is a beautiful companion to more traditional feathery types. Plant 24 in. apart. See Recommended Ferns, *Cyrtomium falcatum*, p. 104.

G Japanese autumn fern (use 12)
This gorgeous plant displays coppery new growth among bright-green leaves. See *Dryopteris erythrosora*, p. 104.

H Japanese painted fern (use 3)
This delicate, low-growing fern has silvery fronds edged in maroon. See *Athyrium niponicum* 'Pictum', p. 104.

I Mondo grass (as needed)
This evergreen woodland perennial resembles grass but never needs mowing. Plant 10 in. apart. It spreads quickly into a soft carpet of ultrathin leaf blades. See *Ophiopogon japonicus*, p. 113.

J Patio
Try flagstones for a texture and feel that are different from those of precast pavers. See p. 138.

See p. 69 for the following:

K Water feature

B Lady palm

E Cast-iron plant

F Holly fern

This dining area with container plants up-close-and-personal is the focal point of the garden.

VARIATIONS ON A THEME

Located away from the house, these patios and plantings afford opportunities for relaxing and entertaining.

Backed by small trees and the giant leaves of elephant's ears, sitters here can enjoy the view and pleasant sound of a small fountain.

Floriferous containers can be moved on a whim if more guests arrive.

Formal Outdoor Living

A PATIO AND A SHADY PERGOLA PROVIDE OPEN-AIR OPPORTUNITIES

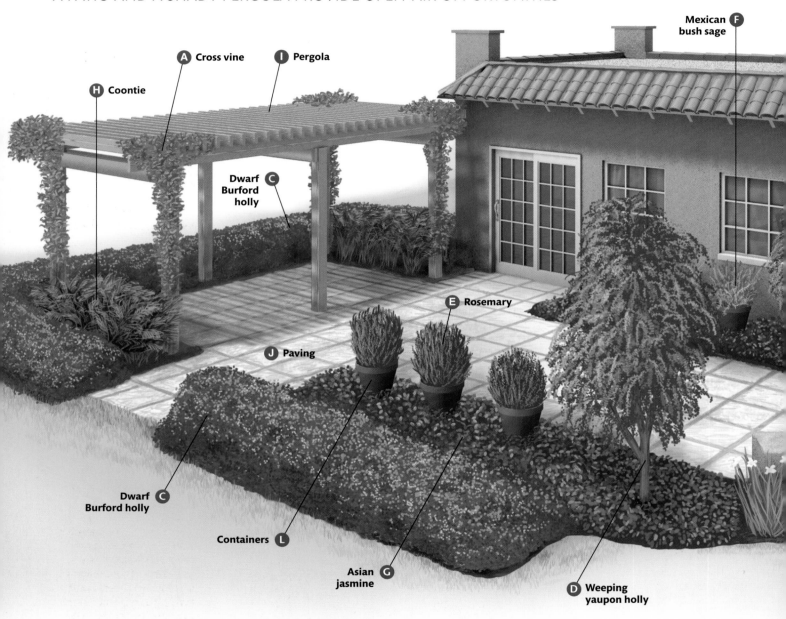

Throughout the South, opportunities for year-round outdoor living abound. This design demonstrates how a patio next to the house can become a true extension of your living space with the addition of a pergola and plants that create an attractive setting.

At one end of a formal patio, a vine-covered pergola provides a shady, cool spot for dining or relaxing. At the opposite end, a sitting-height curved wall invites informal gatherings when the heat of the day has passed.

A neatly trimmed dwarf holly hedge, weeping upright trees,

and shrubs in terra-cotta pots reinforce the formality of the grid-work paving, while ground covers spilling onto the pavement soften the effect. Backing the curved seating wall, a loose hedge of African iris is an informal echo of its dwarf holly counterpart. Easily reached and viewed from the house, the pergola, patio, and plants nicely mingle the "indoors" with the "outdoors."

Scale is particularly important when you're landscaping near the house. This design can be adapted to suit houses and properties in a range of sizes. The grid-work patio can be altered by adding or removing rows of pavers.

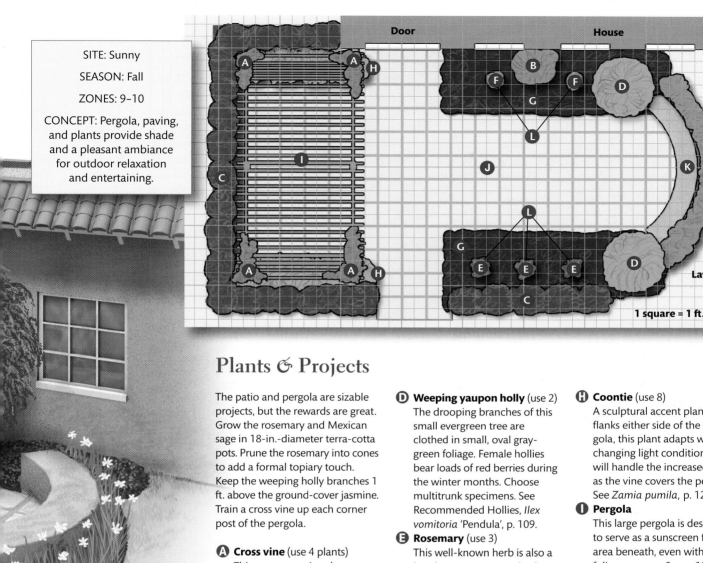

SITE: Sunny

SEASON: Fall

ZONES: 9–10

CONCEPT: Pergola, paving, and plants provide shade and a pleasant ambiance for outdoor relaxation and entertaining.

Door

House

Lawn

1 square = 1 ft.

B White African iris

K Seating wall

Plants & Projects

The patio and pergola are sizable projects, but the rewards are great. Grow the rosemary and Mexican sage in 18-in.-diameter terra-cotta pots. Prune the rosemary into cones to add a formal topiary touch. Keep the weeping holly branches 1 ft. above the ground-cover jasmine. Train a cross vine up each corner post of the pergola.

Ⓐ Cross vine (use 4 plants)
This evergreen vine showcases trumpet-shaped flowers of yellow to red-orange in the spring. Twist and tie the young tendrils up each pergola post to eventually cover and provide shade. See *Bignonia capreolata*, p. 99.

Ⓑ White African iris (use 9)
This iris for the Southeast reaches 24 to 30 in. high sporting white flowers with violet and yellow throats in the spring. Flowers will be easily seen above the seating wall. See *Dietes vegeta*, p. 103.

Ⓒ Dwarf Burford holly (use 21)
This dense evergreen shrub can be clipped to create a formal square-cornered hedge of 24 in. high. For Zone 10, substitute with *Carrisa macrocarpa* (p. 102). See Recommended Hollies, *Ilex cornuta*, p. 109.

Ⓓ Weeping yaupon holly (use 2)
The drooping branches of this small evergreen tree are clothed in small, oval gray-green foliage. Female hollies bear loads of red berries during the winter months. Choose multitrunk specimens. See Recommended Hollies, *Ilex vomitoria* 'Pendula', p. 109.

Ⓔ Rosemary (use 3)
This well-known herb is also a handsome evergreen shrub. Its gray-green, needlelike leaves are fragrant and tasty. Plant one in each container, and trim into a pointed cone. See Recommended Herbs, *Rosmarinus officinalis*, p. 107.

Ⓕ Mexican bush sage (use 2)
This beautiful evergreen perennial adds soft texture and blue flower color to the two containers placed strategically in front of the two windows. This velvety plant can be seen from inside the house. See *Salvia leucantha*, p. 120.

Ⓖ Asian jasmine (use 28)
This evergreen vine creates a dense mat of shiny leaves that smothers most weeds and holds up well under foot traffic. This "carpet" will contrast well with the terra-cotta pots. See *Trachelospermum asiaticum*, p. 122.

Ⓗ Coontie (use 8)
A sculptural accent plant that flanks either side of the pergola, this plant adapts well to changing light conditions and will handle the increased shade as the vine covers the pergola. See *Zamia pumila*, p. 123.

Ⓘ Pergola
This large pergola is designed to serve as a sunscreen for the area beneath, even without a foliage canopy. See p. 159.

Ⓙ Paving
Use flagstone pavers, 24 in. square. See p. 133.

Ⓚ Seating wall
This 18-in.-high wall provides seating and should be constructed with stucco over concrete block or a material to match the house. If your budget doesn't allow hiring a mason, buy commercially made curved wooden or precast concrete benches.

Ⓛ Containers (use 5)
Select matching terra-cotta containers that are 18 in. tall and wide. Place each on a level stepping-stone, set on compacted soil that is free of organic material.

VARIATIONS ON A THEME

Each of these outdoor rooms achieves privacy through adjacent structures and lush plantings.

A simple trapezoidal fabric canopy creates shelter from the elements for grilling and dining.

A vine-covered pergola provides a shady retreat from the summer sun.

Several patio rooms extend along the side of this house. Crushed rock lined with flagstones makes a stunning centerpiece to the design.

Tropical sanctuary

This low-water-use design creates an ocean-side outdoor room with the feel of a lush south-Florida oasis. A formal "grove" of bottle palms is the most striking element. With their long arching fronds, the palms provide dappled shade as well as character. A silver buttonwood hedge screens the patio from neighboring properties and creates a sense of enclosure, aided by two low stucco walls that double as casual seating.

The flagstone paving is roomy enough for several groups of tables, chairs, and shade umbrellas. A vine-draped pergola frames the view beyond the garden. If you're ambitious, add a small pond or fountain to enhance the oasis theme.

Free-form beds wrap around the patio. Foliage is a year-round attraction here. Mounding shrubs and carpet-forming beach sunflower add softer outlines. The fragrant white flowers of the Natal plum are a heady enticement to linger on the patio.

Plants & Projects

Ⓐ Foxtail agave (use 3 plants)
This spineless agave is perfect for coastal gardens. The sculptural look is set off nicely by the ground-hugging beach sunflower. See *Agave attenuata*, p. 95.

Ⓑ Bougainvillea (use 1)
A vigorous vine with bright purple bracts that last for months. Train up the arbor by tying young branches to the frame to cover. Each spring, prune to remove dead wood and keep vine within 18 in. of the frame. See *Bougainvillea spectabilis*, p. 99.

Ⓒ Natal plum (use 13)
This evergreen shrub offers shiny dark-green leaves, fragrant star-shaped flowers that bloom throughout the year, and bright-red edible fruits. See *Carissa macrocarpa*, p. 102.

Ⓓ Silver buttonwood (use 3)
The silvery foliage of this attractive shrub is an ideal contrast to other colors in the garden. Hand-prune this hedge to just below the height of the wall, keeping the top of the hedge narrower than the bottom. See *Conocarpus erectus* var. *sericeus*, p. 103.

Ⓔ Pencil tree (use 1)
This evergreen succulent is sure to catch everyone's interest when they visit. A leafless, multi-trunked tree that is sculptural, it will provide the perfect focal point for this tropical sanctuary. See *Euphorbia tirucalli*, p. 103.

F Beach sunflower (use 17)
Underground runners will quickly fill in to form a dense, dark-green carpet covered with miniature yellow sunflowers throughout the year. Butterflies are attracted to their nectar. See *Helianthus debilis*, p. 105.

G Bottle palm (use 4)
This palm is aptly named for its swollen, bottle-shaped trunk and will enclose the patio space with their dark-green, featherlike fronds. Plant palms with the same height from the ground to the bottom of the lowest frond. See *Hyophorbe lagenicaulis*, p. 108.

H Trailing lantana (use 7)
This low-spreading evergreen perennial produces dark-green leaves and numerous clusters of tiny lavender flowers. Each cluster is a landing pad for butterflies and moths. See *Lantana montevidensis*, p. 110.

I Indian hawthorn (use 13)
Pink or white flowers cover the dark foliage of this low, spreading evergreen shrub in spring, followed by blue berries. Select any compact cultivar. See *Rhaphiolepis indica*, p. 118.

J Pergola
A vine-covered pergola announces the entrance to this tropical garden. See p. 159.

K Containers (use 3)
Select matching terra-cotta containers that are 20 in. square and high. Square bases make these containers less likely to blow over in the wind.

See page 73 for the following:

L Rosemary (use 2)

M Coontie (use 14)

N Paving

O Seating wall

See site plan for **K**.

SITE: Sunny

SEASON: Summer

ZONES: 10–11

CONCEPT: This tropical patio features salt-tolerant and low-water-use plantings.

1 square = 1 ft.

Seaside Front Door

ENHANCE YOUR MAIN ENTRY IN A WEEKEND

Sometimes the simplest landscaping projects pack a surprisingly big punch. This design uses only a few plants and can be easily installed in a single weekend. Yet this small investment of time and money can transform one of the most important parts of your property, welcoming visitors to your home as well as presenting a pleasing face to passersby.

Small plantings often suffer from busyness—too many different kinds of plants in too little space. This design with moderate salt tolerance and low water use makes a bold display with just five different plants. Potted shrubs and upright hollies with a skirt of lily of the Nile frame the doorway, while low pockets of orange bulbine border the walkway. There are pretty flowers and a variety of foliage textures to catch the eye, as well as the scent of rosemary. The planting is enticing to visitors, but not overpowering. And it offers a pleasant spot to chat as guests enter or leave the house.

Coontie **E**

Dwarf Burford holly **C**

Orange bulbine **B**

Lily of the Nile **A**

House

Stoop

D

D

E

E

C

C

B

B

Walkway

A

A

1 square = 1 ft.

Lawn

SITE: Sunny

SEASON: Spring

ZONES: 9–10

CONCEPT: A few well-chosen low-water-use and moderate-salt-tolerant plants and a few hours' work can invigorate a nondescript entry.

Rosemary **D**

A Lily of the Nile

B Orange bulbine

C Dwarf Burford holly

Coontie **E**

Plants & Projects

This simple planting is easy to maintain. Clip the lily of the Nile after its spring bloom, and you may remove spent bulbine flower stalks to keep them tidy. As the years pass, you may need to prune the holly in spring or fall.

A **Lily of the Nile** (use 8 plants) This popular perennial bulb bears blue or white pom-pom-like flowers that float above the neat mounds of straplike leaves. Enjoy these blossoms in late spring to early summer. See Recommended Bulbs, *Agapanthus africanus*, p. 100.

B **Orange bulbine** (use 10) The low grasslike mounds of bulbine will soon fill in to create a low mat covered with tall spikes covered in clusters of tiny orange-yellow flowers from spring to fall. See *Bulbine frutescens* 'Hallmark', p. 100.

C **Dwarf Burford holly** (use 2) This dense evergreen shrub can be easily pruned to create a rounded specimen 30 in. high. For Zone 10, substitute with *Ilex vomitoria*, 'Nana', *Ilex cornuta*, p. 109.

D **Rosemary** (use 2) This well-known kitchen herb can be easily pruned as a topiary. Its gray-green, needlelike leaves are fragrant as well as tasty. Plant one in each container, and trim into a pointed cone. See Recommended Herbs, *Rosmarinus officinalis*, p. 107.

E **Coontie** (use 8) A sculptural accent plant that flanks either side of the front stoop, this plant adapts well to changing light conditions and can handle the shade from house eaves. See *Zamia pumila*, p. 123.

On the shady side

The concept here is the same as for the preceding design—rejuvenate your home's entrance with a limited number of plants and just a few hours' labor. The difference is that these plants will thrive in partial-shade conditions.

The planting offers a variety of foliage texture and color and is an enticement to linger at the doorstep. The foliage is a constant and attractive presence. Providing subtle contrasts and complements in color and texture, all the leaves are evergreen where winters are mild. Protect the aloe when freezing temperatures are forecast.

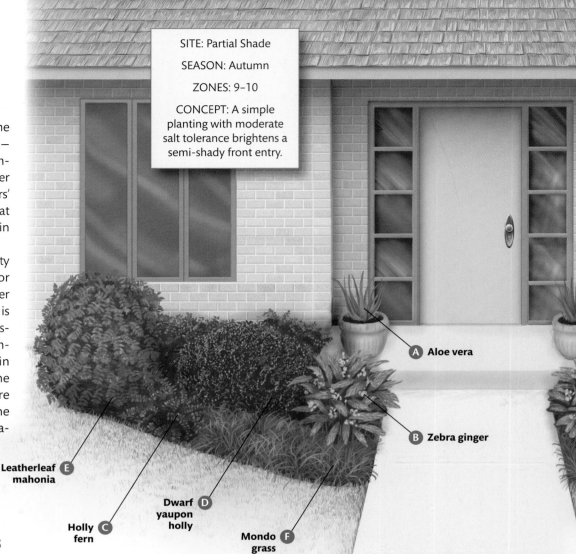

SITE: Partial Shade

SEASON: Autumn

ZONES: 9–10

CONCEPT: A simple planting with moderate salt tolerance brightens a semi-shady front entry.

A Aloe vera

B Zebra ginger

Leatherleaf E mahonia

Dwarf D yaupon holly

Holly C fern

Mondo F grass

Plants & Projects

A Aloe vera (use 2 plants)
The thick, fleshy leaves of this aloe create a unique statement in the matching containers at the front door. See *Aloe vera*, p. 95.

B Zebra ginger (use 2)
The variegated straplike leaves of this ginger will brighten any shady entrance. In summer the clusters of hanging flowers will add a light, spicy scent to the air. See *Alpinia zerumbet* 'Variegata', p. 95.

C Holly fern (use 2)
Glossy, coarse-textured leaves distinguish this dark-green fern. It makes a handsome companion to the finely textured dwarf yaupon holly. See *Cyrtomium falcatum*, p. 104.

D Dwarf yaupon holly (use 2)
This small evergreen shrub forms compact mounds of small gray-green leaves and

stays just the right size for the front porch. See Recommended Hollies, *Ilex vomitoria* 'Nana', p. 109.

E Leatherleaf mahonia (use 4)
This upright, straight-stemmed evergreen shrub is ideal for tight, shady spaces. Dark blue-green leaves set off the fragrant yellow flowers in late winter and early spring. Soon, sky blue berries ripen and last through fall. In Zone 10, substitute with *Pittosporum tobira* 'Variegata' (p. 116). See *Mahonia bealei*, p. 112.

F Mondo grass (use 16)
The thin, leathery, grassy leaves of this evergreen perennial create an attractive deep-green mass along the walk. See *Ophiopogon japonicus*, p. 113.

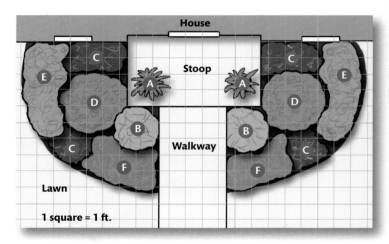

House

Stoop

Walkway

Lawn

1 square = 1 ft.

E **Leatherleaf mahonia**

D **Dwarf yaupon holly**

C **Holly fern**

VARIATIONS ON A THEME

The entryway gardens shown here demonstrate the appeal of asymmetrical designs. These plantings are tied into more-extensive landscapes but would also look good on their own.

Front-door plantings for this shady north-facing entry are all in containers set on pot feet for easy maintenance.

Evergreen shrubs, palms, and ground covers complement this brick path. A few dashes of bright red deliver a big punch among the greenery.

Garden of Texture

EXTEND A FRIENDLY WELCOME

Many suburban developments crowd larger homes onto smaller and smaller lots. This design confronts the problem by placing a courtyard garden that invites gathering or relaxing outside right at the front door. Shaded by the canopy of a small tree, enclosed by a low wall that does not block breezes, and soothed by the trickle of a water feature, the courtyard can be enjoyed by family and friends year-round.

This garden can be located within blocks of the beach and celebrates low-maintenance and low-water-use principles. The moderately salt-tolerant plants featured here contribute distinctive forms, textures, and colors. Grouped together, they create dramatic compositions. Spiky agave, yucca, and saw palmetto are boldly paired with the loosely arching bougainvillea and low-spreading lantana. The deciduous chaste tree allows in the warming winter sun but offers shade in the summer. The flowers in this planting bloom during the warm months, and they are a spectacular sight.

Plants & Projects

Installing the paving, wall, and fountain are the biggest jobs here, though not beyond the means of a resourceful do-it-yourselfer. Once established, the plants will thrive with occasional watering and just seasonal care.

Ⓐ **Pineapple guava** (use 1 plant) This large shrub of silver-green foliage will produce white and red flowers in the spring and small green fruits in the summer. See *Acca sellowiana*, p. 94.

Ⓑ **Twin-flower agave** (use 5) This unusually fine-textured agave has narrow, succulent leaves that form a perfect

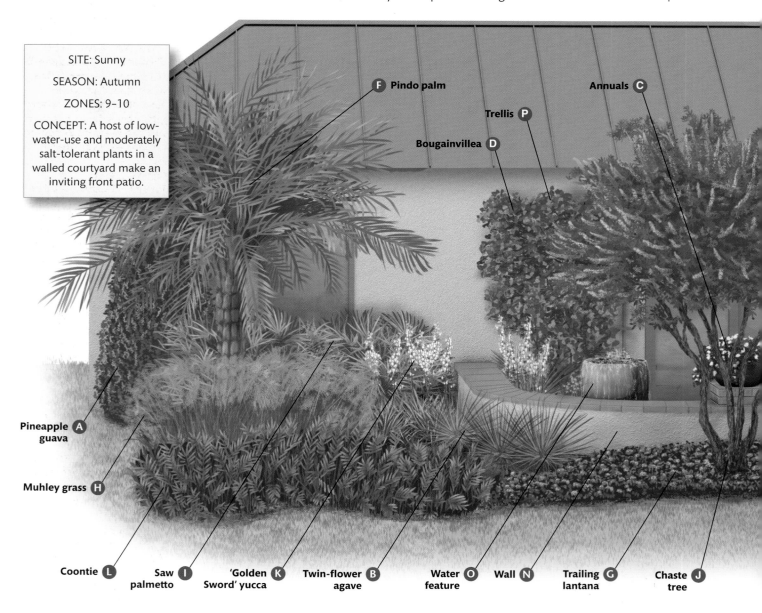

SITE: Sunny

SEASON: Autumn

ZONES: 9–10

CONCEPT: A host of low-water-use and moderately salt-tolerant plants in a walled courtyard make an inviting front patio.

Pindo palm Ⓕ

Trellis Ⓟ

Annuals Ⓒ

Bougainvillea Ⓓ

Pineapple Ⓐ guava

Muhley grass Ⓗ

Coontie Ⓛ   Saw Ⓘ palmetto   'Golden Ⓚ Sword' yucca   Twin-flower Ⓑ agave   Water Ⓞ feature   Wall Ⓝ   Trailing Ⓖ lantana   Chaste Ⓙ tree rosette 2 to 3 ft. in diameter. See *Agave geminiflora*, p. 95.

C Annuals (as needed)
A collection of colorful Madagascar periwinkle, globe amaranth, and moss rose adds a festive look to a stone container resting on the wall. See Recommended Annuals, p. 96.

D Bougainvillea (use 1)
Trained on a trellis, this evergreen vine's lavish display of purple flowers will be eye-catching from any seat.

Blooms spring and summer. See *Bougainvillea spectabilis*, p. 99.

E Orange bulbine (use 20)
The low grasslike mounds of bulbine will soon fill in to create a low mat with tall spikes covered in clusters of tiny orange-yellow flowers from spring to fall. See *Bulbine frutescens* 'Hallmark', p. 100.

F Pindo palm (use 1)
This sturdy palm will mature into a canopy of gray-green

fronds, each up to 5 ft. long. Its stout trunk is decorated with the bases of old fronds and can reach 10 to 20 ft. Slow growing. See *Butia capitata*, p. 102.

G Trailing lantana (use 8)
Small lavender flowers brighten this low-spreading perennial's dark-green leaves; evergreen and ever-blooming where winters are mild. See *Lantana montevidensis*, p. 110.

H Muhley grass (use 6)
In the fall, this ornamental

grass will bloom with fantastic purple flowers held above the fine-textured leaves. See *Muhlenbergia capillaries*, p. 112.

I Saw palmetto (use 2)
This hardy, low clumping palm forms a dense ground cover that needs no maintenance. Ideal for coastal gardens, the silver form (*S. repens* 'Cinerea') is unique to Florida's coast. See *Serenoa repens*, p. 121.

J Chaste tree (use 1)
Choose a multitrunk small tree with a good branch structure. In summer through fall, this tree's attractive clusters of purple flowers will provide fragrance and attract butterflies. In Zone 10 substitute with *Euphorbia tirucalli* (p. 103). See *Vitex agnus-castus*, p. 122.

K 'Golden Sword' yucca (use 3)
This shrubby perennial offers sword-shaped evergreen leaves striped with yellow and gold. It bears showy clusters of creamy flowers on tall stems in summer. See *Yucca filamentosa*, p. 123.

L Coontie (use 3)
A sculptural accent plant that will contrast with the fine textured muhley grass, this plant adapts well to changing light conditions and will handle the increased shade as the pindo palm grows. See *Zamia pumila*, p. 123.

M Paving
Clay brick in 4 x 8-in. pavers, shown in a basketweave pattern, are the right size for this small courtyard. See p. 133.

N Wall
This low stucco wall with matching brick cap allows in the breezes and doubles as a seat. See p. 144.

O Water feature
Water is a wonderful focal point. Use a glazed jar and a self-contained fountain kit to create your own oasis.

P Trellis
You can support the bougainvillea with the sturdy wood trellis shown here, or buy a ready-made one from the garden center. See p. 154.

B Twin-flower agave

E Orange bulbine

A trio of containers and hedging enclose a garden space that can be enjoyed from the front porch.

VARIATIONS ON A THEME

These gardens use heavy plantings to create enclosure and privacy.

This seaside overlook blends contemporary elements with textural salt-tolerant plants.

Loose mounds of foliage and a liberal sprinkling of flowers flank a gravel walk in this "cottage" garden.

Seaside perch

Plant this highly salt-tolerant garden right on the back side of a dune where it is exposed to a bit of salt spray, and you won't be disappointed with its performance. Place it miles from the sea, and it won't mind. Hold back on the water, and you will still be pleased because these plants require little water once established.

Take a stroll out the back door. The patio has enough space for a grill and a café table with chairs. Stepping-stones lead to a bench, under the shady canopy of a multitrunked Japanese ligustrum tree. At the bench, the surrounding coonties and saw palmettos provide privacy.

Linger awhile because this low-maintenance garden doesn't need mowing, and the plants barely need trimming.

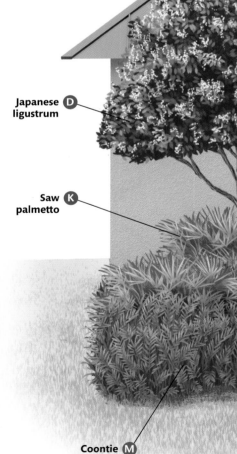

Japanese ligustrum **D**

Saw palmetto **K**

Coontie **M**

Plants & Projects

A **Foxtail agave** (use 1 plant)
This spineless agave is perfect for coastal gardens. The sculptural look is set off nicely by the ground-hugging beach sunflower. See *Agave attenuata*, p. 95.

B **Aloe vera** (use 1)
The bright yellow-green fleshy leaves with white spots will contrast well with a brightly colored glazed pot. See *Aloe vera*, p. 95.

C **Beach sunflower** (use 30)
Underground runners will quickly fill in to form a dense, dark-green carpet covered with miniature yellow sunflowers throughout the year. Butterflies are attracted to their nectar. See *Helianthus debilis*, p. 105.

D **Japanese ligustrum** (use 1)
The dark-green, waxy leaves of this small broad-leaved evergreen tree are a perfect background for the fragrant white flowers it bears in early summer. Dark-blue berries follow in fall and winter. It grows quickly; prune lower branches as necessary to accommodate visitors using the bench. See *Ligustrum japonicum*, p. 111.

E **Paving**
The irregular flagstone paving in muted beach tones will provide an attractive and level surface for the patio and walks. See p. 133.

F **Bench**
Extend your seating from the patio with a comfortable bench in the shade overlooking the beach.

G **Container**
Choose a brightly colored glazed urn to complement the patio stones. Be sure to drill a drainage hole in the bottom if it does not come with one.

See p. 80–81 for the following:

H **Twin-flower agave** (use 3)
I **Bougainvillea** (use 1)
J **Orange bulbine** (use 14)
K **Saw palmetto** (use 3)
L **'Golden Sword' yucca** (use 3)
M **Coontie** (use 10)
N **Trellis**

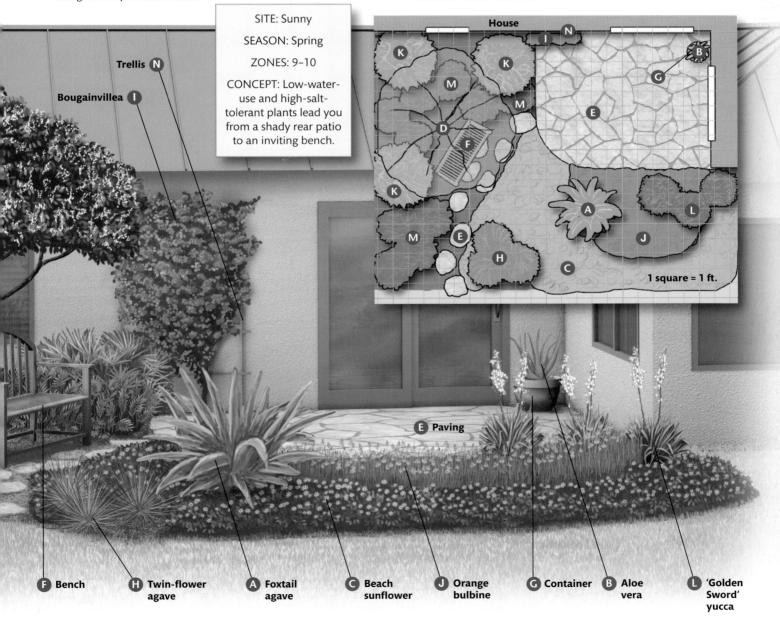

SITE: Sunny

SEASON: Spring

ZONES: 9–10

CONCEPT: Low-water-use and high-salt-tolerant plants lead you from a shady rear patio to an inviting bench.

House

1 square = 1 ft.

Trellis **N**
Bougainvillea **I**
E Paving

F Bench   **H** Twin-flower agave   **A** Foxtail agave   **C** Beach sunflower   **J** Orange bulbine   **G** Container   **B** Aloe vera   **L** 'Golden Sword' yucca

Landscape a Low Wall

A TWO-TIERED GARDEN REPLACES A BLAND SLOPE

Some things may not love a wall, but plants and gardeners do. For plants, walls offer warmth for an early start in spring and good drainage for roots. Gardeners appreciate the rich visual potential of composing a garden on two levels, as well as the practical advantage of working on two relatively flat surfaces instead of a single sloping one.

This design places complementary plantings above and below a wall bounded at one end by a set of steps. While each bed is relatively narrow, when viewed from the lower level, the two combine to form a border more than 10 ft. deep. Two other design features add depth to the display. A jog in the wall creates a niche for a splashy evergreen paspalum grass, and the beds are rounded rather than linear. Together with a selection of billowy plants, these features soften the face of the wall and offer pleasing views from many vantage points.

Building the wall that makes this impressive sight possible doesn't require the time or skill it once did. Nor is it necessary to scour the countryside for tons of fieldstone or to hire an expensive contractor. Thanks to precast retaining-wall systems, anyone with a healthy back (or access to energetic teenagers) can install a knee-high do-it-yourself wall in as little as a weekend or two.

Retaining wall **H** and steps

Plants & Projects

This planting showcases colorful flowers against curtains of soft silvery green foliage. All the plants require only moderate water and need only a little care to keep them performing at their best. The Mexican bush sage will benefit from pruning in late spring and again in midsummer to keep them dense and full.

A **Orange bulbine** (use 10 plants)
The low grasslike mounds of bulbine will soon fill in to create a mat with tall spikes covered in clusters of tiny orange-yellow flowers from spring to fall. In Zone 10 substitute with Stoke's aster (see p. 121). See *Bulbine frutescens* 'Hallmark', p. 100.

B **White African iris** (use 3)
This iris for the South reaches 24 to 30 in. high, sporting white flowers with violet and yellow throats in the spring. Flowers will contrast well against the wall. See *Dietes vegeta*, p. 103.

C **Trailing lantana** (use 5)
This low, spreading evergreen perennial produces dark-green leaves and numerous clusters of tiny lavender flowers. Each cluster provides an endless source of nectar for butterflies and moths. See *Lantana montevidensis*, p. 110.

D **Compact Texas sage** (use 3)
A native evergreen shrub with small woolly leaves and a billowy shape, it bears masses of orchid-pink flowers after summer rains. See *Leucophyllum frutescens* 'Compactum', p. 111.

E **Evergreen paspalum grass** (use 1)
This fine-textured ornamental grass forms an attractive dense mound that sways easily in the breeze. Tall spikes of small flowers appear in spring. See *Paspalum quadrifarium*, p. 113.

F **Mexican bush sage** (use 1)
This big bushy perennial anchors the end of the border and echoes the arching habit of the paspalum grass. Slender branches bear gray-green foliage. In spring and autumn, long wands of small purple and white flowers bloom from branch tips. See *Salvia leucantha*, p. 120.

G **Asian jasmine** (use 5)
This evergreen vine creates a dense mat of shiny leaves that smothers most weeds and provides a dark-green contrast to the slivery foliage of the Mexican bush sage. See *Trachelospermum asiaticum*, p. 122.

H **Retaining wall and steps**
Prefabricated wall systems make this project easy to install. See p. 144.

I **Path**
We've shown concrete pavers here, but use any materials that you feel complement the wall. See p. 133.

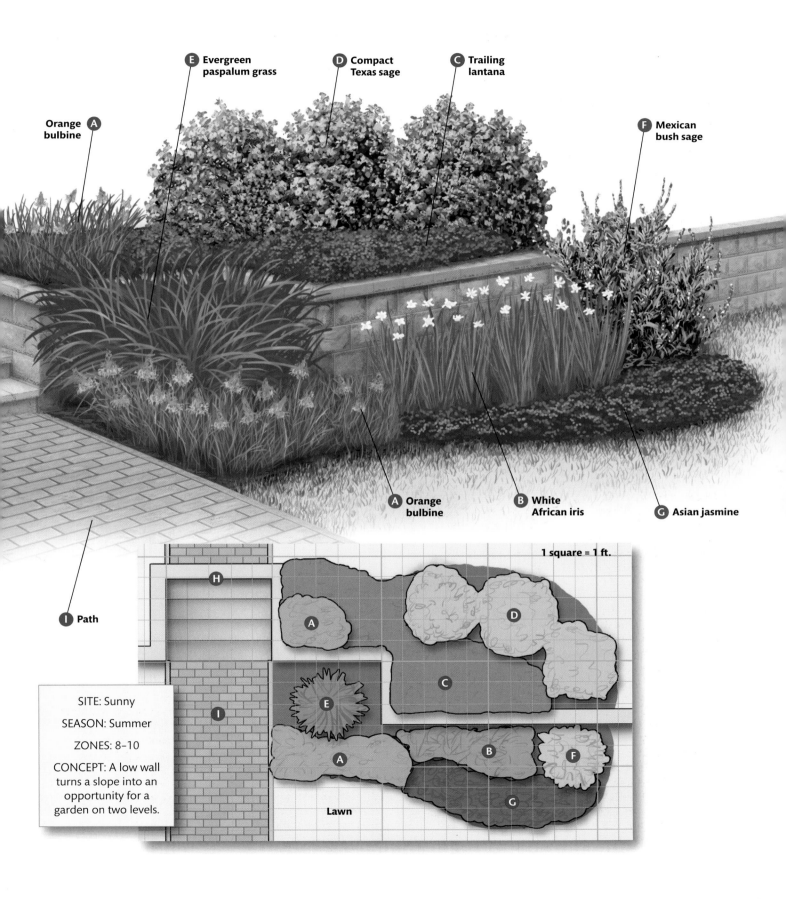

E Evergreen paspalum grass

D Compact Texas sage

C Trailing lantana

A Orange bulbine

F Mexican bush sage

A Orange bulbine

B White African iris

G Asian jasmine

I Path

1 square = 1 ft.

H

A

D

C

E

I

A

B

F

G

Lawn

SITE: Sunny

SEASON: Summer

ZONES: 8–10

CONCEPT: A low wall turns a slope into an opportunity for a garden on two levels.

VARIATIONS ON A THEME

Low garden retaining walls provide dual-level landscaping opportunites.

A retaining wall stepped back from the sidewalk creates a natural space for a garden on two levels. Plants that drape or cascade over the wall are particularly effective.

On a steeply sloped backyard, a hillside garden is a lot more fun than a lawn. This one includes a little patio retreat created by a low retaining wall.

A small patio is incorporated into this retaining wall.

Salty coastal

A retaining-wall planting at the beach can be colorful and sensual. This design relies on the same wall-and-step system but uses high-salt-tolerant and low-water-use plants that will do equally well far inland. Bold saw palmettos on both levels break up the retaining wall's horizontal plane while bringing the garden together as a whole. The muhley grass provides graceful foliage and pink cloudlike flowers.

Plants & Projects

Ⓐ **Aloe vera** (use 6)
The bright yellow-green fleshy leaves with white spots will contrast well with the dark-green leaves of the nearby beach sunflower. See *Aloe vera*, p. 95.

Ⓑ **Beach sunflower** (use 15)
Underground runners will quickly fill in to form a dense, dark-green carpet covered with miniature yellow sunflowers throughout the year. Butterflies are attracted to their nectar. See *Helianthus debilis*, p. 105.

Ⓒ **Yaupon tree** (use 1)
This small-leafed evergreen tree has a vase-shaped form, contoured trunks, and a dense crown of leathery gray-green leaves. Female hollies produce masses of bright-red berries that last into winter. See Recommended Hollies, *Ilex vomitoria*, p. 109.

Ⓓ **Muhley grass** (use 1)
In the fall, this ornamental grass will bloom with fantastic purple flowers held above the fine-textured leaves. See *Muhlenbergia capillaris*, p. 112.

Ⓔ **Saw palmetto** (use 3)
This hardy, low, clumping palm forms a dense ground cover that needs no maintenance. Ideal for coastal gardens, look for the silver form, *S. repens* 'Cinerea', to add a great contrast to the holly tree's dark-green foliage. See *Serenoa repens*, p. 121.

See p. 84 for the following:

Ⓕ **Retaining wall and steps**

Ⓖ **Path**

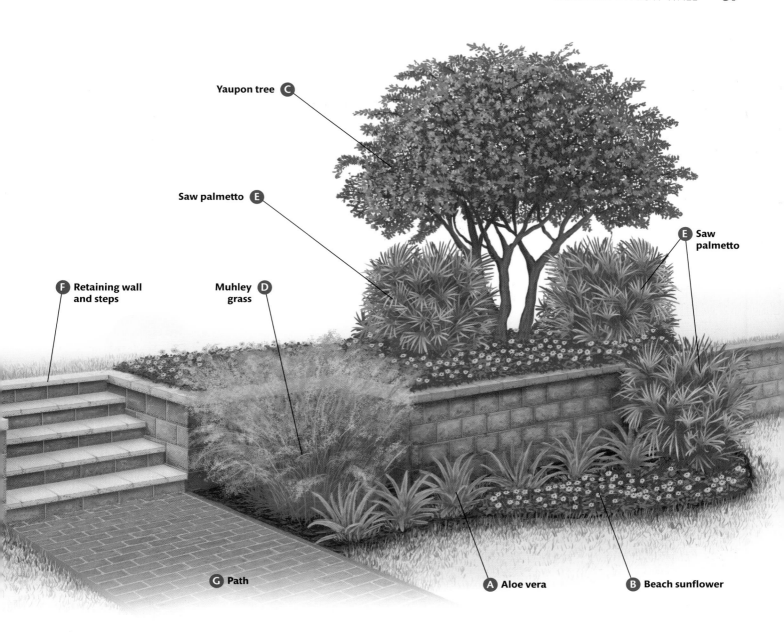

Yaupon tree **C**

Saw palmetto **E**

E Saw palmetto

F Retaining wall and steps

Muhley grass **D**

G Path

A Aloe vera

B Beach sunflower

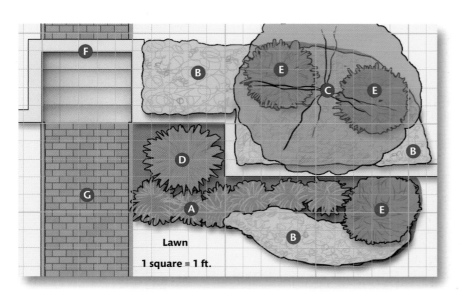

F

B

E

C

E

D

B

G

A

E

B

Lawn

1 square = 1 ft.

SITE: Sunny

SEASON: Autumn

ZONES: 9–10

CONCEPT: High-salt tolerant and low-water-use plants surround a garden wall in a sunny site.

An Outdoor "Living" Room

PATIO AND SHADY ARBOR PROVIDE OPEN-AIR OPPORTUNITIES

Opportunities for outdoor living abound. This design demonstrates how a patio next to the house can become a true extension of your living space with the addition of a pergola, a fence, and plants that create an attractive setting.

At one end of an informal patio, a vine-covered pergola, anchored by a small tree, provides a cool shady spot for dining or relaxing. At the opposite end, a wooden fence and plantings offer privacy as well as a colorful display to be enjoyed from the patio or the house. Together, the fence, pergola, patio, and plants nicely mingle the "indoors" with the "outdoors." From early spring to late fall, the plantings will provide colorful accompaniments to your patio activities. Blossoms of fragrant jasmine open first. By May the patio will be in full swing with long-lasting flowers and nectar-seeking hummingbirds.

Scale is particularly important when you're landscaping near the house, and the vine-covered pergola creates a comfortable link. This design can be adapted to suit houses and properties in a range of sizes. The flagstone patio can be altered by adding or removing irregular pavers. And the plantings can be extended or reduced along the edges. Don't expect to water these low-to-moderate-water-use plants often.

SITE: Sunny

SEASON: Spring

ZONE: 9

CONCEPT: Pergola, paving, and moderately-salt-tolerant plants provide ambiance for outdoor relaxation.

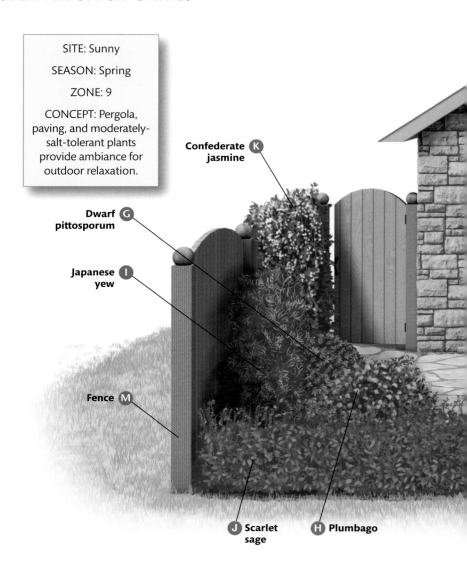

Confederate jasmine **K**

Dwarf pittosporum **G**

Japanese yew **I**

Fence **M**

J Scarlet sage

H Plumbago

Plants & Projects

This design features plants with moderate salt tolerance and low-to-moderate water use. The planting is also quite carefree.

A **Cross vine** (use 2 plants)
This evergreen vine showcases trumpet-shaped flowers of yellow to red-orange in the spring. Train the young tendrils up two pergola posts. See *Bignonia capreolata*, p. 99.

B **Holly fern** (use 4)
This unusual fern, with coarse-textured evergreen fronds re-

sembling holly leaves, provides a dense, knee-high border under the shade of the pergola. See Recommended Ferns, *Cyrtomium falcatum*, p. 104.

C **Dwarf Burford holly** (use 5)
This dense evergreen shrub can be easily pruned to create an informal, solid hedge 30 in. high. See Recommended Hollies, *Ilex cornuta*, p. 109.

D **'New Gold' lantana** (use 12)
Clusters of rich orange-yellow flowers top this evergreen perennial almost year-round.

Enjoy the evening show as night-flying moths are attracted to the nectar. See *Lantana 'New Gold'*, p. 111.

E **Japanese ligustrum** (use 1)
The waxy dark-green leaves of this small broad-leaved evergreen tree are a perfect background for the fragrant white flowers it bears in early summer. Dark-blue berries follow in fall and winter. Grows quickly; prune lower branches as necessary to accommodate ground plantings underneath.

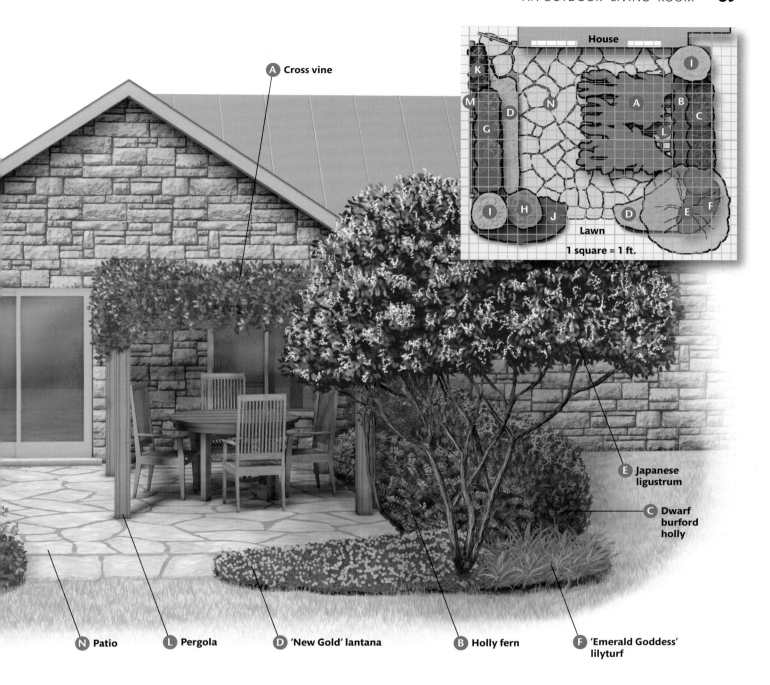

A Cross vine

House

K
M
G
D
N
A
B
C
L
I
H
J
D
E
F
I

Lawn

1 square = 1 ft.

E Japanese ligustrum

C Dwarf burford holly

N Patio   L Pergola   D 'New Gold' lantana   B Holly fern   F 'Emerald Goddess' lilyturf

See *Ligustrum japonicum*, p. 111.

F **'Emerald Goddess' lilyturf** (use 3) Grasslike clumps of 2-ft.-high evergreen leaves make an attractive year-round groundcover. Purple flower spikes appear in summer. See *Liriope muscari*, p. 111.

G **Dwarf pittosporum** (use 4) This evergreen shrub makes a lush, dressy hedge with shiny green leaves that does not need shearing. Its creamy

white flowers scent the air in early summer. See *Pittosporum tobira* 'Wheeleri', p. 116.

H **Plumbago** (use 1) The slender stems and small green leaves of this shrub are hidden for months under a cover of sky blue flowers. The heavy bloom is even more eye-catching with the bright-red salvia. See *Plumbago auriculata*, p. 117.

I **Japanese yew** (use 2) These evergreen sentinels define the patio and balance the ligustrum tree. Trim into a 3-

ft.-wide column to 6 ft. high. See *Podocarpus macrophyllus*, p. 117.

J **Scarlet sage** (use 6) A bushy perennial often grown as an annual, its bright-red flowers heat up the patio for months in the summer and fall. See *Salvia coccinea*, p. 120.

K **Confederate jasmine** (use 1) On early summer evenings you can sit on the patio and enjoy the fragrance of this evergreen vine's white flowers. Twining stems of glossy dark-

green leaves will cover the fence. See *Trachelospermum jasminoides*, p. 122.

L **Pergola** This large pergola will serve as a sunscreen for the patio even before the cross vine covers it. See p. 148.

M **Fence** A simple structure creates an attractive support for the confederate jasmine as well as a screen for privacy. See p. 157.

N **Patio** Flagstones set on a sand-and-gravel base make a durable patio. See p. 138.

VARIATIONS ON A THEME

Whether by day or night, enjoy a garden that's just the right size.

A dense hedge along the property line and vine covered trellises on the walls create privacy and soften the patio space.

The fieldstone patio beneath this vine-covered rustic arbor has ample room for a gathering of friends and family.

Lighting highlights plants and a water feature to extend the use of this garden into the evening hours.

Butterfly zone

This design creates an outdoor room that beckons butterflies along with friends and family. The yaupon holly will provide pleasant shade for a portion of the patio, and it won't get too large to shade out the plantings. Long-blooming flowers are a feast for the eye and roving butterflies. Other plants play their part, too. Hollies and holly fern shelter butterflies from storms, and pots of leafy edibles, such as dill, parsley, and fennel, give the caterpillars something to munch.

Here are a few tips to increase your butterfly population once they discover your patio. Place decorative rocks or logs in the flower beds as places where butterflies can rest and spread their wings. Butterflies need to soak up warmth from the sun to become active. Protect their life stages—egg, caterpillar, and pupa—by eliminating the use of pesticides on plants. And remember, some leaf eating is desirable, expected, and beneficial in a butterfly garden. Leaves with holes are a sure sign of success.

Plants & Projects

This design features butterfly-attracting plants with low-to-moderate water use. The planting is also quite carefree.

A **'Silky Gold' milkweed**
(use 8 plants)
Monarch butterflies flock to this plant, not only for its nectar-rich gold flowers but to lay eggs so that the caterpillars can munch away. See *Asclepias curassavica* 'Silky Gold', p. 98.

B **'Moonbeam' coreopsis** (use 3)
This perennial will produce hundreds of small daisylike flowers from spring until fall, which will keep butterflies very happy. See *Coreopsis verticillata* 'Moonbeam', p. 114.

C **Firebush** (use 1)
This evergreen shrub won't attract butterflies, but it will bring in migrating hummingbirds. Bright-red tubular flowers in the warm months make this a favorite. In areas with mild winters, it can be grown into a small tree. See *Hamelia patens*, p. 105.

D **Burford holly** (use 1)
This evergreen shrub is easily maintained in a columnar form by pruning or shearing. Its dark- green leaves are a great backdrop for a fine show of red winter berries. See Recommended Hollies, *Ilex cornuta*, p. 109.

E **Dwarf Burford holly** (use 3)
This smaller cousin of the Burford holly can be easily maintained as an informal or sheared hedge 30 in. high. See Recommended Hollies, *Ilex cornuta*, p. 109.

F **Yaupon tree** (use 1)
This small-leafed evergreen tree has a vase-shaped form, contoured trunks, and a dense crown of leathery gray-green leaves. Female hollies produce masses of bright-red berries that last into winter. The birds will love this garden, too. See Recommended Hollies, *Ilex vomitoria*, p. 109.

G **Trailing lantana** (use 8)
This evergreen shrub's weeping branches are laden with clusters of small lavender-purple flowers in summer. It's another great pit stop for butterflies. See *Lantana montevidensis*, p. 110.

H **Pentas** (use 4)
This perennial, with its nectar-rich flowers that bloom almost year-round, is a favorite of butterfly lovers . Choose pink, lavender, white, or red blooming varieties. See Recommended Perennials, *Pentas lanceolata*, p. 115.

I **Containers** (as needed)
Plant dill, parsley, and fennel to attract swallowtail butterflies. (See Recommended Herbs, p. 106.) Grow passion vine on a support for gulf fritillary butterflies. (See *Passiflora* x 'Amethyst', p. 113.)

J **Water basin**
A shallow dish makes an ideal birdbath for butterflies. Place some sand in the bottom; add a few pebbles on which butterflies can land fill it with water; and watch what happens.

K **Paving**
Shown here is a brick patio laid in a simple basketweave pattern. See p. 133.

See p. 88–89 for the following:

L **Holly fern** (use 5)

M **Scarlet sage** (use 3)

SITE: Sunny

SEASON: Summer

ZONES: 8–9

CONCEPT: A butterfly garden brings this outdoor room to life.

See site plan for **B**.

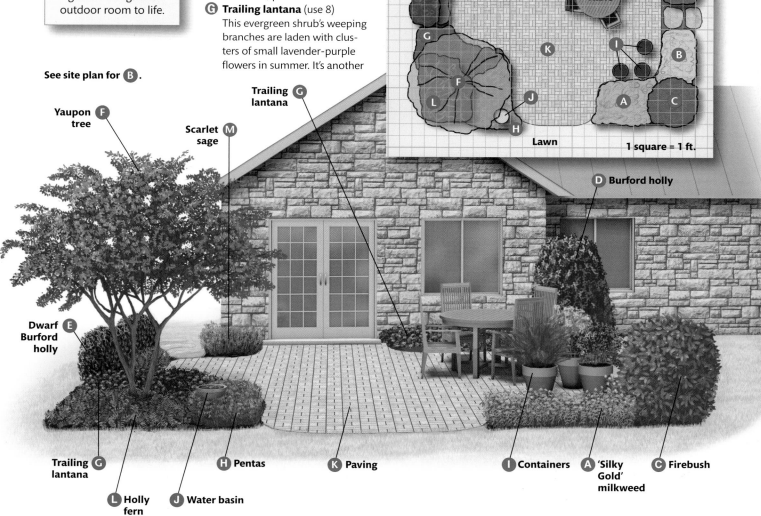

Plant Profiles

Plants are the heart of the designs in this book. In this section, you'll find descriptions of all the plants used in the designs, along with information on planting and maintaining them. These trees, shrubs, perennials, grasses, bulbs, and vines have all proved themselves as dependable performers in the region. They offer a wide spectrum of lovely flowers and fruits, handsome foliage, and striking forms. Most contribute something of note in at least two seasons. You can use this section as an aid when installing the designs in this book and as a reference guide for other landscaping projects.

Key to plant symbols

LIGHT
Full sun .... ☀
Partial shade .... ◗
Shade .... ●

WATER USE
Low water use... **L**
Moderate water use.. **M**
High water use .... **H**

SALT TOLERANCE
High salt tolerance .... ▲
Moderate salt tolerance .... ◆
Low salt tolerance.. ▼

Using the plant profiles

All of these plants are proven performers in many of the soils, climates, and other conditions commonly found in the Southeast Coastal region. But they will perform best if planted and cared for as described in the Guide to Installation. Please refer to the Hardiness Zones map for the Southern Coastal region on page 13 to determine your zone. Each plant is listed here with its Hardiness Zone range, which will help guide you in selecting the best suited plants for your zone.

Please refer to the symbol legend for each plant's requirements for sun, water, and tolerance to salt. Here, "full sun" means a site that gets at least eight hours a day of direct sun throughout the growing season. "Partial shade" refers to sites that get direct sun for part of the day but are shaded the rest of the time by a building, fence, or trees. "Shade" means sites that do not receive direct sunlight. Most plants require regular watering when they are first planted. Here, the plant's water needs once established are noted. "Low water use" refers to plants that are drought tolerant. Those labeled "moderate water use" perform best with regular watering but tolerate drying out between watering. "High water use" plants perform best in constantly moist soils.

Soils in coastal areas are generally high in excess soluble salts. These locations can also be inundated with salt spray and have salt intrusion into irrigation water sources. (See page 166 for more tips on coastal landscaping.) Here, "high salt tolerance" defines plants that are resistant to extreme coastal conditions, including exposed locations with salt spray. Those labeled "moderate salt tolerance" need protection from salt spray, but they will tolerate some inundations from storms. These grow best protected by buildings, fences, or other high salt-tolerant plants. Those labeled "low salt tolerance" must be protected from salt spray and used away from exposed areas.

The plants are organized here alphabetically by their scientific name followed by their common name. While many plants are sold by common name, scientific names help ensure that you get what you want. Familiarize yourself with a plant's scientific name. You will be surprised at how many you know already. If you're browsing, page references direct you to the designs in which the plants appear.

Acca sellowiana
PINEAPPLE GUAVA

Acer palmatum
JAPANESE MAPLE

Acca sellowiana

PINEAPPLE GUAVA **Zones 9–11** ☀ ◗ **L** ◆ This semitropical guava's evergreen foliage is a semiglossy gray-green on top and a downy silver-gray underneath and often finds its way into flower arrangements. The showy, fragrant flowers bloom in the spring. Each flower sports edible, fleshy, white petals with a purple tint and dark red centers. Pluck the white petals and add to salads or ice cream for a sweet treat. The pineapple-flavored small green fruits are also edible and can be made into jelly. The pineapple guava can be maintained as a 4-to-6-ft.-high shrub or allowed to grow into an 8-to-10-ft.-high and wide spreading ornamental multitrunk tree. Pages: 20, 80.

Acer palmatum

JAPANESE MAPLE **Zones 5–9** ☀ ◗ **M** ▼ Neat, small deciduous trees with delicate-looking leaves that have jagged edges. There are many kinds, growing 10 to 25 ft. tall and wide, with foliage that is green, bronze, or red in summer and red or scarlet in fall. They need shade from the midday sun and rich, moist soil covered with a layer of mulch. Water deeply once a week during dry weather. These maples grow slowly, so buy the biggest tree you can afford. Prune only to remove weak, damaged, or crossing limbs. Will not thrive in the warmer portions of Zone 9. Pages: 16, 19, 22.

Achillea spp.

YARROW **Zones 3–9** ☀ **L** ◆ These long-blooming perennials produce showy, flat clusters of small flowers on stiff stalks 1 to 3 ft. tall. The foliage has finely divided gray-green leaves that release a pungent aroma when crushed. Apple blossom yarrow (*Achillea millefolium* 'Apple Blossom',) has pink flowers on 2-to-3-ft.-tall stalks. Other popular varieties include Coronation Gold (*A. filipendulina* 'Coronation Gold') with 2-to-3-ft.-high stalks of yellow-gold flowers and 'Moonshine' (*Achillea* x 'Moonshine') with lemon yellow flowers on 1-to-2-ft. stalks. Cut off old flower stalks when the blossoms fade, and use in dried flower arrangements. Divide every few years in spring or fall. Pages: 47, 48.

Achillea spp.
YARROW

Agave attenuata

FOXTAIL AGAVE **Zones 9–11** ☀ ◗ **L ▲** This beautiful soft green agave is spineless and performs well in coastal gardens. The wide, pliable leaves arise from a stout gray stem in rosettes, appearing like large green flowers, up to 4 ft. wide. The common name foxtail agave arises from its flower stalks that appear on mature plants. This 5-to-10-ft. stalk flexes up and down to resemble a fox's tail. The multiple flowers are pale green to yellow and will soon develop seed pods and small plantlets. After flowering, the agave will die so collect the plantlets to start anew. Pages: 74, 83.

Agave geminiflora

TWIN FLOWERED AGAVE **Zones 9–11** ☀ **L ▲** This compact, diminutive succulent forms a tight rosette, 2 to 3 ft. wide, of stiff, narrow, green leaves, each tipped with a single spine. As many as 200 leaves will develop in a single rosette. Mature plants may develop white filaments along their leaf margins that peel away in loose, decorative spirals. Most plants mature in 10 years and produce an 8-to-12-ft.-tall stalk with paired yellow flowers up and down the stalk. After flowering, the plant will die and must be replaced. *Agave geminiflora* is also an excellent choice for containers. Page: 81

Alocasia x amazonica 'Polly'

DWARF AFRICAN MASK **Zones 9–11** ◗ ● **M H ▼** A colorful dwarf version of an evergreen perennial, it has large, tropical foliage that often resembles elephant ears. This cultivar bears dark-green arrow-shaped leaves up to 1 ft. long, featuring silver veins and purple undersides. Leaf stalks emerge directly from the ground, forming a clump 18 in. wide and up to 24 in. tall. In Zones 9 and 10, the foliage disappears during the winter, reappearing when evening temperatures reach the 70s. Prefers well-drained moderately fertile soil and is happiest with only morning sun. Remove dead foliage to reduce bacterial soft rot and fungal diseases. The sap is mildly irritating. Page: 63.

Aloe vera

ALOE VERA **Zones 9–11** ☀ ◗ ● **L ▲** This succulent is a short-stemmed plant that grows up to 2 ft. tall and spreads by forming small plants at its base. The leaves are thick and fleshy with a gray-green to yellow-green color and small white flecks. The leaf margins are serrated with small white fleshy teeth. In summer, they may produce flower spikes up to 3 ft. tall with yellow tubular flowers. Heralded for its medicinal qualities, its gelatinous sap is often used to promote the healing of wounds and burns. However, the skin of the aloe vera can be an irritant. This plant likes sandy soils and is a great addition to low water-use gardens. Pages: 78, 83, 86.

Alpinia zerumbet 'Variegata'

ZEBRA GINGER **Zones 9–11** ☀ ◗ ● **L ◆** An evergreen perennial that brightens shady spots in a tropical garden. Grows from ginger-scented rhizomes to form clumps of long, straplike, yellow-and-green-striped leaves on strong, but slender stems. In summer, it bears hanging clusters of slightly fragrant bell-shaped white flowers with yellow-and-red-striped lips. Flowers can be cut for indoor arrangements. Remove frost-damaged leaves in spring and apply water and fertilizer monthly until bloom. Pages: 62, 66, 70, 78.

Alpinia zerumbet 'Variegata'
ZEBRA GINGER

Agave attenuata
FOXTAIL AGAVE

Agave geminiflora
TWIN FLOWERED AGAVE

Alocasia x *amazonica* 'Polly'
DWARF AFRICAN MASK

Aloe vera
ALOE VERA

Annuals

Gardeners in the South use annuals generously to provide bright patches of colorful flowers throughout the year. They're fast-growing plants that bloom abundantly for months, and when they are finished blooming, or become ragged, it's easy to uproot them and replace them with something else. One of the fun things about growing annuals is that you can try different kinds from year to year, choosing varieties with small or large flowers in a wide range of colors, or plants that range in height from 6 to 30 in.

Most annuals can be divided into two groups. Cool-season annuals are planted when the weather starts to cool in autumn. They bloom during the autumn months, live through the winter, perhaps blooming off and on, and put on a show again in spring, before hot weather starts. This group includes pansies, snapdragons, petunias, dianthus, and dusty miller. Hot-season annuals are planted after the last frost in spring. They grow and bloom throughout the heat of summer, usually continuing until the first frost in fall. This group includes begonias, Madagascar periwinkle, globe amaranth, impatiens, moss rose, and annual salvia. (See Recommended Annuals for details on popular plants.)

Some annual wildflowers, such as Indian blanket and garden phlox, are easily grown from seed. Prepare the soil for planting and sow the seeds in late fall or early spring. Water as needed to keep the seeds and little seedlings from drying out. They will grow quickly in the spring, bloom in early summer, then set seed and die in late summer or fall. Once established, they self-sow and bloom year after year, as in the roadside plantings that are so popular throughout the Southeast.

Artemisia 'Powis Castle'

POWIS CASTLE ARTEMISIA **Zones 5–9** ☀ **L** ◆ A shrubby perennial that forms a dome-shaped mound 2 to 3 ft. tall and 4 to 5 ft. wide. The finely divided gray-green leaves have a pleasant aroma and are evergreen in mild winters. Prune hard every spring, cutting stems back by about one-half their height. Pages: 47, 48.

Artemisia 'Powis Castle' POWIS CASTLE ARTEMISIA

Recommended annuals

Begonia semperflorens WAX LEAF BEGONIA

Begonia semperflorens

WAX LEAF BEGONIA ☀ ◗ **M** ▼ A fleshy green or bronze-leafed begonia with small white, pink, or red flowers that bloom from early spring to late fall. Plants reach 6 to 12 in. high and should be spaced 6 to 12 in. apart. In frost-free areas, wax leaf begonia can grow as a perennial. Pages: 22, 42.

Catharanthus roseus

MADAGASCAR PERIWINKLE ☀ ◗ **L** ◆ ▲ This annual can grow as a semi-woody perennial in many parts of the Southeast. The shiny dark green leaves give rise to numerous five-petaled flowers from white to shades of lavender and pink. Cultivars vary from spreading carpet-like to mounding upright forms. Space 8 to 20 in. apart in moderately fertile soil. Periwinkles bloom best during the hot months, but establish new plants in the spring or fall. Page: 81.

Gaillardia pulchella INDIAN BLANKET

Impatiens wallerina
IMPATIENS

Gaillardia pulchella

INDIAN BLANKET ☀ L ▲ This sturdy North American native thrives in the heat and humidity and is an excellent choice for the coastal Southeast. It reseeds itself, forming 12- to 24-in. mounding clumps of silvery-gray foliage and single to bicolored flowers of yellow, orange, and red. The long flower stalks attract butterflies and make this wildflower ideal for cutting. Establish in the spring, 12 to 18 in. apart, for bloom almost year-round.

Gomphrena globosa

GLOBE AMARANTH ☀ L ◆ This mounding annual reaches 18 in. tall and produces small, globe-shaped flowers in shades of purple, pink, yellow, or white. Space 12 to 18 in. apart for mass plantings or use in containers or small pocket plantings. Flowers can be dried for indoor use if cut just before they open.. Globe amaranth tolerates heat and prefers to stay dry. Page: 81.

Impatiens walleriana

IMPATIENS ◗ ● H ▲ Known as Busy Lizzy, this shade-loving annual continues to grow, spread, and re-seed in warmer regions of the Southeast. The five-petaled, spurred flowers come in white and shades of red, purple, and orange. Some cultivars have been selected for higher light and heat tolerance. Impatiens perform best in consistently moist soils. Space 12 to 18 in. apart, and pinch the tips to encourage bushiness. Pages: 22, 42.

Phlox drummondii

GARDEN PHLOX ☀ L ▲ This native wildflower of Texas has been bred for garden use to produce numerous sizes (6 to 18 in. high) and colors including shades of red, lavender, and white in single and bicolors. Flower clusters are held above the foliage and not much is more breathtaking than a mass planting of Phlox. It is ideal for naturalizing in large open, sunny areas, and its sweetly-scented blossoms attract butterflies and make great cut flowers. Space 12 to 18 in. apart.

Portulaca grandiflora

MOSS ROSE ☀ L M ▲ This ground cover annual loves hot, dry areas in the garden. The small, flat leaf gives rise to a profusion of jewel-tone flowers that close in the evening and on cloudy days. Plants grow 6 to 10 in. high and should be spaced 12 to 18 in. apart. Freezing temperatures will take plants to the ground that resprout in the spring as well as reseed. Establish in the spring or fall for best results. Pages: 22, 42, 81.

Salvia splendens

ANNUAL SALVIA ☀ L M ▲ A popular garden annual that provides color year-round in the Southeast. Salvia bears spikes of red, purple, pink, salmon, white, or bicolored flowers. Plants typically grow 12 to 18 in. tall and should be spaced 12 in. apart. Some cultivars can grow to 36 in. high. Be sure to remove spent flower spikes before they produce seeds to continue the flower show. Pages 25, 33.

Portulaca grandiflora
MOSS ROSE

Aspidistra elatior
CAST-IRON PLANT

Asclepias curassavica 'Silky Gold'
SILKY GOLD MILKWEED

Aucuba japonica 'Variegata'
GOLD-DUST AUCUBA

Bambusa multiplex
HEDGE BAMBOO

Asclepias curassavica 'Silky Gold'

SILKY GOLD MILKWEED **Zones 4–10** ✳ **L** ▼ Often planted to attract monarch butterflies, this evergreen perennial offers a new twist on the beloved milkweed. Small, star-shaped flowers form clusters of pure yellow-gold, instead of the traditional orange-yellow, from spring to autumn. Grows into an upright bushy plant 3 ft. tall and half as wide, bearing narrow pointed leaves. Adult butterflies feast on the flower nectar; caterpillars prefer the foliage, often leaving flowers perched on naked stalks. But don't worry; plants recover quickly, ensuring more foliage and flowers for you and food for future generations of butterflies. Aphids also love milkweed, but resist spraying them with anything stronger than a blast of water or mild soap spray. Grows in a wide range of soils. Pages: 69, 90.

Aspidistra elatior

CAST-IRON PLANT **Zones 7–11** ◗ ● **L M** ▼ An unusual perennial with underground stems and stiff, dark evergreen leaves about 24 in. tall and 4 in. wide. Flowers are inconspicuous. Spreads slowly to form a dense, weed-proof ground cover. This plant is absolutely carefree. Pages: 40, 63, 66, 70.

Aucuba japonica 'Variegata'

GOLD-DUST AUCUBA **Zones 6–10** ◗ ● **M** ▼ An evergreen shrub with thick, erect stems. Grows 6 to 10 ft. tall, and at least 5 ft. wide. Large, toothed, leathery leaves are dark green and speckled with yellow dots. Female plants bear cherry red berries, if there's a male plant nearby. One of the best shrubs for dark shady sites. Prune in late winter, if desired. Pages: 22, 40.

Bambusa multiplex

HEDGE BAMBOO **Zones 8–11** ✳ ◗ **L M** ◆ Noninvasive evergreen bamboo that grows quickly to heights of 10 to 25 ft., screening a two-story house in two seasons. Ideal as a tall privacy hedge in areas too small for shade trees. Grows in clumps of erect, 1-in. stems (culms) bearing pairs of lance-shaped leaves at each node. As the culms mature and thicken, they "knock" in the wind, adding another dimension to the landscape. For more color, try 'Alphonse Karr', a cultivar with yellow-and-green-striped culms. Hedge bamboo prefers fertile well-drained soil. Young culms can be easily removed if they creep out of bounds. Plants are sometimes also sold as *B. glaucescens*. Page: 58.

Betula nigra

RIVER BIRCH **Zones 3–9** ☀ ◗ **M H** ◆ A multi-trunked, deciduous tree with very attractive beige, tan, or coppery bark that peels loose and curls back similar to the pages of a book that's gotten wet. The leaves are glossy green all summer and turn tan or gold in fall. Grows 1 to 2 ft. a year, reaching 60 ft. tall and almost that wide when mature. Prefers moist soil but adapts to drier sites. Subject to various diseases and insects, but usually the damage is minor. Wind resistant, but train young trees to eliminate narrow crotches, which can break apart in storms. Page: 16.

Bignonia capreolata

CROSS VINE **Zones 7–10** ☀ ◗ **M H** ▼ A Southeast native vine of quilted, lance-shaped, evergreen leaves. In spring, the entire plant turns into a mass of beautiful trumpetlike yellow-to-orange flowers with reddish throats, a welcome sight for winter-weary eyes and a source of nectar for migrating hummingbirds. Scattered bloom continues through the growing season. Train the vine on fences, trellises, or arbors for a colorful focal point. If left unattended, this vigorous climber can reach a height of 30 ft. Prune as needed, at least annually. Pages: 16, 19, 57, 73, 88.

Bougainvillea spectabilis

BOUGAINVILLEA **Zones 9–11** ☀ **L** ▲ One of the most spectacular flowering plants, with colorful bracts (modified leaves) in striking shades of white, pink, red, orange, yellow, or purple seen periodically throughout the year. Habit varies by variety from sprawling, shrubby vines that can spread over 20 ft. wide to low ground covers. The true species (*B. spectabilis*) has purple bracts and is the most common bougainvillea found and one of many vigorous types that need the support of a strong fence or trellis. 'Barbara Karst' has red bracts and is also a shrubby vine but can be used as a ground cover on banks. 'New Gold' is bronzy yellow and grows 5 to 6 ft. tall with the support of a trellis. Bougainvilleas are hardy in Zones 10 and 11 but are often grown in warmer portions of Zone 9 with protection during freezes or removal of die back in the spring. Bougainvillea is very thorny, and eye protection, gloves, and long sleeves are recommended when pruning. Be careful not to damage roots when planting. Water during the summer until the plants are established. Pages: 74, 81.

Betula nigra
RIVER BIRCH

Bignonia capreolata
CROSS VINE

Bougainvillea spectabilis
BOUGAINVILLEA

Bulbs

The bulbs recommended in this book are perennials that bloom in spring, early summer, or late fall in the Southeast. Some lose their foliage and go dormant when out of their bloom cycle, while others are evergreen. To get started, you can purchase bulbs from a catalog or potted plants from a garden center. Plant them promptly in a bed with well-prepared soil. In subsequent years, all you have to do is pick off the faded flowers and remove (or ignore, if you choose) the old leaves after they turn brown. Most bulbs can be divided every few years if you want to make more plants. Dig them up after they bloom or as the foliage is turning yellow; shake or pull them apart; and replant them right away. For more information on specific bulbs, see Recommended Bulbs.

Bulbine frutescens 'Hallmark'

ORANGE BULBINE **Zones 8–11** ☀ ◗ **L M** ◆ This great succulent ground cover should be in every water-wise garden in the Southeast. It is drought tolerant and hardy to 20°F, and it flowers from early spring to fall. The handsome, fleshy linear leaves are 6 to 12 in. long and ¼ in. wide, forming mounded clumps that slowly spread by rhizomes. Flower stalks arise above the foliage and are topped with multiple, six-petal, star-shaped flowers that bloom sequentially from the bottom to the top. 'Hallmark' bulbine's flowers are orange with yellow centers. Remove spent flower stalks to keep plants looking tidy. Plant 18 in. apart and divide after 3 to 4 years. Pages: 34, 55, 77.

Bulbine
frutescens
'Hallmark'
ORANGE BULBINE

Recommended bulbs

Agapanthus africanus

LILY OF THE NILE **Zones 8–10** ☀ ◗ **L M** ◆ This is a great flowering bulb with arching, straplike leaves and ball-shaped clusters of blue or white flowers in late spring and early summer. Most varieties grow 2 to 3 ft. tall and bear flower clusters on stalks 3 to 5 ft. high. Agapanthus 'Peter Pan' is a dwarf variety with leaves only reaching 12 in. tall and blue flowers on stalks 18 in. high. In warmer regions of the Southeast, Lily of the Nile prefers afternoon shade and well-drained soils. All grow best with regular watering but can tolerate dry periods. This lily stays evergreen in mild winters and goes dormant in colder climes. Space 12 to 18 in. apart with the neck of the bulb just above the soil line. Divide when crowded, every five to seven years. A great choice for pots and near pools. Pages: 38, 77.

Caladium x hortulanum

CALADIUM **Zones 9–11** ☀ ◗ ● **L** ▼ (Light needs vary with varieties) The colorful, arrow-shaped foliage of the caladium comes in a variety of color combinations, leaf sizes, and heights to make this shade-loving plant a must in Southeast gardens. Caladium is most effective in masses planted within existing beds of green ground covers, such as mondo grass, lilyturf, or cast-iron plant. When early summer evening temperatures reach 70°F, caladiums awake from their winter slumber to add drama to a dark, shady garden. As temperatures cool in the fall, the foliage fades. Tubers should be planted 3 to 5 in. deep with the "eye," or growing tip, pointing up. Tubers or potted plants should be spaced 8 to 12 in. apart. Page: 38.

Agapanthus
africanus
LILY OF THE NILE

Caladium x *hortulanum*
CALADIUM

Hippeastrum x *hybridum*
AMARYLLIS

Hippeastrum x hybridum

AMARYLLIS **Zones 8–10** ❋ ◗ **M** ▼ A semievergreen bulb in Zone 8, evergreen in Zones 9 -11, the amaryllis is well known for its tall flower stalk held well beyond its straplike leaves. Borne in clusters of 2 to 5, the trumpet-shaped blooms appear in spring in various shades and colors. The bulbs or grown plants can be scattered singly for splashes of color or planted in mass, spaced 12 to 18 in. apart with the neck of the bulb just above the top of the soil.

Lycoris radiata

HURRICANE LILY **Zones 8–10** ❋ ◗ **M** ▲ This lily is also called the "surprise lily" due to its fall flower. After the heavy summer rains, slender 12-to-24-in.-tall stalks give rise to 8-in. clusters of tubular red flowers. After flowering, the long, narrow strap leaves emerge and persist until spring. Resist the temptation to remove yellowing leaves and allow them to die back naturally. This summer dormant bulb is best planted in late summer or fall with the neck of the bulb just below the soil surface, 12 in. apart. Potted plants can be added to the garden any time of year.

Zephyranthes atamasca

RAIN LILY **Zones 7–11** ❋ ◗ **M H** ▼ This Southeast native bulb can be easily spotted after a spring rain along roadsides. Dotted among mown areas, you'll find

Zephyranthes atamasca
RAIN LILY

masses of star-shaped, crocus-like flowers of white, pink, or yellow. Choose the rain lily for sunny or shady areas, planted within other low ground covers as these bulbs go dormant in the winter. Blooms only last a few days, but successive rains bring more blooms. Collect the seeds to germinate or allow them to naturalize beds in your garden. Flowers of *Z. atamasca* are white that fade to light pink on 10-in. stalks. Plant bulbs or young plants 12 in. apart with the bulb just below the soil surface. Page 38.

Butia capitata
PINDO PALM

Buxus microphylla
LITTLELEAF BOXWOOD

Carrisa macrocarpa
NATAL PLUM

Butia capitata

PINDO PALM **Zones 8–10** ☀ ◗ **L** ◆ This slow-growing palm of feather-like, blue-gray fronds can reach a height of 10 to 20 ft. and a spread of 8 to 10 ft. Old fronds can be trimmed close to the trunk to create a diamond pattern and an interesting texture. Choose a palm with at least 3 ft. of trunk height; a young palm lacks this characteristic trunk, and once a trunk is visible, the growth rate slows to less than 1 ft. per year. In spring, pindo palm produces clusters of small creamy yellow flowers that mature into pineapple-scented fruits that are yellow to bright orange. Fruits can be eaten fresh or used to make jellies. This palm adapts to a wide range of soils and tolerates high rainfall or drought conditions. This is a superior wind-resistant palm for the Southeast and the coast. Pages: 34, 57, 81.

Buxus microphylla

LITTLELEAF BOXWOOD **Zones 6–10** ☀ ◗ **L M** ▼ Very popular and highly prized shrub that forms a dense mass of neat, small, glossy evergreen leaves. The leaves, and the small spring flowers, have a distinct fragrance. Boxwood forms soft mounded shapes if left alone or can be sheared into formal globes, cones, hedges, or topiary. There are many kinds of boxwood, differing in rate of growth, size of leaf, and natural habit (upright or spreading). Most cultivars of littleleaf boxwood, *B. microphylla*, have small, bright-green leaves and form compact globes up to 4 ft. tall. English boxwood, *B. sempervirens*, has larger, darker-green leaves; can grow quite large, up to 20 ft. tall; and is only recommended for Zones 6 through 8. Boxwoods grow slowly, so buy the largest plants you can afford. They need well-drained soil covered with a layer of mulch. Shear in early summer if desired. Pages: 18, 20, 26, 53.

Camellia sasanqua 'Shishigashira'

SHISHIGASHIRA CAMELLIA **Zones 7–9** ☀ ◗ **M** ▼ Evergreen shrub with glossy foliage and rose-colored, semidouble flowers that bloom in early winter. Like all sasanqua camellias, 'Shishigashira' adapts to full sun as well as partial shade but remains as a low, compact shrub of only 3 to 4 ft. height and spread. They are relatively pest-free and easier to care for than *C. japonica*. They prefer moist, well-drained, acid soil with a layer of mulch. Prune and fertilize with an acid fertilizer immediately after flowering if desired. Pages: 22, 42, 44.

Camellia sasanqua 'Shishigashira'
SHISHIGASHIRA CAMELLIA

Carrisa macrocarpa

NATAL PLUM **Zones 10–11** ☀ ◗ **L** ▲ Evergreen shrub that grows up to 10 ft. in height. The natal plum has glossy, dark-green rounded leaves and small fragrant white flowers that bloom spring, summer, and fall. The flowers are followed by small green fruits that ripen to red. The birds love the fruits, but you can also collect them for making jellies. Stems generally have forked spines, so take care when pruning. 'Emerald Beauty' is a dense, spreading cultivar that only reaches 12 to 18 in. in height. Taller varieties can be "limbed up" to produce decorative small trees. Pages: 33, 53, 55, 73, 74.

Cephalotaxus harringtonia 'Prostrata'

PROSTRATE JAPANESE PLUM YEW **Zones 6–9** ☀ ◗ **M** ▼ An evergreen conifer with shiny dark-green needles. Spreads to form a low mound 2 to 3 ft. tall and wide. Grows slowly and needs little pruning. An excellent conifer for the South and substitute for the traditional yew (*Taxus* spp.), it is very tolerant of hot weather and resists pests, including deer. It's not commonly grown, so you may have to ask your local nursery to order one for you. Prune only when needed to correct its shape. Shearing is not recommended. Page: 40.

Cercis canadensis

REDBUD **Zones 4–9** ☀ ◗ **L** ▼ A small deciduous native tree that produces clusters of tiny bright-pink-purple flowers on its bare branches in early spring. Heart-shaped leaves appear after blooming and are medium green all summer, turning gold in fall. This wind-resistant tree may reach 20 to 25 ft. tall and wide. Redbud prefers well-drained soil and performs best in Zone 9 with afternoon shade. Available with single or multiple trunks, redbud grows quickly, so it's reasonable to start with a small plant. Prune every summer, removing limbs that hang too low and dead twigs that accumulate inside the crown. Pages: 18, 31.

Cephalotaxus harringtonia 'Prostrata'
PROSTRATE JAPANESE PLUM YEW

Cercis canadensis
REDBUD

Cornus florida
DOGWOOD

Conocarpus erectus var. sericeus

SILVER BUTTONWOOD **Zones 10–11** ☀ **L** ▲ A low-branching, multitrunked, evergreen shrub to small tree with beautiful silvery leaves due to silky hairs that cover the leaf surface. The small, greenish flowers appear in dense cone-like heads in spring followed by ½-in. red-brown fruits. The attractive dark-brown bark is ridged and scaly adding interest to the garden. This wind-resistant tree can reach 15 to 20 ft. in height and spread. It needs little pruning to develop a good structure. However, with regular pruning you can create an attractive hedge. Native to Florida's southernmost coast, it will often take on a picturesque, contorted appearance when exposed to constant seashore winds, creating an attractive specimen. Pages: 34, 74.

Cornus florida

DOGWOOD **Zones 4–9** ☀ ◗ **H** ▼ Dogwood is a very popular native deciduous tree with showy flowers in spring, red berries that attract birds in fall, and crimson autumn foliage. Grows up to 25 ft. tall and wide, with a rounded crown. Typically has white flowers, but some cultivars have pink flowers instead. In Zone 9, it prefers partial shade. Small trees transplant better than large specimens. Plant when dormant in early spring or late fall, not in the heat of summer. Prune in early summer, right after it blooms, only to remove weak, crossing, or lower limbs. Wind resistant. Pages: 19, 38.

Cryptomeria japonica 'Yoshino'

YOSHINO JAPANESE CEDAR **Zones 5–9** ☀ **M** ▼ A fast-growing conifer that forms a neat cone-shaped tree with needle-like fragrant foliage that is bright green in summer and bronzy in winter. Grows to 30 ft. or taller. Requires no care at all. Page: 25.

Dichorisandra thyrsiflora

BLUE GINGER **Zones 9–11** ◗ **M** ▼ This shade-loving evergreen perennial is a perfect jungle specimen for a tropical garden. Lustrous succulent leaves are arranged in spirals on stems, forming a dark-green patchwork 5 to 8 ft. tall and 4 ft. wide. Dense clusters of deep violet flowers, the size of hyacinths, bloom at the top of the plant in autumn. Prefers well-drained, fertile soil. Water plentifully during warm months but sparingly in winter. Remove frost-damaged foliage in early spring, and apply a liquid fertilizer monthly. Page: 62.

Dietes vegeta

WHITE AFRICAN IRIS **Zones 8–10** ☀ ◗ **L** ▼ An evergreen perennial grown as a ground cover. Forms clumps of stiff, bladelike, gray-green foliage 18 to 24 in. tall and wide. From spring through summer, branching flower stalks bear 2-in.-diameter irislike white flowers with violet and yellow throat marks. It prefers well-drained soil and is drought tolerant once established. Remove spent flower stalks to encourage blooms. Divide clumps every 3 to 4 years in late summer or late winter. Also known as *D. iridoides*. Pages: 50, 53, 59, 61, 65, 73, 84.

Euphorbia tirucalli

PENCIL TREE **Zones 10–11** ☀ **L** ▲ An evergreen succulent that has thin, usually leafless, light-green stems. Older branches turn reddish brown, and the flowers are inconspicuous. Trees can be single or multitrunked, and older specimens can reach 20 to 30 ft. high and 6 to 10 ft. wide. All parts of the plant ooze a milky sap when cut. Caution: this sap can be a skin and eye irritant. In Zones 8 and 9, this tree can be grown in a container and moved to a protected area during frost or freezes. Makes a great specimen or dense hedge. Pages: 74, 81.

Dichorisandra thyrsiflora
BLUE GINGER

Dietes vegeta
WHITE AFRICAN IRIS

Ferns

Ferns are carefree, long-lived perennials for shady sites. Despite their delicate appearance, they're among the most durable and trouble-free plants you can grow. Almost all ferns need shade from the midday and afternoon sun. They grow best in soil that's been amended with extra organic matter. You can divide them every few years in early spring if you want more plants, or leave them alone for decades. They need no routine care. See Recommended Ferns for more information on specific ferns.

Recommended ferns

Athyrium niponicum
'Pictum'
JAPANESE PAINTED FERN

Athyrium niponicum 'Pictum'

JAPANESE PAINTED FERN **Zones 4–9** ◗ ● **M** ▼ A colorful fern that forms rosettes of finely cut fronds marked in shades of green, silver, and maroon. They look almost iridescent. Remove fronds damaged by frost and freezes in spring. Grows 1 to 2 ft. tall and 2 ft. wide. Pages: 18, 22, 38, 40, 44, 71.

Cyrtomium falcatum
HOLLY FERN

Cyrtomium falcatum

HOLLY FERN **Zones 9–10** ◗ ● **M** ◆ A showy evergreen fern with fronds divided into large, glossy, hollylike leaflets. Forms clumps about 2 ft. tall and 3 ft. wide. Pages: 39, 40, 44, 63, 66, 71, 78, 88.

Dryopteris erythrosora
AUTUMN FERN

Dryopteris erythrosora

AUTUMN FERN **Zones 9–11** ◗ ● **M H** ▼ Beautiful glossy fronds start out coppery colored and then turn medium green as they mature. Evergreen in mild winters, but may freeze to the ground in cold years. Remove damaged fronds in the spring. Forms erect clumps 2 to 3 ft. tall and 2 ft. wide. Pages: 40, 63, 67, 71.

Osmunda cinnamomea
CINNAMON FERN

Osmunda cinnamomea

CINNAMON FERN **Zones 3–10** ◗ ● **H** ▼ A native fern that forms erect clumps of finely divided deciduous fronds. Grows 2 to 3 ft. tall and spreads to form small colonies. Needs consistently moist soil. For drier conditions in Zone 8, substitute with the similar-looking interrupted fern, *O. claytoniana*. Page: 39.

Polystichum polyblepharum

TASSEL FERN **Zones 5–9** ◗ **M H** ▼ An evergreen fern with stiff, glossy, finely divided fronds. Needs consistently moist soil. Forms a clump about 2 ft. tall and 3 to 4 ft. wide. Page: 39.

Fortunella spp.
KUMQUAT

Gelsemium sempervirens
CAROLINA JASMINE

Hamelia patens
FIREBUSH

Fortunella spp.

KUMQUAT **Zones 9–11** ✳ **M** ◆ Kumquats are one of the cold-hardiest of the citrus family (to 20° F) and are a great landscape or patio tree for the Southeast. These evergreen shrubs to small trees rarely reach over 10 ft. The fragrant creamy flowers appear in May, well after the threat of frost, and the small green fruits ripen to a golden orange in late November. *F. margarita*, or the 'Nagami' kumquat, has oval fruits with a sweet-tart taste. *F. crassifolia*, or the 'Meiwa', has a round fruit that is sweeter. Both are eaten whole. Pick the fruit by clipping them from the tree because pulling results in a torn peel which quickly dries out the fruit. Fertilize every 4 to 6 weeks with a citrus fertilizer from February to September. Kumquats grafted on Flying Dragon rootstock are a popular dwarfing choice for container-grown plants. Page: 47.

Gelsemium sempervirens

CAROLINA JASMINE **Zones 7–9** ✳ ◗ **M** ▼ An evergreen vine native to the Southeast and beloved throughout the region for its showy display of fragrant yellow bell-shaped flowers in early spring. The neat small leaves are dark green all summer, maroon in winter. This vine can climb trees, but it is usually trained against a fence, trellis, or post. Prune annually (right after it blooms) to keep it under 10 ft. tall. Can also be used as a ground cover. Page: 23.

Hamelia patens

FIREBUSH **Zones 9–11** ✳ ◗ **L** ◆ A native Florida evergreen shrub that brings color, texture, and hummingbirds to the garden. Bright red, tubular flowers bloom from March to November and mature into glossy black berries. Large compound leaves acquire a red tinge as autumn approaches. Grows 6 to 8 ft. tall and 4 to 5 ft. wide. Prefers full sun but adapts to partial shade. Grow it in moderately-to-well-drained soil. Hard freezes will knock it back to the ground. Remove cold-damaged or dead branches prior to new spring growth. Pages: 58, 61, 69, 91.

Helianthus debilis

BEACH SUNFLOWER **Zones 8–10** ✳ **L** ▲ A spreading perennial ground cover with attractive, small sunflower-like flowers throughout the year. The foliage is small, dark green with leaf edges that are irregularly lobed and toothed. Beach sunflower grows to an 18-in. height. This plant spreads by underground runners and will quickly fill in an area if provided with occasional irrigation. Over-irrigation can slow growth and cause plant decline. This Florida native attracts butterflies and can be used in mass plantings or cascading over walls. Pages: 75, 83, 86.

Hemerocallis cvs.

DAYLILY CULTIVARS **Zones 3–9** ✳ **L** ▲ Among the most reliable and popular perennials, with large lilylike flowers in summer held above dense clumps of grassy arching leaves. Each clump produces several flower stalks 2 to 4 ft. tall, bearing up to a dozen or more flowers apiece. Hundreds of cultivars produce flowers in shades of orange, gold, yellow, cream, pink, red, or purple, each blooming for a few weeks or more during June or July. 'Stella d'Oro' is especially popular because it blooms almost continuously from late spring until hard frost, with golden yellow flowers on stalks about 2 ft. tall. Cut off flower stalks after blooming is finished. Divide every few years in late summer. Pages: 17, 25, 29, 37.

Helianthus debilis
BEACH SUNFLOWER

Hemerocallis cvs.
DAYLILY CULTIVARS

Herbs

Nothing is more satisfying than when in the midst of preparing a meal, you can take a quick walk out into the garden to snip a few fresh herbs to add to your dish. Most herbs prefer full sun to create those volatile oils that make them so fragrant and tasty (basil, oregano, parsley, and rosemary), but a few can also take partial shade (mint, chives, and thyme). Herbs grown in the Southeast prefer moderately fertile, well-draining soil and regular watering. Most perform very well in containers; we recommend growing a selection in the ground as well as in containers so that you can judge for yourself. Terra-cotta containers are best for keeping roots cooler in the summer months.

Fertilize regularly February to September with a general-purpose fertilizer, and trim often to keep plants nicely shaped and provide new cooking opportunities. Don't forget, if an herb is edible, so is it's flower. See Recommended Herbs for more information on specific herbs for the region.

Hosta sieboldiana 'Elegans'

ELEGANS HOSTA **Zones 3–8** ● **M** ▼ Long-lived, care-free perennial with large, round, puckered leaves with a blue-gray color and waxy texture. Stalks of white flowers appear in mid- to late summer. Cut off flower stalks before seedpods ripen. Clumps can be divided in early spring if you want to make more plants; otherwise, leave them alone. This slug-resistant hosta forms an impressive clump, 2 to 3 ft. tall, up to 8 ft. wide. Pages: 19, 31, 42.

Hosta sieboldiana 'Elegans'
ELEGANS HOSTA

Recommended herbs

Allium schoenoprasum

ONION CHIVES **Zones 3–9** ✳ ◗ **M** ▼ This perennial herb can be started from seed, but starting with young plants is faster. The hollow, tubular leaves are harvested at the plant's base and used fresh in dressings, soups, omelets, and so much more. Divide by digging up the plants, pulling them apart, and replanting them every 3 to 4 years.

Mentha spp.

MINT **Zones 6–11** ✳ ◗ **M** ▼ One of the easiest perennial herbs to grow. Spearmint (*M. spicata*) and peppermint (*M. piperita*) are two of the most popular. Start from cuttings or small plants. Harvest the leaves and flowering tops to be used either fresh or dried. Mints can be aggressive if planted in the ground, so containers are highly recommended. Withholding water will also slow down their growth.

Ocimum basilicum
SWEET BASIL

Origanum vulgare
OREGANO

Ocimum basilicum

SWEET BASIL Annual ☀ M ▼ A popular annual herb that is the main ingredient in pesto. There are many types, from large to small leaved, with leaf colors ranging from green to purple to variegated. Start from seed, and harvest the young leaf tips often to encourage bushiness and discourage flowering. Start new plants every few weeks so that you never run out.

Origanum vulgare

OREGANO Zones 7–10 ☀ L M ◆ A low growing perennial ground cover for well-draining soils. The leaves have the best flavor when the flowers are just beginning to bloom. Oreganos make a great ground cover to use on slopes where erosion is a problem.

Petroselinum spp.

PARSLEY Zones 5–9 Biannual ☀ ◗ M ▼ Curly parsley (*P. crispum*) and Italian parsley (*P. crispum* var. *neapolitanum*) are both staples in the herb garden. This biannual takes two years to flower and produce seed. Shortly thereafter, the plant will die, so replace it quickly so you never run out. The black swallowtail butterfly will lay its eggs on parsley, so don't be alarmed if you see dozens of white, black, and yellow striped caterpillars munching away. The plant will recover after the caterpillars turn to butterflies, but plant more so there is enough for everyone. Page: 91.

Rosmarinus officinalis

ROSEMARY Zones 7–10 ☀ L ◆ An evergreen shrub with gray-green needle-like leaves that combine a lovely fragrance with a tasty flavor. Small blue, lilac, or white flowers bloom in late winter and early spring. Grows upright and bushy, 3 to 4 ft. tall. 'Arp' is the hardiest cultivar of this popular herb and survives outdoors throughout the Southeast (pp. 47, 73, 77). Prune or shear in spring or summer.

Thymus vulgaris

THYME Zones 4–8, annual elsewhere ☀ ◗ L M ▲ A shrubby perennial that usually grows no more than 8 to 10 in. tall, with very tiny green-to-gray-green leaves. Purplish flowers are formed at the ends of the stems. To harvest, remove the top one-third portion

Petroselinum crispum var. *neapolitanum* ITALIAN PARSLEY

Rosmarinus officinalis ROSEMARY

Thymus x *citriodorus* VARIEGATED LEMON THYME

of the plant when in full bloom and use fresh or spread on newspaper to dry. Thyme can be grown from seed, or purchase young plants to set in the spring or fall. *T. citriodorus*, lemon thyme, has yellow variegated leaves and can only be propagated by cuttings.

Hydrangea quercifolia
OAKLEAF HYDRANGEA

Hyophorbe lagenicaulis
BOTTLE PALM

Illicium parviflorum
YELLOW ANISE

Hydrangea quercifolia

OAKLEAF HYDRANGEA **Zones 5–9** ✻ ❱ **M H** ▼ A deciduous shrub native to the Southeast and well adapted to hot, humid weather. Large lobed leaves emerge pale green in spring, turn dark in summer, and display winelike shades of red and purple in fall. Grows fairly quickly, reaching at least 8 ft. tall and wide. The stems have peeling, cinnamon-colored bark that's attractive in winter. Clusters of papery white flowers top the stems in late spring, then turn beige or pink-tan and last through the summer and fall. Snow Queen has larger-than-average flowers, and Snowflake has double flowers. Water during dry spells. Page: 38.

Hyophorbe lagenicaulis

BOTTLE PALM **Zones 10–11** ✻ ❱ **L** ▲ This tropical wind-resistant palm is known for its characteristic swollen, bottle-shaped trunk, up to 2 ft. in diameter. It grows slowly up to 15 ft. high and develops 4 to 8 featherlike (pinnate) leaves each up to 9 to 12 ft. long. Cream-colored flowers on long stalks develop just below the crownshaft, where the lowest frond base meets the trunk. Its high salt tolerance makes the bottle palm a unique specimen for southernmost coastal gardens. Pages: 34, 75.

Hollies

A versatile group of evergreen shrubs and trees used for foundation plantings, hedges, and specimens. The stiff-textured leaves can be small or large, smooth or spiny, dull or glossy. Holly plants are either male or female. Females typically bear heavy crops of small round berries that ripen in fall and last through the next spring. All tolerate sun or partial shade. Prune or shear at any season to keep them at the desired size. See Recommended Hollies for more information on specific hollies.

Illicium parviflorum

YELLOW ANISE **Zones 7–9** ✻ ❱ **M L** ◆ A native evergreen shrub often grown as a hedge because of its dense, uniform habit. The thick yellow-green matte foliage reaches 4 to 10 ft. high, staying full to the ground. Leaves release a licorice scent when cut or crushed. The flowers are inconspicuous. Yellow anise performs well in full sun or partial shade and tolerates wet soil and short periods of drought. It responds well to hand pruning. Trim the top narrower than the base to allow light to reach the lower limbs. Pages: 47, 66, 70.

Recommended hollies

Ilex cornuta
'Burforii Nana' HOLLY

Ilex x *attenuata* 'Foster #2'
FOSTER HOLLY

Ilex cornuta
'Burfordii' HOLLY

Ilex x *attenuata* 'Foster #2'

FOSTER'S HOLLY **Zones 7–10** ☀ ◗ **M** ◆ A slim, columnar or conical tree, growing about 25 ft. tall and 10 to 15 ft. wide, with shiny leaves and lots of red berries. *I.* x *attenuata* 'Foster #2' is a popular cultivar with slender leaves. *I.* x *attenuata* 'Savannah' is similar but has larger leaves and berries. Best grown in Zone 8 and upper portion of Zone 9. Pages: 26, 53.

Ilex cornuta

EVERGREEN HOLLY **Zones 7–9** ◗ ◗ **L** ◆ A large, dense, bushy shrub with glossy foliage. *I. cornuta* 'Burfordii' or Burford holly, grows 15 to 20 ft. tall, has large leaves with few spines, and bears abundant crops of red berries. *I. cornuta* 'Burfordii Nana' or dwarf Burford holly only grows to 10 ft. but is easily clipped to keep it shorter. *I. cornuta* 'Needlepoint' can reach 10 ft. tall and wide but is often kept smaller by shearing. It has lobed leaves, and bright red-orange berries. Pages: 17, 26, 33, 47, 53, 73, 77, 88, 91.

Ilex crenata

JAPANESE HOLLY **Zones 6–9** ☀ ◗ **L** ◆ A dense twiggy shrub with small dark green leaves and inconspicuous dark berries. 'Compacta' grows about 6 ft. tall and wide, with glossier-than-average leaves. 'Helleri' reaches only 4 ft. tall and wide and has dull leaves. Both are often sheared, but they don't need it, as their

natural growth habit is very neat and compact. Japanese hollies need acid soil; where the soil is alkaline, plant dwarf yaupon holly instead. Pages: 17, 20, 26.

Ilex vomitoria

YAUPON HOLLY **Zones 7–10** ☀ ◗ ● **L** ▲ A wind-resistant native tree with small, shiny, spineless leaves and juicy red berries. Grows about 15 to 20 ft. tall, usually with multiple trunks and is easily trained and pruned. *I. vomitoria* 'Pendula' is a weeping form and is used as a unique columnar specimen tree. Dwarf yaupon holly, *I. vomitoria* 'Nana', or the schillings holly, is a low, compact, shrubby form that grows 3 to 5 ft. tall and wide. This holly is propagated from male plants, so it never flowers, thus produces no berries. All yaupon hollies are very tough, adaptable, and easy to grow. Pages: 23, 27, 37, 47, 53, 65, 70, 73, 77, 78, 86, 91.

Ilex cornuta
'Needlepoint' HOLLY

Ilex vomitoria
YAUPON HOLLY

Ilex vomitoria
'PENDULA' HOLLY

Juniperus chinensis
'TORULOSA'
HOLLYWOOD JUNIPER

Juniperus davurica
'EXPANSA'
PARSON'S JUNIPER

Justicia carnea
JACOBINEA

Juniperus chinensis 'Torulosa'

HOLLYWOOD JUNIPER **Zones 4–10** ☀ **L ◆** A small evergreen tree with an interesting irregular profile and bright green, fine-textured foliage. Grows 15 to 20 ft. tall, 4 to 8 ft. wide. Prune only if needed to remove damaged shoots. A carefree plant specimen or screen. Pages: 25, 27.

Juniperus davurica 'Expansa'

PARSON'S JUNIPER **Zones 4–9** ☀ **L ▲** A low evergreen shrub with gray-green foliage. Grows about 2 ft. tall and can spread several feet wide but is often pruned to keep it narrower. One of the best shrubby junipers for Southeast gardens. Pages: 25, 29.

Justicia carnea

JACOBINEA **Zones 8–11** ◗ **H ▼** An erect, sparsely branching, evergreen shrub grown for its irresistible hot-pink flowers. Also known as "Brazilian plume" or "flamingo flower." Clusters of tubular flowers open in feathery plumes against a backdrop of dark-green oblong leaves in summer. Grows 6 ft. tall and 3 ft. wide. Plant in bright filtered sunlight or partial shade, but always protect it from hot sun. Prune the tips of young plants in spring to promote bushiness. Frost and freezes will knock the plant to the ground. Remove damaged leaves and stems in the spring. Pages: 39, 40, 63.

Lagerstroemia indica

CRAPE MYRTLE **Zones 7–10** ☀ **L ▼** Small, often multi-trunked, deciduous trees with handsome bark, rounded leaves, and clusters of frilly-edged flowers. Unlike old-fashioned crape myrtles, the cultivars listed below are resistant to powdery mildew, and their foliage looks nice throughout the growing season. 'Natchez' grows 20 to 25 ft. tall and blooms all summer, bearing large clusters of papery-textured white flowers atop each stem. Leaves turn bright red, orange, or purplish in fall, and the flaking cinnamon-colored trunk bark is very attractive in winter. 'Acoma' (*L. indica* x *fauriei*, p. 61) is a white semidwarf slightly weeping cultivar, growing 10 to 12 ft. tall and 7 to 8 ft. wide. Crape myrtle flowers appear in late spring to early summer, followed by rounded seedpods. Removing pods as they develop encourages a second and even a third bloom. Crape myrtles need well-drained soil. Prune in spring. Never commit "crape murder"; trim healthy branches only if they are smaller than the diameter of a pencil. Select multitrunked trees if possible.

Crape myrtles may suffer frost damage in severe winters, but they soon recover. Wind resistant. Pages: 20, 25, 61.

Lantana montevidensis

TRAILING LANTANA **Zones 8–11** ☀ **L ▲** A low-growing, trailing, evergreen shrub that forms a dense mat 2 to 4 ft. wide and up to 3 ft. high of slender, hairy stems and dark-green toothed leaves. Tiny lavender to violet flowers bloom in tight domed heads, making perfect sipping stations for butterflies and moths. The heaviest bloom is in summer, but it will bloom year-round in coastal areas and in mild winters elsewhere. A good choice for hot sites and poor soils. Prune stem tips in early spring and fall to encourage bushiness and new blooms. Pages: 61, 65, 69, 75, 81, 84, 91.

Lagerstroemia indica
CRAPE MYRTLE

Lantana montevidensis
TRAILING LANTANA

Lantana 'NEW GOLD'
NEW GOLD LANTANA

*Leucophyllum
frutescens*
'COMPACTUM'
COMPACT TEXAS SAGE

Lantana 'New Gold'

NEW GOLD LANTANA **Zones 8–11** ✷ ◗ L ▲ A low-growing compact evergreen ground cover with dark-green saw-toothed leaves. Clusters of tiny five-petaled flowers are a rich, clear orange-yellow and provide a great source of nectar for butterflies and night moths. Grows 12 to 18 in. high and spreads 30 in. wide. It is drought-tolerant once established. Prune lightly in early spring and again in early fall to encourage more flowers. Blooms almost year-round in warmer regions of the Southeast. Pages: 34, 37, 48, 53, 59, 61, 69, 88.

Leucophyllum frutescens 'Compactum'

COMPACT TEXAS SAGE **Zones 8–10** ✷ L ◆ A dwarf cultivar of the striking, silver-leaved, drought tolerant Texas-native shrub. It has a dense, slightly irregular shape and reaches 3 to 4 ft. tall and wide. Following summer rains, it becomes flushed with small orchid-pink flowers. Texas sage demands excellent drainage and requires little, if any, supplemental watering. Expect few insect or disease problems. Page: 84.

Ligustrum japonicum

JAPANESE OR WAX-LEAF LIGUSTRUM **Zones 7–11** ✷ ◗ L ▲ A fast-growing evergreen shrub or small tree with very glossy bright-green leaves, clusters of heavy-scented white flowers in early summer, and dark blue-black berries in fall and winter. This small tree develops a graceful shape if you leave it alone. It can reach 15 to 20 ft. tall, or you can prune it however (and whenever) you choose. Shearing is not recommended. Pages: 29, 33, 44, 65, 69, 83, 88.

Liriope muscari

LILYTURF **Zones 5–10** ✷ ◗ ● L ◆ A perennial that forms clumps about 1 to 2 ft. tall and wide of grasslike evergreen leaves. Bears spikes of small violet, purple, or white flowers in late summer,

followed by pea-size black berries. Often used as a ground cover. 'Super Evergreen Giant' is one of the largest cultivars, growing as much as 2 ft. tall and bearing ½-in.-wide dark-green leaf blades. 'Emerald Goddess' is a recently introduced lilyturf that is resistant to crown rot and similar in looks to 'Super Evergreen Giant'. Mow or shear off the old foliage in early spring only if it is damaged. Lilyturf can be divided every few years. Pages: 23, 53, 55, 57, 59, 65, 89.

Liriope spicata

CREEPING LILYTURF **Zones 7–10** ✷ ◗ ● L ▲ Resembles regular lilyturf, but it spreads quickly by underground runners to form a dense patch of foliage, not just clumps. It also has narrower leaves, and the flowers are less conspicuous than those of regular lilyturf. The grassy-looking foliage stays dark green throughout the year. Makes a good ground cover for shady sites. Mow or shear off old foliage in early spring if it becomes damaged. Can be divided every few years to make more plants. Pages: 17, 20, 31, 37.

Liriope muscari
LILYTURF

Ligustrum japonicum
JAPANESE OR WAX-LEAF LIGUSTRUM

Loropetalum chinense var. *rubrum*
RUBY LOROPETALUM

Magnolia grandiflora
'Little Gem'
LITTLE GEM MAGNOLIA

Mahonia bealei
LEATHERLEAF MAHONIA

Loropetalum chinense var. *rubrum*

RUBY LOROPETALUM **Zones 8–10** ☀ **M** ▼ Also known as "fringe flower," this small shrub bears fluffy clusters of lovely dark-pink or rose flowers among layers of oval evergreen burgundy leaves. Blooms mostly in spring but occasionally in summer and fall. Grows about 4 ft. tall, up to 5 ft. wide, with arching limbs. Ruby loropetalum prefers acid soil. Hand-prune lightly after spring bloom to maintain a rounded shape and encourage flower bud development. Shearing is not recommended. Trouble-free. Pages: 20, 57, 65.

Magnolia grandiflora 'Little Gem'

LITTLE GEM MAGNOLIA **Zones 8–10** ☀ ◗ **L** ◆ Popular southern evergreen trees with showy flowers in spring or summer. Little Gem magnolia blooms in late spring, early summer with large, cup-shaped flowers in creamy white that are lemony scented. Its large oblong leaves are a deep, glossy green with rich red-brown undersides. This slow-growing, wind-resistant tree can eventually reach 20 to 25 ft. tall and 10 to 15 ft. wide. Use this diminutive southern belle in areas too small for a large shade tree. Plant in spring, being careful not to damage the roots, which are brittle. If you don't prune them, magnolias retain their lower limbs and form impressive specimens that are bushy all the way to the ground. If you want to shape them into a tree with a trunk and open up the space underneath the boughs, prune in midsummer. Pages: 20, 44.

Mahonia bealei

LEATHERLEAF MAHONIA **Zones 6–9** ◗ ● **L** ◆ An evergreen shrub whose large compound leaves with hollylike leaflets radiate from a clump of stout, erect, usually unbranched, stems. Dense clusters of fragrant golden-yellow flowers in early spring are followed by grape-like clusters of blue berries that birds enjoy. Grows upright, 8 to 10 ft. tall and 3 to 4 ft. wide. Prefers well-drained soil. Groom in early spring, removing tattered or discolored leaves. To prune, remove old, weak, or broken stems at ground level. Pages: 19, 40, 44, 78.

Muhlenbergia capillaris

MUHLEY GRASS **Zones 7–11** ☀ **L** ▲ A fine-textured ornamental grass, native to the Southeast. Muhley grass forms rounded clumps, 24 to 30 in. overall and each fall produces multiple purple plumes held above the foliage. It can tolerant a wide range of soils conditions; from moist to dry, acidic to alkaline, and sandy to marl. It needs little supplemental water, once established. Propagate new plants from seed, or divide large clumps in the spring. If the foliage looks tired, trim it back to 8 in. above the ground in early spring to rejuvenate. Pages: 81, 86.

Nandina domestica

HEAVENLY BAMBOO **Zones 7–10** ☀ ◗ **L** ▼ An evergreen shrub that forms a clump of slender erect stems. Fine-textured compound leaves change color from green to gold to red with the seasons. Common nandina grows 4 to 6 ft. tall, 2 to 3 ft. wide. Invasive in Zone 10. Bears fluffy clusters of white flowers in summer followed by long-lasting red berries. 'Harbour Dwarf', which works in Zones 6–9, forms bushy mounds 18 to 24 in. tall and wide, with fine-textured foliage that turns bright crimson in winter. Prune in spring, removing old, weak, or winter-damaged stems. Pages: 17, 20, 25, 29, 50, 57, 65.

Muhlenbergia capillaris
MUHLEY GRASS

Nandina domestica
HEAVENLY BAMBOO

Odontonema cuspidatum
FIRESPIKE

Odontonema cuspidatum

FIRESPIKE **Zones 8–11** ☀ ◗ **M** ▼ A tropical evergreen shrub with rigid upright stems and glossy, deep-green, wavy leaves. Each stem is topped with showy clusters of tubular crimson flowers in winter, in time for hummingbirds returning south. Blooms continue through the spring. If left unpruned, firespike will grow 6 ft. tall or more and 4 ft. wide. Remove dead or winter-damaged stems at ground level in spring to encourage new growth. Also sold as *O. strictum*. Page: 69.

Ophiopogon japonicus

MONDO GRASS **Zones 8–10** ◗ ● **L** ▲ A perennial ground cover with shiny dark green leaves about ⅛ in. wide and up to 1 ft. long. A mature bed of mondo resembles flowing underwater grass. The flowers are inconspicuous. Do not grow in full sun, as the foliage will burn. A patch fills in better if you start with several small plants instead of a few large ones. Rake out dead foliage in early spring. Fresh, new growth will keep the bed neat the rest of the year. Pages: 19, 38, 40, 44, 63, 67, 71, 78.

Ophiopogon japonicus
MONDO GRASS

Osmanthus fragrans

TEA OLIVE **Zones 7–9** ☀ ◗ **L** ▼ An evergreen shrub with stiff, dark-green hollylike leaves and white flowers that are tiny but very sweet-scented. Blooms in late fall to spring. It is usually grown as an upright, informal shrub up to 12 ft. tall and 6 ft. wide. However, older specimens can be shaped into a small ornamental tree. In Zone 9, tea olive prefers to grow in partial shade. A great addition for winter fragrance. Pages: 23, 39, 40.

Paspalum quadrifarium

EVERGREEN PASPALUM GRASS **Zones 8–11** ☀ **L** ▲ A fine-textured ornamental grass with yellow-green to blue-green arching leaf blades. It forms a graceful mound 3 to 4 ft. tall and wide and is attractive as a single specimen or in a mass planting. Slender flower heads rise above the foliage. Foliage normally needs no winter pruning but may be cut back to 8 in. above the ground in early spring to rejuvenate. Pages: 33, 59, 84.

Passiflora x 'Amethyst'

AMETHYST PASSION FLOWER **Zones 9–11** ☀ ◗ **M** ◆ A favorite evergreen vine of butterfly enthusiasts. It climbs with slender stems and delicate tendrils to heights of 12 ft. or more. Star-shaped flowers with purple-blue centers and green anthers look spectacular against rich green-lobed leaves from late spring through autumn. This vine attracts gulf fritillary butterflies, which lay single golden eggs that hatch into orange-and-black-striped caterpillars. Well-established vines can easily support their voracious appetites. Vines may be stripped of foliage but will quickly recover. Resist the urge during the growing season to trim young growth, which will remove potential blooms and egg-laying sites. For renewed growth, cut back severely in early spring. Also sold as *P.* x 'Lavender Lady'. Pages: 69, 91.

Osmanthus fragrans
TEA OLIVE

Paspalum quadrifarium
EVERGREEN PASPALUM GRAS

Passiflora × 'Amethyst'
AMETHYST PASSION FLOWER

Perennials

Flowering perennials can provide Southeast gardeners long-lived color just about all year. If you are from the North, what you used as annuals may be a great perennial for the South and vice-versa. Our milder winters make all of the difference in the longevity of these flowering plants. Choose well-established plants in 1-to 3-gallon pots. Check the foliage and stems for leafspots and under leaves for hitchhiking insects. Slip the plant out of its pot, and inspect the roots. Is the root system sparse or potbound? Do they look healthy and free from rot? Often, the success of a perennial is found in a healthy root system.

Spring and fall are the best times to plant perennials in the garden. Know their mature width and space them accordingly in the garden to avoid crowding. Give them ample water until they are established and showing new growth. To keep plants healthy, water during the summer and fertilize every other month from spring until fall. Most perennials in the Southeast prefer minimal water during the winter months.

All perennials benefit from periodic "deadheading," or removal of spent flower stalks. This often generates new flower buds and more color. Each spring and fall, give your perennials a good grooming, removing up to one-third the volume of the plant to shape it and promote new growth. See Recommended Perennials for more information on perennials popular in the region.

Coreopsis verticillata 'Moonbeam'
MOONBEAM COREOPSIS

Recommended perennials

Coreopsis verticillata 'Moonbeam'
MOONBEAM COREOPSIS   **Zones 4–9** ☀ ◗ **L** ◆ A long-blooming perennial that bears hundreds of small lemon-yellow daisylike blossoms. Blooming starts in late spring, repeating until fall if you shear off the old flowers from time to time. The dark-green leaves are short and threadlike. Grows about 18 in. tall and wide. Spreads by underground runners, but it is not invasive. Attracts butterflies. Page: 91.

Echinacea purpurea
PURPLE CONEFLOWER   **Zones 3–10** ☀ **L** ▼ A prairie wildflower that thrives in gardens and blooms for several weeks in midsummer. Large rosy-pink daisylike blossoms are held on stiff branching stalks about 3 ft. tall, above a mound of dark-green basal foliage about 2 ft. wide. Cut back flower stalks if you choose, or let the seed heads ripen for winter interest. May self sow, but is not weedy. Older plants can be divided in early spring. Attracts butterflies.

Echinacea purpurea
PURPLE CONEFLOWER

Evolvulus glomeratus
BLUE DAZE   **Zones 8–11** ☀ ◗ **L** ▲ A finely textured, dense, low-growing perennial with gray-green leaves accented with a profusion of clear-blue flowers. Blue daze works well as an edging plant, and will cascade over the side of a raised planter, container, or hanging basket. The small flowers close in the late afternoon, and new ones open in the morning. Space 18 in. apart, and prune back in the spring or early fall to generate new growth and blooms. Blue daze may not survive a hard freeze in Zone 8. Page: 48.

Lysimachia nummularia
MONEYWORT   **Zones 3–10** ☀ ◗ **M** ▼ A creeping, clinging perennial that forms a carpet of round coin-size leaves. Cheerful yellow flowers last for a month or so in summer. Tolerates full sun if the soil is moist, but also does well in full shade. Buy one to start, and divide it later if you want more plants. Spreads quickly, up to 1 ft. per year. Normally has medium-green leaves, but 'Aurea' has golden-yellow leaves.

Lysimachia nummularia
MONEYWORT

Pentas lanceolata

PENTAS **Zones 8–11** ☀ ☽ **L M** ◆ This upright 1-to-4-ft.-tall perennial blooms most of the year with clusters of nectar-rich flowers of white, pink, red, and lavender. Hummingbirds enjoy red varieties; while butterflies will visit any color. The dark-green foliage is heavily veined and covered in fine hairs. Plant 18 to 24 in. apart, and remove spent flowers to encourage repeat blooming. In Zone 8, treat pentas as an annual. Pages: 33, 91.

Rudbeckia fulgida 'Goldsturm'

GOLDSTURM CONEFLOWER **Zones 3–9** ☀ **L** ◆ An improved form of a popular perennial wildflower. Bears hundreds of gold-and-brown flowers, often called black-eyed Susans, for several weeks in late summer. Forms a robust clump about 3 ft. tall and wide, with large dark-green leaves at the base and stiff branching flower stalks. Cut down the flower stalks in fall or spring, as you choose. Divide every few years in early spring. Attracts butterflies. Page: 48.

Salvia farinacea

MEALY BLUE SAGE **Zones 8–10** ☀ **L** ▲ A perennial Texas wildflower. Grows 2 to 3 ft. tall and wide, with a bushy habit and slender, glossy green leaves. Blooms all summer and fall, with dense spikes of violet, blue, or white flowers on slender stiff stalks. Often sold as a bedding plant but overwinters in the Southeast. Cut down old stalks in fall or spring. Care free and attracts butterflies.

Scaevola aemula

FAIRY FAN-FLOWER **Zones 9–11** ☀ **L** ▲ A low-growing, shrubby, evergreen perennial used as a bedding plant in containers and hanging baskets. Leaves are medium green and lance-shaped forming a low carpet, topped with white, blue, or pink fan-shaped flowers that bloom throughout the warm months. 'Blue Wonder' is a favorite selection for Southeast gardens.

Solenostemon scutellarioides

COLEUS **Zones 10–11** ☀ ☽ ◉ **M, H** ▼ (Light levels depend on variety.) For spectacular, year-round

Rudbeckia fulgida 'Goldsturm'
GOLDSTURM CONEFLOWER

Scaevola aemula 'BLUE WONDER'

color, nothing beats the striking foliage of coleus. This perennial comes in a variety of color combinations, leaf sizes, heights, and degree of light tolerance. Once reserved for shady areas of the garden, many of today's cultivars can take full sun. Space 12 to 24 in. apart (depending on cultivar), and pinch young growing tips and flower spikes to encourage bushiness.

Petrea volubilis
QUEEN'S WREATH

Philodendron 'Xanadu'
XANADU PHILODENDRON

Pittosporum tobira
'VARIEGATA'

Petrea volubilis

QUEEN'S WREATH **Zones 10–11** ☀ ◗ **M** ◆ Queen's wreath is a tropical evergreen, twining vine with large, rough-surfaced, dark-green leaves and a very showy display of purplish blue, star-shaped flowers in hanging clusters. It blooms from late winter through summer, but for several weeks in the spring, flowers literally cover the vine. It can be easily trained to cover a fence, pergola, arbor, or trellis. It is important to protect young vines from frost. Page: 34.

Philodendron 'Xanadu'

XANADU PHILODENDRON **Zones 9–11** ◗ **M** ▲ A well-behaved cousin of the familiar philodendron, this compact, nonvining shrub forms a slow-growing mound that won't overrun the landscape. Reaches a maximum height and spread of 4 ft. Deeply split evergreen leaves are smaller and narrower than those of common philodendron. Remove dead or damaged growth in early spring. Pages: 63, 66.

Pittosporum tobira

PITTOSPORUM **Zones 8–11** ☀ ◗ **L** ▲ An evergreen shrub with tufts of glossy leaves, fragrant white flowers in early summer, and a rounded bushy habit. The most popular cultivars are 'Variegata,' variegated pittosporum, which has gray-green leaves with white edging and grows about 6 ft. tall and wide, and 'Wheeleri,' dwarf pittosporum, which has bright green leaves and grows only 3 to 4 ft. tall and wide. Both adapt to sun or shade and need only minimal pruning. Pages: 17, 20, 25, 27, 37, 78, 89.

Plumbago auriculata
PLUMBAGO

Podocarpus macrophyllus
JAPANESE YEW

Pittosporum tobira
'WHEELERI'

Plumbago auriculata

PLUMBAGO **Zones 9–11** ☀ **L** ◆ A semitropical semievergreen shrub that forms a rounded mound 3 to 5 ft. high and wide of slender whip-like stems and oblong leaves. In many parts of the Southeast, it will be smothered in clusters of clear blue flowers from summer to frost. In Florida, it blooms nearly year-round. Plumbago needs fertile, well-drained soil. Lightly prune in early spring and early fall to rejuvenate tired plants. Remove dead stems in early spring.. Pages: 33, 35, 55, 61, 89.

Podocarpus macrophyllus

JAPANESE YEW **Zones 8–11** ☀ ◗ ● **L** ◆ This versatile evergreen is typically grown as a dense screen or hedge but can easily be trained and sheared into topiaries or a beautiful wind-resistant ornamental tree, up to 40 ft. high. The neat, yewlike, dark-green foliage covers the densely limbed trunk to the ground. In lower light, branching becomes less dense and more open. When maintaining as a hedge or column, be sure to keep the lower growth wider than the top to prevent shading. Pages: 33, 89.

Rhaphiolepis indica
INDIAN HAWTHORN

Rhapis excelsa
LADY PALM

Rhaphiolepis indica

INDIAN HAWTHORN **Zones 8-11** ☀ ◗ **L** ▲ A low, spreading evergreen shrub with thick-textured dull-green leaves, small pink or white flowers in spring, and blue berries that last through the summer and fall. Grows 2 to 4 ft. tall, 3 to 6 ft. wide. There are many fine cultivars, including 'Majestic Beauty', 'Snow White', and 'Ballerina', a dwarf cultivar with dark pink flowers. Requires minimal pruning or care. Pages: 25, 29, 37, 75.

Rhapis excelsa

LADY PALM **Zones 9-11** ◗ ● **L** ◆ A small palm with delicate hand-like fronds. Grows slowly, forming a clump of slender, reed-like stems and deeply lobed, lustrous, dark-green leaves, often a foot long. Well-established clumps may achieve a height of 7 ft. Clusters of tiny cream-colored flowers bloom among the foliage in summer. Grows in moderately fertile but well-drained soil. Pages: 62, 66, 70.

Rhododendron

Rhododendron and azalea is an especially diverse and popular group of shrubs with very showy flowers in spring or fall. The leaves can be small or large, deciduous or evergreen. The plants can be short, medium, or tall, with spreading, mounded, or erect habits. They do best with partial shade and need fertile, moist, well-drained soil.

Plant rhododendrons and azaleas in spring or early fall. Don't plant them too deep—the top of the root ball should be level with, or a little higher than, the surrounding soil. When planting them with solid root balls, it's very important that you make a few deep cuts down the root ball and tease apart some of the roots; otherwise they will not root well into the surrounding soil.

Use a layer of mulch to keep the soil cool and damp around your azaleas and rhododendrons, and water the plants during any dry spell for the first few years. Prune or shear off the flower stalks as soon as the petals fade to prevent seed formation and to neaten the plants. Pruning later will reduce next season's flowering. Prune or shear to control plant size and shape at the same time. See Recommended Rhododendrons and Azaleas, opposite, for more information on specific varieties.

Recommended rhododendrons and azaleas

Rhododendron 'George Lindley Taber'
GEORGE LINDLEY TABER AZALEA

Rhododendron prunifolium
PLUMLEAF AZALEA

Rhododendron 'Fiedlers White'

FIEDLERS WHITE AZALEA **Zones 7–9** ☀ ◗ **M** ◆ A vigorous evergreen shrub, 7 to 8 ft. tall, with lovely single white flowers in mid-spring. This Southern Indica hybrid is popular in mass as well as standards, espaliers, and single specimens.

Rhododendron 'George Lindley Taber'

GEORGE LINDLEY TABER AZALEA **Zones 7–10** ☀ ◗ **M** ◆ Another Southern Indica hybrid selected for its vigor and sun tolerance. An evergreen shrub, 7 to 8 ft. tall, with beautiful pale-pink flowers in mid-spring. Page: 44.

Rhododendron hybrids

GUMPO AZALEAS **Zones 6–9** ☀ ◗ **M** ◆ Low, spreading shrubs, 2 to 3 ft. tall and wide, with small evergreen leaves. 'Gumpo' has white flowers; 'Gumpo Pink' has rose pink flowers. These Satsuki hybrids are selected for later bloom. Pages: 19, 31.

Rhododendron prunifolium

PLUMLEAF AZALEA **Zones 5–8** ◗ **M** ▼ A deciduous native azalea that bears its orange-red flowers in midsummer, long after other azaleas have finished blooming. Grows 8 to 10 ft. tall and wide. Page: 44.

Rhododendron 'Roseum Elegans'

ROSEUM ELEGANS RHODODENDRON **Zones 5–9** ☀ ◗ **M** ▼ A fast-growing shrub with large, glossy, evergreen leaves and rounded clusters of pink or pink-purple flowers in late spring. Grows about 6 ft. tall and wide. Tolerates long, hot summers up to Zone 9. Pages: 19, 39.

Rhododendron hybrids
GUMPO AZALEAS

Rhododendron 'Roseum Elegans'
ROSEUM ELEGANS RHODODENDRON

Sabal palmetto
SABAL PALM

Salvia coccinea
SCARLET SAGE

Salvia greggii
AUTUMN SAGE

Salvia leucantha
MEXICAN BUSH SAGE

Serenoa repens
SAW PALMETTO

Sabal palmetto

SABAL PALM **Zones 8–11** ☀ ◗ **L** ▲ A popular wind-resistant native palm of the Southeast. Grows slowly (about 6 in. a year), reaching a mature height of 100 ft. and a spread of 8 ft. Leaf stalks bear impressive fan-shaped leaves up to 6 ft. long. Frond bases remain on the trunk after they die, forming characteristic "boots." For a cleaner look, you can remove them with a sharp shovel. Large clusters of small cream-colored flowers bloom among the leaves in summer. They can be removed before the seeds mature to prevent sprouting palm seedlings. Sabal palm grows in a range of soils from well to poorly drained. Pages: 35, 55, 58, 61.

Salvia coccinea

SCARLET SAGE **Zones 7–11** ☀ **L** ◆ A perennial Texas and Florida wildflower that grows about 2 ft. tall and wide, with a bushy habit, heart-shaped green leaves, and flower stalks at the top of every stem. Blooms for months throughout the summer and fall attracting butterflies and hummingbirds. 'Lady in Red' is a popular cultivar with bright red flowers; although sold as a bedding plant, it often overwinters in the Southeast. Pages: 53, 89.

Salvia greggii

AUTUMN SAGE **Zones 6–11** ☀ **L** ▼ A shrubby perennial with small semievergreen leaves. Grows about 2 to 3 ft. tall and wide. Blooms throughout the summer and fall. The butterfly-attracting flowers are typically bright red, but they can be pink, salmon, or white. 'Cherry Chief' has cherry red flowers. In spring, prune or shear off any weak, damaged, or frozen stems. Pages: 25, 27, 48.

Salvia leucantha

MEXICAN BUSH SAGE **Zones 8–10** ☀ ◗ **L** ▼ This shrubby perennial blooms best in autumn and spring, producing hundreds of spikes of purple and white flowers above gray-green foliage. The nectar-rich blossoms attract bees, butterflies, and occasionally hummingbirds. Grows into a mound 3 to 4 ft. high and 2 to 3 ft. wide. Young stems and leaves are covered with a downy growth, and even the flowers sport soft, velvety hairs. It has very few pests and needs little watering. To rejuvenate, cut back to 8 in. above the ground in late summer and again in early spring. Pages: 29, 47, 69, 73, 84.

Stachytarpheta jamaicensis
BLUE PORTERWEED

Stokesia laevis
STOKE'S ASTER

Ternstroemia gymnanthera
CLEYERA

Serenoa repens

SAW PALMETTO **Zones 8–11** ☀ ☽ L ▲ An extremely sturdy, low, clumping, bushy palm with great texture that works well in natural or seaside landscapes. A single saw palmetto can reach 5 to 10 ft. high and wide and live hundreds of years. The leaves are large, green fan-shaped fronds that create a dense ground cover. *S. repens* 'Cinerea' has silver-blue leaves and can be found along the east coast of Florida. Three-foot-long flower stalks appear in spring, covered with small, yellow-white, fragrant flowers. Bees love the blossoms. The following yellow berries turn black in the fall, a great food source for birds. Choose young plants, and place 4 to 5 ft. apart to establish a mass planting, or plant singly for a unique specimen. Pages: 35, 37, 55, 81, 86.

Stachytarpheta jamaicensis

BLUE PORTERWEED **Zones 9–11** ☀ ☽ M ▼ A sprawling native shrub with light-blue flowers on long spikes that attract butterflies. Grows 3 to 4 ft. tall and wide. The gray-green leaves may have a purplish blush, and the leaf surfaces are flat. Avoid planting the non-native porterweed that has dark-blue flowers with white centers, dark-green leaves, and raised-leaf surfaces. It can invade natural areas and hybridize with native populations. Page: 69.

Stokesia laevis

STOKE'S ASTER **Zones 5–10** ☀ ☽ L ▼ A native perennial wildflower that blooms from June until frost, with flowers like large flat bachelor's buttons; they make excellent long-lasting cut flowers. 'Blue Danube' has sky-blue flowers on stalks 12 to 18 in. tall. The basal foliage is evergreen. Needs well-drained soil. Pick the flowers regularly to promote continuous bloom. Divide every few years in spring or fall. Pages: 48, 84.

Ternstroemia gymnanthera

CLEYERA **Zones 7–11** ☀ ☽ L ▼ A neat, compact evergreen shrub with glossy leaves in changeable colors; they can be red, gold, green, or purple, depending on stage of growth, season, and light level. Red berries, which ripen in fall, are attractive, too. Grows about 4 ft. tall and 3 ft. wide. 'Bronze Beauty' (p. 57) has bronzy new foliage that turns a dark glossy green with a mature height of 8 ft. Cleyera prefers acid soil, requires minimal pruning, and is trouble-free. Pages: 57, 65.

Trachelospermum asiaticum
ASIAN JASMINE

Trachelospermum jasminoides
CONFEDERATE JASMINE

Vitex agnus-castus
CHASTE TREE

Trachelospermum asiaticum

ASIAN JASMINE **Zones 8–10** ✺ ◗ ● **L** ◆ A creeping, non-flowering vine commonly used as a ground cover. Grows less than 1 ft. tall and spreads to about 3 ft., forming a thick mat of small, shiny evergreen leaves. Many variegated cultivars display mahogany to cream colored and pinkish young growth. Asian jasmine requires watering only when it's dry and the leaves turn dull green. Low water use makes this a good choice to compete with tree roots. Plant in full sun or in the shade of tree canopies. Fills in completely in two to three years, keeping out most weeds. Shear the edges and top of the foliage as needed to keep the plant tidy. Pages: 27, 47, 50, 53, 57, 61, 65, 73, 84.

Trachelospermum jasminoides

CONFEDERATE JASMINE **Zones 8–10** ✺ ◗ ● **L** ◆ The woody twining stems of this evergreen vine are lined with pairs of small, leathery oval leaves. Bears dangling clusters of cream-colored, sweet-scented flowers in early summer. Climbs 10 to 15 ft. or more in height. Prune at least once a year, cutting out older stems and cutting new ones back partway. Take care when pruning; the stems contain a milky sap that can stain clothes and surfaces. Pages: 20, 23, 44, 61, 89.

Verbena bonariensis

PURPLE VERBENA **Zones 7–10** ✺ ◗ **M** ▼ A perennial that thrives in hot weather and blooms from June or July until frost. Forms a low mound of basal foliage topped by a thicket of stiff, many-branched but almost leaf-less flower stalks, 3 to 4 ft. tall. Bears countless small clusters of small purple flowers that butterflies love. Care free; simply cut down old stalks in winter or spring. May self sow but isn't weedy. Pages: 25, 61, 69.

Vitex agnus-castus

CHASTE TREE **Zones 7–9** ✺ ◗ **L** ◆ A large, deciduous, multistemmed shrub or small tree 10 to 15 ft. tall and 15 to 20 ft. wide. It is noteworthy for its showy late spring to summer display of fragrant clusters of lavender blooms, which attract butterflies. The sage-scented leaves are hand shaped and green to blue-green. Prune when young to develop a strong structure. Chaste tree seeds itself into landscaped beds and can become somewhat weedy. Page: 81.

Verbena bonariensis
PURPLE VERBENA

Yucca filamentosa 'Golden Sword'
GOLDEN SWORD YUCCA

Zamia maritima
CARDBOARD PLANT

Yucca filamentosa 'Golden Sword'

GOLDEN SWORD YUCCA **Zones 7–10** ✱ ◗ **L** ▲
An unusual shrub or perennial with ever-green daggerlike leaves, 2 ft. long that stick out in all directions from a short thick trunk. Leaves have a broad yellow stripe down the middle and green edges; although lovely, this cultivar grows more slowly than the common all-green form. Grows 2 to 3 ft. high and wide. Blooms in late spring with large creamy-white flowers on stiff branching stalks, 4 to 6 ft. tall. The woody seedpods are decorative, too. Cut down the old flower stalks, and peel dead leaves from around the base of the plant. Once established, it lives for decades and shouldn't be moved, although you can dig up the baby plants that form around the base and transplant them. Page 81.

Zamia maritima

CARDBOARD PLANT **Zones 9–11** ✱ **L** ▲ This prehistoric cycad, also known as cardboard palm, makes a dramatic specimen in a tropical garden. It produces a rosette of thick, palm-like, evergreen leaves 3 to 4 ft. high and 6 to 8 ft. in diameter. The new leaves appear to be covered in red felt and unfurl from an underground trunk, stiffening and turning green as they mature. Male or female cones appear at the base of the clump in summer. It prefers moderate-to-well-drained soil. Give it plenty of room, and keep it tidy by removing unsightly fronds from the base. Also sold as *Z. furfuracea*. Page: 58.

Zamia pumila

COONTIE **Zones 8–11** ✱ ◗ **L** ▲ A Florida native cycad and smaller cousin to the card-

Zamia pumila
COONTIE

board plant (*Z. maritima*). It has a mounding habit and is often grown as a ground cover, reaching a height and spread of 3 ft. Stiff featherlike fronds emerge from an underground stem, unfurling in the spring like fern fiddleheads. Bears either male or female cones in summer. Also known as *Z. floridana*. Pages: 33, 55, 57, 73, 77, 81.

Zamioculcas zamiifolia

ZZ **Zones 9–11** ◗ ● **L** ◆ An African jewel that resembles a cycad and performs equally well indoors and out; in a container, or as a tropical accent in the landscape in Zones 10–11. Thick underground rhizomes bear large stemless leaves that are glossy and evergreen. Grows 3 ft. tall and wide. Requires well-drained soil and shade from the hot sun but not much else. Tolerates very low light and low watering. Divide the plant when it becomes crowded or if you want more plants. Page: 63.

Zamioculcas zamiifolia
ZZ

Guide *to* Installation

In this section, we introduce the hard but rewarding work of landscaping. Here you'll find information on all the tasks you need to install any of the designs in this book, organized in the order in which you'd most likely tackle them. Clearly written text and numerous illustrations help you learn how to plan the job; clear the site; construct paths, patios, fences, pergolas, arbors, and trellises; and prepare the planting beds and install and maintain the plantings. Roll up your sleeves and dig in. In just a few weekends you can create a landscape feature that will provide years of enjoyment.

Organizing Your Project

If your gardening experience is limited to mowing the lawn, pruning the shrubs, and growing some flowers and vegetables, the thought of starting from scratch and installing a whole new landscape feature might be intimidating. But in fact, adding one of the designs in this book to your property is completely within reach, if you approach it the right way. The key is to divide the project into a series of steps and take them one at a time. This is how professional landscapers work. It's efficient and orderly, and it makes even big jobs seem manageable. This is the way we do it in our own gardens.

On this and the facing page, we'll explain how to think your way through a landscaping project and anticipate the various steps. Subsequent topics in this section describe how to do each part of the job. Detailed instructions and illustrations cover all the techniques you'll need to install any design from start to finish.

The step-by-step approach
Choose a design and adapt it to your site. The designs in this book address parts of the home landscape. In the most attractive and effective home landscapes, all the various parts work together. Don't be afraid to change the shape of beds; alter the number, kinds, and positions of plants; or revise paths and structures to bring them into harmony with their surroundings.

To see the relationships with your existing landscape, you can draw the design on a scaled plan of your property. Or you can work on the site itself, placing wooden stakes, pots, tricycles, or whatever is handy to represent plants and structures. With a little imagination, either method will allow you to visualize basic relationships.

Lay out the design on site. Once you've decided what you want to do, you'll need to lay out the paths and structures and outline the beds. Some people are comfortable laying out a design "freehand," pacing off distances and relying on their eye to judge sizes and relative positions. Others prefer to transfer the grid from the plan full size onto the site in order to place elements precisely. (Garden lime, a grainy white powder available at nurseries, can be used like chalk on a blackboard to "draw" a grid or outlines of planting beds, or use a garden hose.)

Clear the site. (See pp. 128–129) Sometimes you have to work around existing features—a nice big tree, a building or

DIGGING POSTHOLES

AMENDING SOIL

fence, a sidewalk—but it's usually easiest to start a new landscaping project if you clear as much as possible down to ground level. That means removing unwanted structures or pavement and killing, cutting down, or uprooting all the plants. Needless to say, this can generate a lot of debris, and you'll need to figure out how to dispose of it all. Still, it's often worth the trouble to make a fresh start.

Make provisions for water. (See pp. 130–131.) In the South, a well-thought-out irrigation strategy will provide your plants with the water they need and help conserve this precious resource as well. Some parts of most watering systems should be installed before other landscape features.

Build the "hardscape." (See pp. 132–159.) "Hardscape" means anything you build as part of a landscape—a fence, trellis, arbor, retaining wall, walkway, edging, outdoor lighting, or whatever. If you're going to do any building, do it first, and finish the construction before you start

any planting. That way you won't have to worry about stepping on any of the plants, and they won't be in the way as you work. Just remember not to install a fence or gate that limits the work.

Prepare the soil. (See pp. 160–163.) On most properties, it's uncommon to find soil that's as good as it should be for growing plants. Typically, the soil around a house is shallow, compacted, and infertile. It may be rocky or contain buried debris. Some plants tolerate such poor conditions, but they don't thrive. To grow healthy, attractive plants, you need to improve the quality of the soil throughout the entire area that you're planning to plant.

Do the planting and add mulch. (See pp. 165–168.) Putting plants in the ground usually goes quite quickly and gives instant gratification. Spreading mulch over the soil makes the area look neat and "finished" even while the plants are still small.

Maintain the planting. (See pp. 169–172.) Most plantings need regular watering and occasional weeding for the first year or two. After that, depending on the design you've chosen, you'll have to do some routine maintenance—pruning, shaping, cutting back, and cleaning up—to keep the plants looking their best. This may take as little as a few hours a month or as much as an hour or two every week throughout the growing season.

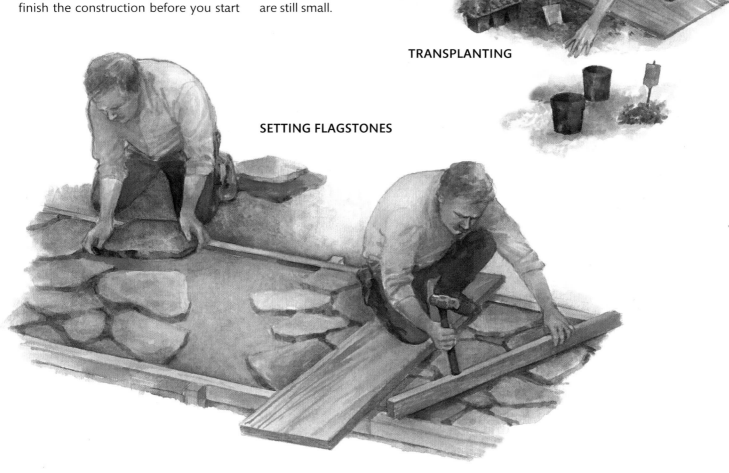

TRANSPLANTING

SETTING FLAGSTONES

Clearing the Site

The site you've chosen for a landscaping project may or may not have any man-made objects (fences, old pavement, trash, etc.) to be removed, but it will almost certainly be covered with plants.

Before you start cutting down plants, try to find someone—a friend or neighbor who enjoys gardening—to identify them for you. As you walk around together, make a sketch that shows which plants are where, and attach labels to the plants, too. Determine if there are any desirable plants worth saving—mature shade trees that you should work around, shapely shrubs that aren't too big to dig up and relocate or give away, worthwhile perennials and ground covers that you could divide and replant, healthy sod that you could lay elsewhere. Likewise, decide which plants have to go—diseased or crooked trees, straggly or overgrown shrubs, weedy brush, invasive ground covers, tattered lawn.

You can clear small areas yourself, bundling the brush for pickup and tossing soft-stemmed plants on the compost pile, but if you have lots of woody brush or any trees to remove, you might want to hire someone else to do the job. A crew armed with power tools can turn a thicket into a pile of wood chips in just a few hours. Have them pull out the roots and grind the stumps, too. Save the chips; they're good for surfacing paths or you can use them as mulch after they age.

Working around trees

If there are any large, healthy trees on your site, be careful as you work around them. It's okay to prune off some of a tree's limbs, as shown on the facing page, but respect its trunk and its roots. Try to never cut or wound the bark on the trunk (don't nail things to a tree), as that exposes the tree to disease organisms. Don't pile soil or mulch against the trunk, because it keeps the bark wet and can make it rot.

Killing perennial weeds

Some common weeds or invasive plants that sprout back from perennial roots or runners are bindweed, blackberry and other briers, Johnson grass, kudzu, nutsedge, potato vine, and poison ivy. Once they become established, perennial weeds are hard to eliminate. You can't just cut off the tops, because they keep sprouting back. The only sure way to rid your landscape of them is to dig the weeds out, smother them with mulch, or kill them with an herbicide, and it's better to do this before rather than after you plant a bed.

Smothering weeds

This technique is easier than digging, particularly for eradicating large infestations, but much slower. First mow or cut the tops of the weeds as close to the ground as possible ❶. Then cover the area with sections from the newspaper, overlapped like shingles ❷, or use flattened-out cardboard boxes. Top with a layer of mulch, such as straw, grass clippings, tree leaves, wood chips, or other organic material spread several inches deep ❸.

Smothering works by excluding light, which stops photosynthesis. If any shoots reach up through the covering and produce green leaves, pull them out immediately. Wait a few months, until you're sure the weeds are dead, before you dig into the smothered area and plant there.

SMOTHERING WEEDS

❶ Smothering kills weeds by depriving them of light. Cut the tops off close to the ground.

❷ Cover with thick newspaper or cardboard.

❸ Top with several inches of mulch. Wait a few months to be sure weeds are dead; then till rotted newspaper and mulch into the soil.

Digging. In many cases, you can do a pretty good job of removing a perennial weed if you dig carefully where the stems enter the ground, find the roots, and follow them as far as possible through the soil, pulling out every bit of root that you find. Some plant roots go deeper than you can dig, and most plants will sprout back from the small bits that you miss, but these leftover sprouts are easy to pull.

Spraying. Herbicides are easy, fast, and effective weed killers when chosen and applied with care. Look for those that break down quickly into more benign substances, and make sure the weed you're trying to kill is listed on the product label. Apply all herbicides exactly as directed by the manufacturer. After spraying, you usually have to wait from one to four weeks for the weed to die completely, and some weeds need repeated applications. Some weeds just "melt away" when they die, but if there are tough or woody stems and roots, you'll need to dig them up and discard them.

Replacing turf

Removing parts of a lawn depends on the condition of the turf and on what you want to put in its place. If the turf is healthy, you can "recycle" it to replace, repair, or extend the lawn on other parts of your property.

The drawing below shows a technique for removing relatively small areas of strong healthy turf for replanting elsewhere. First, using a sharp shovel, cut it into squares or strips about 1 to 2 ft. square (these small pieces are easy to lift) ❶. Then slice a few inches deep under each square and lift the squares, roots and all, like brownies from a pan ❷. Quickly transplant the squares to a previously prepared site; water them well until the roots are established.

If you don't need the turf anywhere else, or if it's straggly or weedy, leave it in place and kill the grass. A single application of herbicide kills some grasses, but you may need to spray vigorous turf twice. Another way to kill grass is to cover it with a tarp or a sheet of black plastic for about four weeks during the heat of summer. After you've killed the grass, dig or till the bed, shredding the turf, roots and all, and mixing it into the soil.

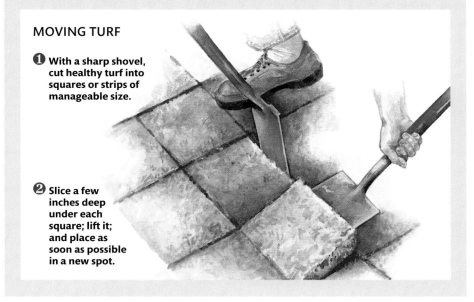

MOVING TURF

❶ With a sharp shovel, cut healthy turf into squares or strips of manageable size.

❷ Slice a few inches deep under each square; lift it; and place as soon as possible in a new spot.

Removing large limbs

If there are large trees on your property, you may want to remove some lower limbs so you can walk underneath them and so light can reach plantings. Major pruning of large trees is a job for a professional arborist, but you can remove limbs smaller than 4 in. in diameter and less than 10 ft. above the ground yourself with a simple bow saw or pole saw.

Use the three-step procedure shown below to remove large limbs. First, saw partway through the bottom of the limb, approximately 1 ft. out from the trunk ❶. This keeps the bark from tearing down the trunk when the limb falls. Then make a corresponding cut down through the top of the limb ❷—be prepared to get out of the way when the limb drops. Finally, remove the stub ❸. Undercut it slightly or hold it as you finish the cut, so it doesn't fall away and peel bark off the trunk. Note that the cut is not flush with the trunk but is just outside the thick area at the limb's base, called the branch collar. Leaving the branch collar helps the wound seal over naturally. Wound dressing is not beneficial to the tree.

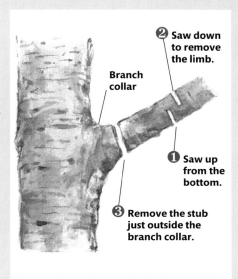

❷ Saw down to remove the limb.

Branch collar

❶ Saw up from the bottom.

❸ Remove the stub just outside the branch collar.

Water for Your Plants

Long, dry summers and droughts make watering a critical concern of gardeners in many areas of the South. Though some plants will survive long dry periods once established, almost all plants will need regular watering the first few years after planting. And most will need watering their entire life during dry periods to look their best.

But there is more at stake than just the survival of plants. Water conservation is a daily obligation in many areas, where water is a valuable and limited resource. Outdoor landscapes use a large portion of drinkable water, so nothing should be wasted. In some regions, mandatory conservation is often strictly enforced either year-round or during periods of drought.

So for your pocketbook, the health of your plants, and for the preservation of a valuable resource, make water conservation part of your landscape planning from the beginning. The box below outlines effective water-saving practices for home landscapes. (See p. 171 for more on when and how much to water.) You can also consult your local water department or water management district for advice about watering gardens and lawns.

High salinity of the water from irrigation wells is an issue in many coastal areas. Make sure to have well water tested for salt content before selecting plants.

Watering systems

One of the best ways to conserve water is to use an efficient delivery system. The simplest watering systems—watering cans and handheld hoses—are also the most limited and inefficient. They can be adequate for watering new transplants or widely separated individual plants. Sprinkling plants in an entire bed with a hose and nozzle for even as long as an hour may provide less water than half an inch of rainfall. And wetting just the top few inches of soil this way encourages shallow root growth, making it necessary to water more frequently. To provide enough water to soak the soil to a depth of a foot or more, you need a system that can run untended for extended periods.

Hose-end sprinklers are easy to set up and leave to soak an area. But they're also inefficient: water is blown away by wind (especially close to the coast). It runs off sloped or paved areas. It is applied unevenly, or it falls too far away from individual plants to be of use to them. And because sprinklers soak leaves as well as soil, the damp foliage may breed fungal diseases.

Low-volume irrigation. For garden beds and landscape plantings, low-volume irrigation systems are the most efficient and offer the most flexibility and control. Frequently called "drip" irrigation systems, they deliver water at low pressure through a network of plastic pipes, hoses, and tubing, and a variety of emitters and microsprinklers. Such systems are designed to apply water slowly and directly to the roots of targeted plants, so very little water is lost or wasted on plants that don't need it. Because water is usually applied at soil level, the risk of foliar diseases is reduced. And because less soil is watered, weeds are also reduced.

Water-wise practices

Group plants with similar water needs. Position plants that require the most water together so that they can be treated equally by hand watering or make up a zone of an automatic system.

Mulch plantings. A 2 to 3 in. layer of mulch reduces evaporation by keeping the soil cool and sheltering it from wind.

Create water-retaining basins. Use these to direct hand-irrigation water to large plants. Make a low soil mound around the plant's root ball perimeter at its drip line. (Basins aren't necessary in drip-irrigated beds.)

Plant in the rainy season. This way, new plants will have the wetter seasons to become established.

Limit lawn size. Lawns demand lots of water. Reduce the size of your lawn by planting beds, borders, and less-thirsty ground covers.

Water in the morning. Lower morning temperatures and less wind mean less water is lost through evaporation.

Adjust watering to conditions. Reduce watering period lengths during cool weather. Turn off automatic timers during rainy periods, and install a rain sensor.

How much did it rain? Get a rain gauge so that you know how much rain fell on your landscape.

Install, monitor, and maintain an irrigation system. Even a simple drip system conserves water. Once it's installed, check and adjust the equipment regularly.

Select an irrigation controller that has multiple programs. This allow you to program different watering plans for each irrigation zone. Fine-tune the zones so that high-water-use zones are separated from low-water-use zones.

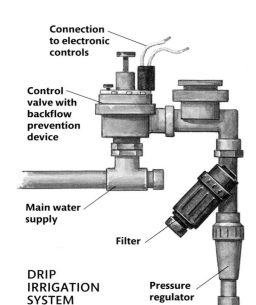

- Connection to electronic controls
- Control valve with backflow prevention device
- Main water supply
- Filter

DRIP IRRIGATION SYSTEM

- Pressure regulator

Basic components of a drip irrigation system are shown here. Individual systems will vary. Several common types of emitters are shown; systems can incorporate others.

Simple low-volume systems can be attached to ordinary outdoor faucets or garden hoses and controlled manually. More-sophisticated systems include their own attachment to your main water supply, a network of valves and buried pipes that allow you to divide your property into zones, and an electronic control device that can automatically water each zone at preset times for preset durations.

A person with modest mechanical skills and basic tools can plan and install a low-volume irrigation system. Extensive multizone systems (particularly those with their own attachment to the main water supply) are more difficult to install. If you do, have a professional review your plans before you start. You can buy kits or individual system components from garden centers, nurseries, or specialty suppliers. (The main components of low-volume systems are illustrated on this page.) All manufacturers provide instructions, but choose from among your local suppliers based on their knowledge of system design and installation and their ability to help you with both.

Low-volume-system components. Any irrigation system connected to a domestic water supply needs a **backflow prevention device** (also called an "antisiphon device") at the point of connection to the water supply to protect drinking water from contamination. Check with local health or building officials about requirements.

Install a **filter** to prevent minerals and flakes that slough off metal water pipes from clogging the emitters. You'll need to clean the filter regularly.

Pressure regulators reduce the mains' water pressure to levels required by the system's low-volume emitters.

Supply lines deliver water from the source to the emitters. Some systems incorporate buried lines of rigid plastic pipe. For aboveground use, you'll need flexible tubing designed specifically for low-volume irrigation.

Emitters and **soaker hoses** deliver the water to the plants. A wide range of emitters are available for different kinds of plants and garden situations. Various drip fittings, bubblers, and micro-sprinklers can be plugged into the flexible plastic tubing. Soaker hoses and "ooze" tubes seep or drip water along their length. Consult with your supplier about which delivery systems best meet your plants' needs. (The high calcium and salt content of some water sources in Texas and other areas can clog drip emitters, so check them regularly.)

A **timer** or **electronic controller** helps ensure efficient water use. Unlike you, a controller won't forget and leave the water on too long. And one equipped with a rain sensor won't run when it rains (required by law in Florida and Georgia). Used in conjunction with zoned plantings, these devices provide control and flexibility to deal with the specific water needs of groups of plants or even individual specimens.

Installation

Lay underground piping that crosses paths, patios, or similar landscape features after the site is cleared but before installing any of these permanent features. It is best to lay pipes in planting areas, including lawns, after you have prepared the soil. That way, you won't damage the piping when digging or rototilling. Install underground pipe in trenches dug to the appropriate depth. Then temporarily cap the ends. Hook up the aboveground tubing and position emitters after planting.

½-in. supply line

Microsprinkler

¼-in. feedline

Stake

Individual emitter

¼-in. connector

Inline emitter

Punch-in emitter

Making Paths and Walkways

Every landscape needs paths and walkways if for no other reason than to keep your feet dry as you move from one place to another. A path can also divide and define the spaces in the landscape, orchestrate the way the landscape is viewed, and even be a key element enhancing its beauty.

Whether it is a graceful curving garden path or a utilitarian slab leading to the garage, a walk has two main functional requirements: durability and safety. It should hold up through seasonal changes. It should provide a well-drained surface that is easy to walk on and to maintain.

A path's function helps determine its surface and its character. In general, heavily trafficked walkways leading to a door, garage, or shed need hard, smooth (but not slick) surfaces and should take you where you want to go fairly directly. A path to a backyard play area could be a strip of soft wood bark, easy on the knees of impatient children. A relaxed stroll in the garden might require only a hop-scotch collection of flat stones meandering from one prized plant to another.

Before laying out a walk or path, spend some time observing existing traffic patterns. If your path makes use of a route people already take (particularly children), they'll be more likely to stay on the path and off the lawn or flowers. Avoid areas that are slow to drain. When determining path width, consider whether the path must accommodate yard carts and wheelbarrows or two strollers walking abreast, or just provide stepping-stone access for maintaining the plants.

Dry-laid paths

You can make a path by laying bricks or spreading wood chips on bare earth. While quick and easy, this method has serious drawbacks. Laid on the surface, with no edging to contain them, loose materials are soon scattered, and solid materials are easily jostled out of place. If the earth base doesn't drain very well, the path will be a swamp after a rainstorm. And in cold-winter areas, repeated expansion and contraction of the soil will heave bricks or flagstones out of alignment, making the path potentially dangerous.

The method we recommend—laying surface material on an excavated sand-and-gravel base—minimizes these problems. The sand and gravel improve drainage and provide a cushion against the freeze-thaw movement of the soil. Excavation can place the path surface at ground level, where the surrounding soil or an installed edging can contain path materials.

All styles, from a "natural" wood-bark path to a formal cut-stone entry walk, and all the materials discussed here can be laid on an excavated base of gravel and sand.

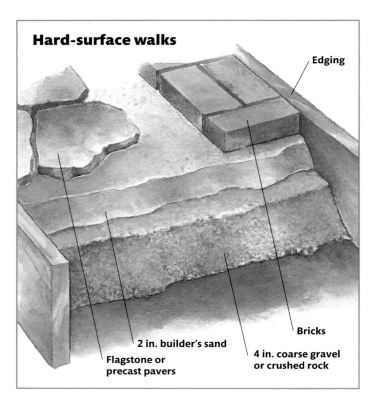

Hard-surface walks

Edging

2 in. builder's sand

Flagstone or precast pavers

Bricks

4 in. coarse gravel or crushed rock

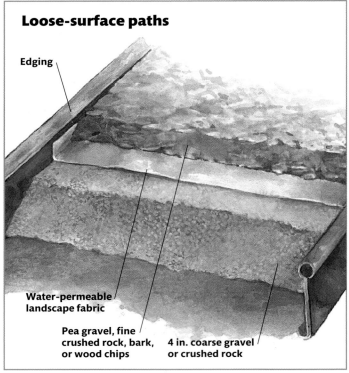

Loose-surface paths

Edging

Water-permeable landscape fabric

Pea gravel, fine crushed rock, bark, or wood chips

4 in. coarse gravel or crushed rock

Choosing a surface

Walkways and paths can be made of either hard or soft material. Your choice of material will depend on the walkway's function, your budget, and your personal preferences.

Soft materials, including bark, wood chips, pine needles, and loose gravel, are best for informal and low-traffic areas. Inexpensive and simple to install, they settle, scatter, or decompose and must be replenished or replaced every few years.

Hard materials, such as brick, flagstone, and concrete pavers, are more expensive and time-consuming to install, but they are permanent, requiring only occasional maintenance. (Compacted crushed stone can also make a hard-surface walk.) Durable and handsome, they're ideal for high-traffic, "high-profile" areas.

Bark, wood chips, and pine needles

Perfect for a "natural" look or a quick temporary path, these loose materials can be laid directly on the soil or, if drainage is poor, on a gravel bed. Bagged materials from a nursery or garden center will be cleaner, more uniform, and considerably more expensive than bulk supplies bought by the cubic yard. Check with local tree services to find the best prices on bulk material.

Gravel and crushed rock

Loose rounded gravel gives a bit underfoot, creating a "soft" but messy path. The angular facets of crushed stone eventually compact into a "hard" and tidier path that can, if the surrounding soil is firm enough, be laid without an edging. Gravel and stone type and color vary from area to area. Buy materials by the ton or cubic yard.

Concrete pavers

Precast concrete pavers are versatile, readily available, and often the least expensive hard-surface material. They come in a range of colors and shapes, including interlocking patterns. Precast edgings are also available. Most home and garden centers carry a variety of precast pavers, which are sold by the piece.

PRECAST PAVERS

Brick

Widely available in a range of sizes, colors, and textures, brick complements many design styles. When carefully laid on a well-prepared sand-and-gravel base, brick provides an even, safe, and long-lasting surface. Buy paving brick instead of the softer "facing" brick, which may break up after a few freeze-thaw cycles. (If you buy used brick, pick the hardest.) Avoid glazed brick; the glaze traps moisture and salts, which will damage the brick.

RUNNING BOND

TWO-BRICK BASKET WEAVE

HERRINGBONE

DIAGONAL HERRINGBONE

Flagstone

"Flagstone" is a generic term for stratified stone that can be split to form pavers. Limestone, sandstone, and bluestone are common paving materials. The surfaces of marble and slate are usually too smooth to make safe paving. Cut into squares or rectangles, flagstone can be laid as individual pieces or in interesting patterns. Flagstones come in a range of colors, textures, and sizes. Flags for walks should be at least 2 in. thick. Purchased by weight, surface area, or pallet load, flagstones are usually the most expensive paving choice.

CUT FLAGSTONE

CUT AND IRREGULAR FLAGSTONE

IRREGULAR FLAGSTONE

Drainage

Few things are worse than a path dotted with puddles or icy patches. To prevent these from forming, the soil around and beneath the path should drain well. The path's location and construction should ensure that rainwater does not collect on the surface. Drainage also affects frost heaving. In cold-winter areas, the soil expands and contracts as the water in it freezes and thaws. As the soil moves, so do path and walkway materials laid on it. The effect is minimal on loose materials such as wood chips or gravel, but frost heaving can shift brick and stone significantly out of line.

Before you locate a path, observe run-off and drainage on your property during and after heavy rains. Avoid routing a path through areas where water courses, collects, or is slow to drain.

While both loose and hard paving can sometimes be successfully laid directly on well-drained soil, laying surface materials on a base of gravel and sand will help improve drainage and minimize frost heaving. In most situations, a 4 in. gravel bed topped with 2 in. of sand will be sufficient. Water moves through these materials quickly, and they "cushion" the surface materials from the expansion and contraction of the underlying soil. Very poorly drained soils may require more gravel, an additional layer of coarse rock beneath the gravel, or even drain tiles. If you suspect your site has serious drainage problems, consult a specialist for advice.

Finally, keep water from pooling on a walk by making its surface higher in the center than at the edges. The center of a 4-ft.-wide walk should be at at least ½ in. higher than its edges. If you're using a drag board to level the sand base, curve its lower edge to create this "crown." Otherwise crown the surface by eye.

Edgings

All walk surfaces need to be contained in some fashion along their edges. Where soil is firm or tightly knit by turf, neatly cut walls of the excavation can serve as edging. An installed edging often provides more effective containment, particularly if the walk surface is above grade. It also prevents damage to bricks or stones on the edges of paths. Walkway edgings are commonly made of 1- or 2-in.-thick lumber, thicker landscaping timbers, brick, or stone.

Wood edging

Wood should be rot-resistant redwood, cedar, or cypress, or pressure-treated for ground-contact use. If you're working in loose soils, fix a deep wooden edging to support stakes with double-headed nails. When the path is laid, pull the nails, and fill and tamp behind the edging. Then drive the stakes below grade. In firmer soils, or if the edging material is not wide enough, install it on top of the gravel base. Position the top of the edging at the height of the path. Dimension lumber 1 in. thick is pliable enough to bend around gradual curves.

Treated dimensional lumber with support stakes   **Landscape timbers with crossties laid on gravel base**

Brick and stone edging

In firm soil, a row of bricks laid on edge and perpendicular to the length of the path adds stability. For a more substantial edging, stand bricks on end on the excavated soil surface, add the gravel base, and tamp earth around the base of the bricks on the outside of the excavation. Stone edgings laid on end can be set in the same way. "End-up" brick or stone edgings are easy to install on curved walks.

Bricks on edge, laid on gravel base   **Bricks on end, laid on soil**

Preparing the base

The initial steps of layout and base preparation are much the same for all surface materials.

Layout

Lay out straight sections with stakes and string. You can plot curves with stakes and "fair" the curve with a garden hose, or you can outline the curve with the hose alone, marking it with lime or sand ❶.

Excavation

The excavation depth depends on how much sand-and-gravel base your soil's drainage calls for, the thickness of the surface material, and its position above or below grade ❷. Mark the depth on a stake or stick, and use this to check depth as you dig. Walking surfaces are most comfortable if they are reasonably level across their width. Check the bottom of the excavation with a level as you dig. If the walk cuts across a slope, you'll need to remove soil from the high side and use it to fill the low side to produce a level surface. If you've added soil or if the subsoil is loose, compact it by tamping.

Edging installation

Some edgings can be installed immediately after excavation; others are placed on top of the gravel portion of the base ❸.

(See the sidebar "Edgings" on the facing page.) If the soil's drainage permits, you can lay soft materials now on the excavated, tamped, and edged soil base. To control weeds, and to keep bark, chips, or pine needles from mixing with the subsoil, you can spread water-permeable landscape fabric over the excavated soil base.

Laying the base

Now add gravel (if required), rake it level, and compact it ❹. Use gravel up to 1 in. in diameter or ¼- to ¾-in. crushed stone, which drains and compacts well. You can rent a hand tamper (a heavy metal plate on the end of a pole) or a machine compactor if you have a large area to compact.

If you're making a loose-gravel or crushed-stone walk, add the surface material on top of the base gravel. (See "Loose materials" p. 136.) For walks of brick, stone, or pavers, add a 2 in. layer of builder's sand, not the finer sand masons use for mixing mortar.

Rake the sand smooth with the back of a level-head rake. You can level the sand with a wooden drag board, also called a screed ❺. Nail together two 1x4s or notch a 1x6 to place the lower edge at the desired height of the sand, and run the board along the path edging. To settle the sand, dampen it thoroughly with a hose set on fine spray. Fill any low spots, rake or drag the surface level, then dampen it again.

PREPARING THE BASE

❶ Lay out the path with stakes, string, garden hose, and lime.

❷ Dig out path between layout string and lime lines.

❸ Install the edging.

❹ Rake out gravel base.

Lay out free-form curved sections with garden hose and mark with lime.

Mark straight sections with 1x2 stakes and string.

Drag board

Edging

❺ Level sand base with a drag board.

Laying the surface

Whether you're laying a loose or hard material, take time to plan your work. Provide access for delivery trucks, and have material deposited as close to the worksite as possible.

Loose materials

Install water-permeable landscape fabric over the gravel base to prevent gravel from mixing with the surface material. Spread bark or wood chips 2 to 4 in. deep. For a pine-needle surface, spread 2 in. of needles on top of several inches of bark or chips. Spread loose pea gravel about 2 in. deep. For a harder, more uniform surface, add ½ in. of fine crushed stone on top of the gravel. You can let traffic compact the top layer of crushed-rock surfaces, or compact them by hand or with a machine.

Bricks and precast pavers

Take time to figure out the pattern and spacing of the bricks or pavers by laying them out on the lawn or driveway, rather than disturbing your carefully prepared sand base. When you're satisfied, begin in a corner, laying the bricks or pavers gently on the sand so the base remains even ❶ while butting the edges together. Lay full bricks first; then cut bricks to fit as needed at the edges. Maintain alignment with a straightedge or with a string stretched across the path between nails or stakes. Move the string as the work proceeds.

As you complete a row or section, bed the bricks or pavers into the sand base with several firm raps of a rubber mallet or a hammer on a scrap 2x4. Check with a level or straightedge to make sure the surface is even ❷. (You'll have to do this by feel or eye across the width of a crowned path.) Lift low bricks or pavers carefully, and fill beneath them with sand; then reset them. Don't stand on the walk until you've filled the tight joints.

When you've finished a section, sweep fine, dry mason's sand into the joints, working across the surface of the path in all directions ❸. Wet thoroughly with a fine spray and let dry; then sweep in more sand if necessary. If you want a "living" walk, space bricks with a piece of wood cut to the joint width and sweep a loam-sand mixture into the joints. Then plant small, tough, ground-hugging plants, such as thyme, in them.

Rare is the brick walk that can be laid without cutting something to fit. To cut brick, mark the line of the cut with a dark pencil all around the brick. With the brick resting firmly on sand or soil, score the entire line by rapping a wide mason's chisel called a "brickset" with a heavy wooden mallet or a soft-headed steel hammer as shown on the facing page. Place the brickset in the scored line across one face and give it a sharp blow with the hammer to cut the brick.

If you have a lot of bricks to cut, or if you want greater accuracy, consider renting a masonry saw. Whether you work by hand or machine, always wear safety glasses.

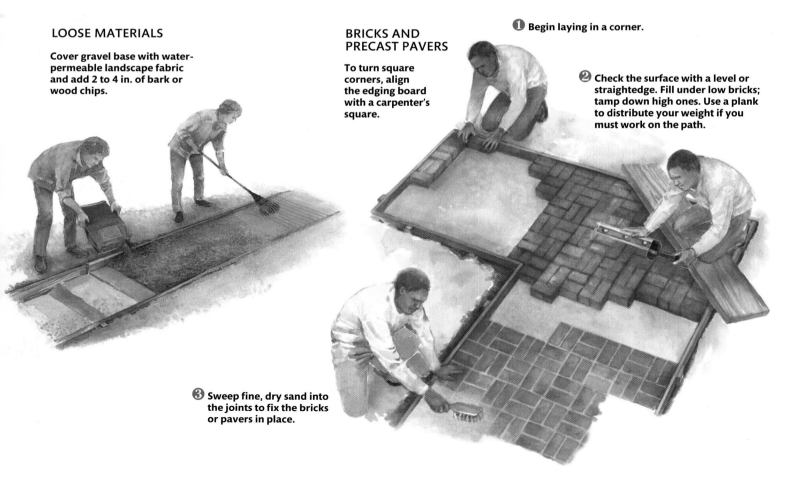

LOOSE MATERIALS

Cover gravel base with water-permeable landscape fabric and add 2 to 4 in. of bark or wood chips.

BRICKS AND PRECAST PAVERS

To turn square corners, align the edging board with a carpenter's square.

❶ Begin laying in a corner.

❷ Check the surface with a level or straightedge. Fill under low bricks; tamp down high ones. Use a plank to distribute your weight if you must work on the path.

❸ Sweep fine, dry sand into the joints to fix the bricks or pavers in place.

Stepping-stones

A stepping-stone walk set in turf creates a charming effect and is very simple to lay. You can use cut or irregular flagstones or fieldstone, which is irregular in thickness as well as in outline. Arrange the stones on the turf; then set them one by one. Cut into the turf around the stone with a sharp flat shovel or trowel, and remove the stone; then dig out the sod with the shovel. Placing stones at or below grade will keep them away from mower blades. Fill low spots beneath the stone with earth or sand so the stone doesn't move when stepped on.

Cut around stepping-stone with shovel or trowel.

Remove sod and soil.

Set in place, filling with sand or soil to bed stone firmly.

Cutting bricks

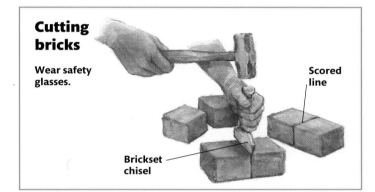

Wear safety glasses.

Scored line

Brickset chisel

Cutting flagstones

Wear safety glasses.

Scored line

Wood batten

Brickset

Flagstones

Install cut stones of uniform thickness as described for bricks and pavers. Working out patterns beforehand is particularly important—stones are too heavy to move around more than necessary. To produce a level surface with cut or irregular stones of varying thickness, you'll need to add or remove sand for each stone. Set the stone carefully on sand; then move it back and forth to work it into place ❶. Lay a level or straightedge over three or four stones to check the surface's evenness ❷. When a section is complete, fill the joints with sand or with sand and loam as described for bricks and pavers.

You can cut flagstone with a technique similar to that used for bricks. Score the line of the cut on the top surface with a brickset and hammer. Prop the stone on a piece of scrap wood, positioning the line of the cut slightly beyond the edge of the wood. Place the brickset on the scored line, and strike sharply to make the cut.

FLAGSTONES

❶ **Set flagstones in place carefully to avoid disturbing the sand base.**

❷ **Extend a straightedge over several stones to check the surface for evenness. Tap high spots to level.**

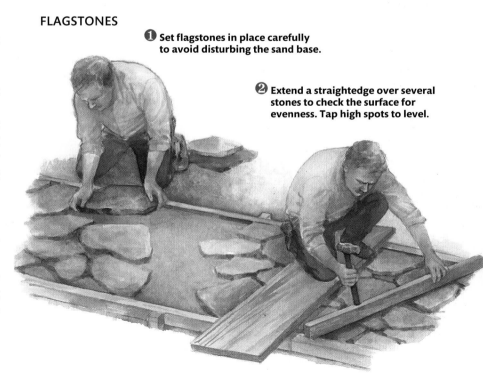

Laying a Patio

You can install a simple patio using the same techniques and materials we have discussed for paths. To ensure good drainage, an even surface, and durability, lay hard surfaces such as brick, flagstone, and pavers on a well-prepared base of gravel, sand, and compacted soil. (Crushed-rock and gravel surfaces likewise benefit from a sound base.) Make sure the surface drains away from any adjacent structure (house or garage); a drop-off of ¼ in. per foot is usually adequate. If the patio isn't near a structure, make it higher in the center to avoid puddles.

Establish the outline of the patio as described for paths; then excavate the area roughly to accommodate 4 in. of gravel, 2 in. of sand, and the thickness of the paving surface. (Check with a local nursery or landscape contractor to find out if local conditions require alterations in the type or amounts of base material.) Now grade the rough excavation to provide drainage, using a simple 4-ft. grid of wooden stakes as shown in the drawings below.

Drive the first row of stakes next to the house (or in the center of a freestanding patio), leveling them with a 4-ft. builder's level or a smaller level resting on a straight 2x4. The tops of these stakes should be at the height of the top of the sand base (finish grade of the patio less the thickness of the surface material) ❶. Working from this row of stakes, establish another row about 4 to 5 ft. from the first. Make the tops of these stakes 1 in. lower than those of the first row, using a level and spacer block, as shown in the boxed drawing below. Continue adding rows of

LAYING A SIMPLE PATIO

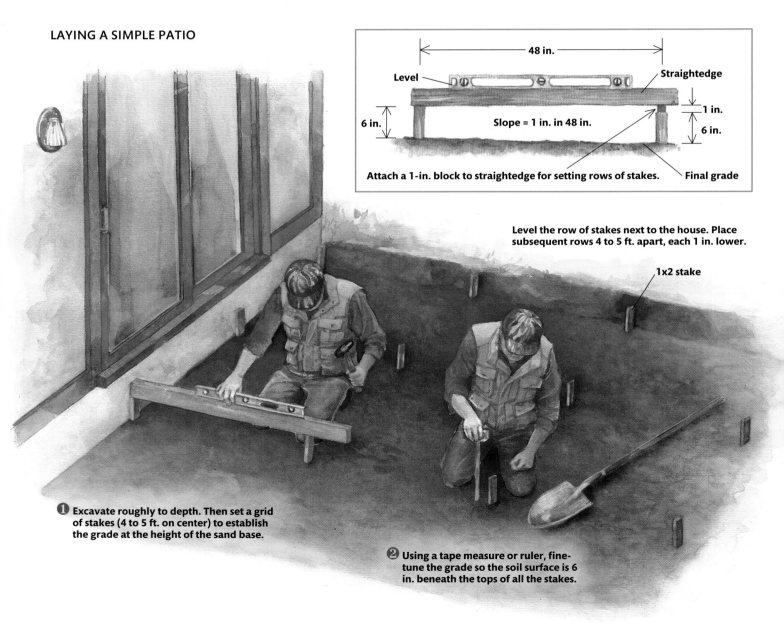

|←——————— 48 in. ———————→|

Level   Straightedge

6 in.   **Slope = 1 in. in 48 in.**   1 in.
                                                       6 in.

Attach a 1-in. block to straightedge for setting rows of stakes.   Final grade

Level the row of stakes next to the house. Place subsequent rows 4 to 5 ft. apart, each 1 in. lower.

1x2 stake

❶ Excavate roughly to depth. Then set a grid of stakes (4 to 5 ft. on center) to establish the grade at the height of the sand base.

❷ Using a tape measure or ruler, fine-tune the grade so the soil surface is 6 in. beneath the tops of all the stakes.

stakes, each 1 in. lower than the previous row, until the entire area is staked. Then, with a tape measure or ruler and a shovel, fine-tune the grading by removing or adding soil until the excavated surface is 6 in. (the thickness of the gravel-sand base) below the tops of all the stakes ❷.

When installing the sand-and-gravel base, you'll want to maintain the drainage grade you've just established and produce an even surface for the paving material. If you have a good eye or a very small patio, you can do this by sight. Otherwise, you can use the stakes to install a series of 1x3 or 1x4 "leveling boards," as shown in the drawing below. (Before adding gravel, you may want to cover the soil with water-permeable landscape fabric to keep perennial weeds from growing; just cut slits to accommodate the stakes.)

Add a few inches of gravel ❸. Then set leveling boards along each row of stakes, with the boards' top edges even with the top of the stakes ❹. Drive additional stakes to sandwich the boards in place (don't use nails). Distribute the remaining inch or so of gravel, and compact it by hand or machine, then the 2 in. of sand. Dragging a straight 2x4 across two adjacent rows of leveling boards will produce a precise grade and an even surface ❺. Wet the sand and fill low spots that settle.

You can install the patio surface as previously described for paths, removing the leveling boards as the bricks or pavers reach them ❻. Disturbing the sand surface as little as possible, slide the boards out from between the stakes, and drive the stakes an inch or so beneath the level of the sand. Cover the stakes, and fill the gaps left by the boards with sand, tamped down carefully; then continue laying the surface. Finally, sweep fine sand into the joints.

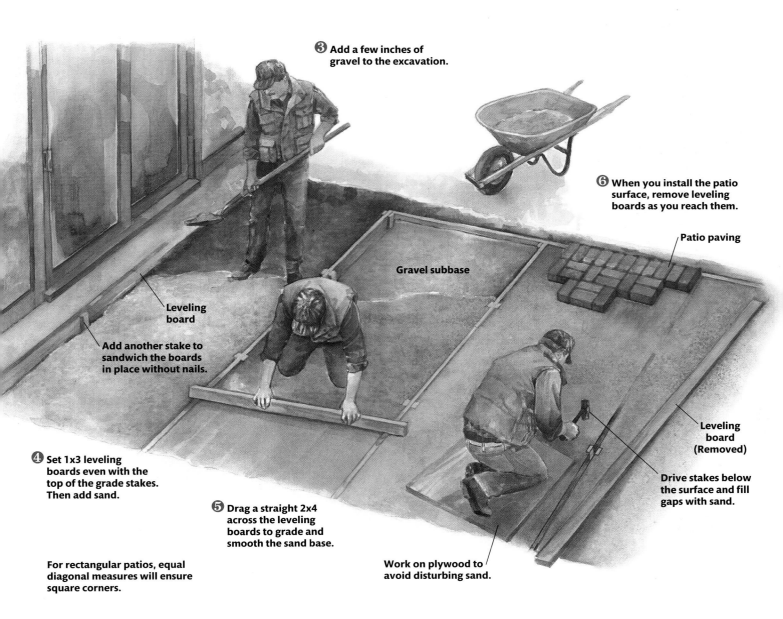

❸ **Add a few inches of gravel to the excavation.**

❻ **When you install the patio surface, remove leveling boards as you reach them.**

Patio paving

Gravel subbase

Leveling board

Add another stake to sandwich the boards in place without nails.

Leveling board (Removed)

Drive stakes below the surface and fill gaps with sand.

❹ **Set 1x3 leveling boards even with the top of the grade stakes. Then add sand.**

❺ **Drag a straight 2x4 across the leveling boards to grade and smooth the sand base.**

Work on plywood to avoid disturbing sand.

For rectangular patios, equal diagonal measures will ensure square corners.

Installing a Pond

It wasn't so long ago that a garden pond required yards of concrete, an expert mason, and deep pockets. Today's strong, lightweight, and long-lasting synthetic liners and rigid fiberglass shells have put garden pools in reach of every homeowner. Installation does require some hard labor, but little expertise: just dig a hole, spread the liner or seat the shell, install edging, and plant. We'll discuss installation of a linered pond in the main text; see below for installing a smaller, fiberglass pool.

Liner notes

More and more nurseries and garden centers are carrying flexible pond liners; you can also buy them from mail-order suppliers specializing in water gardens. Synthetic rubber liners are longer lasting but more expensive than PVC liners. (Both are much cheaper than rigid fiberglass shells.) Buy only liners specifically made for garden ponds—don't use ordinary plastic sheeting. Many people feel that black liners look best; blue liners tend to make the pond look like a swimming pool.

Before you dig

First, make sure you comply with any rules your town may have about water features. Then keep the following ideas in mind when locating your pond. Avoid trees whose shade keeps sun-loving water plants from thriving; whose roots make digging a chore; and whose flowers, leaves, and seeds clog the water, making it unsightly and inhospitable to plants or fish. Avoid the low spot on your property; otherwise your pond will be a catch basin for runoff. Select a level spot; the immediate vicinity of the pond

Small fiberglass pool

A fiberglass shell 2 to 3 ft. wide, 4 to 5 ft. long, and 2 to 3 ft. deep is ideal for a small pool. Garden centers often stock pond shells in a variety of shapes.

Dig a hole about 6 in. wider on all sides than the shell; its depth should equal that of the shell plus 1 in. for a sand base, plus the thickness of the fieldstone edging. Compact the bottom of the hole and spread the sand; then lower the shell into place. Add temporary wedges or props to level the shell. Slowly fill the shell with water, backfilling around it with sand or sifted soil, keeping pace with the rising water. Excavate a wide relief for the edging stones, laying them on a firm base, slightly overhanging the rim of the shell.

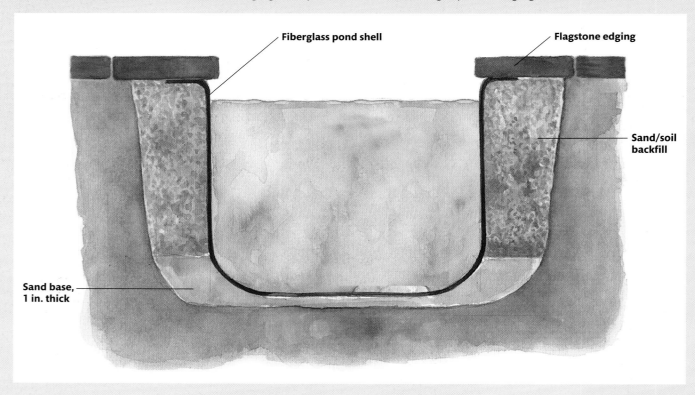

Fiberglass pond shell

Flagstone edging

Sand/soil backfill

Sand base, 1 in. thick

must be level, and starting out that way saves a lot of work. (Remember that you can use excavated soil to help level the site.)

Using graph paper to help you determine the dimensions of the water feature, draw an outline of the water feature you wish to install. If you want a deep pond, or you are interested in growing a variety of water plants or in adding fish, remember that a healthy pond must achieve a balance between the plants and fish and the volume, depth, and temperature of the water. Even if you're planning on adding only a few pond plants and fish, it's a good idea to consult with a knowledgeable person at a nursery or pet store specializing in water-garden plants and animals.

Calculate the liner width by adding twice the maximum depth of the pool plus an additional 2 ft. to the width. Use the same formula to calculate the length. So, for a pond 2 ft. deep, 6 ft. wide, and 17 ft. long, the liner width would be 4 ft. plus 6 ft. plus 2 ft. (or 12 ft.). The length would be 4 ft. plus 17 ft. plus 2 ft. (or 23 ft.).

Water work

Unless you are a very tidy builder, the water you used to fit the liner will be too dirty to leave in the pond. (Spilled mortar can also make the water too alkaline for plants or fish.) Siphon or pump out the water, clean the liner, and refill the pond. If you're adding fish to the pond, you'll need to let the water stand for a week or so to allow any chlorine (which is deadly to fish) to dissipate. Check with local pet stores to find out if your water contains chemicals that require commercial conditioners to make the water safe for fish.

Installing the pond and plants is only the first step in water gardening. It takes patience, experimentation, and usually some consultation with experienced water gardeners to achieve a balance between plants, fish, and waterborne oxygen, nutrients, and waste that will sustain all happily while keeping algae, diseases, insects, and predators at acceptable levels.

Growing pond plants

One water lily, a few upright-growing plants, and a bundle of submerged plants (which help keep the water clean) are enough for a medium-size pond. An increasing number of nurseries and garden centers stock water lilies and other water plants. For a larger selection, your nursery or garden center may be able to recommend a specialist supplier.

These plants are grown in containers filled with heavy garden soil (not potting soil, which contains ingredients that float). You can buy special containers designed for aquatic plants, or simply use plastic pails or dishpans. Line basketlike containers with burlap to keep the soil from leaking out the holes. A water lily needs at least 2 to 3 gal. of soil; the more, the better. Most other water plants, such as dwarf papyrus, need 1 to 2 gal. of soil.

After planting, add a layer of gravel on the surface to keep soil from clouding the water and to protect roots from marauding fish. Soak the plant and soil thoroughly. Then set the container in the pond, positioning it so the water over the soil is 6 to 18 in. deep for water lilies, up to 6 in. for most other plants.

For maximum bloom, push a tablet of special water-lily fertilizer into the pots once or twice a month throughout the summer. Most water plants are easy to grow and carefree, although many are tropicals that die after hard frost, so you'll have to replace them each spring.

PLANTING WATER PLANTS

Set water plants in a container of heavy garden soil. Then cover soil surface with gravel to keep soil from floating away.

Gravel

1- to 3-gal. dishpan or special container

Heavy garden soil

Excavation

If your soil isn't too compacted or rocky, a good-size pond can be excavated with a shovel or two in a weekend ❶. (Energetic teenagers are a marvelous pool-building resource.) If the site isn't level, you can grade it using a stake-and-level system like the one described on pp. 138–139 for grading the patio.

Outline the pond's shape with garden lime, establishing the curves freehand with a garden hose or by staking out a large grid and plotting from the graph-paper plan. The pond shown below has two levels. The broad end, at 2 ft. deep, accommodates water lilies and other plants requiring deeper water as well as fish. Make the narrow end 12 to 16 in. deep for plants requiring shallower submersion. (You can put plant pots on stacks of bricks or other platforms to vary heights as necessary.) The walls will be less likely to crumble as you dig and the liner will install more easily if you slope them in about 3 to 4 in. for each foot of depth. Make the walls smooth, removing roots, rocks, and other sharp protrusions.

Excavate a shallow relief about 1 ft. wide around the perimeter to contain the liner overlap and stone edging. (The depth of the relief should accommodate the thickness of the edging stones.) Somewhere along the perimeter, create an overflow channel to take runoff after a heavy rain. This can simply be a 1- to 2-in. depression 1 foot or so wide spanned by one of the edging stones. Lengths of PVC pipe placed side by side beneath the stone (as shown in the drawing opposite) will keep the liner in place. The overflow channel can open onto a lower area of lawn or garden adjacent to the pond or to a rock-filled dry well.

Fitting the liner

When the hole is complete, cushion the surfaces to protect the liner ❷. Here we show a 1-inch-thick layer of sand on the bot-

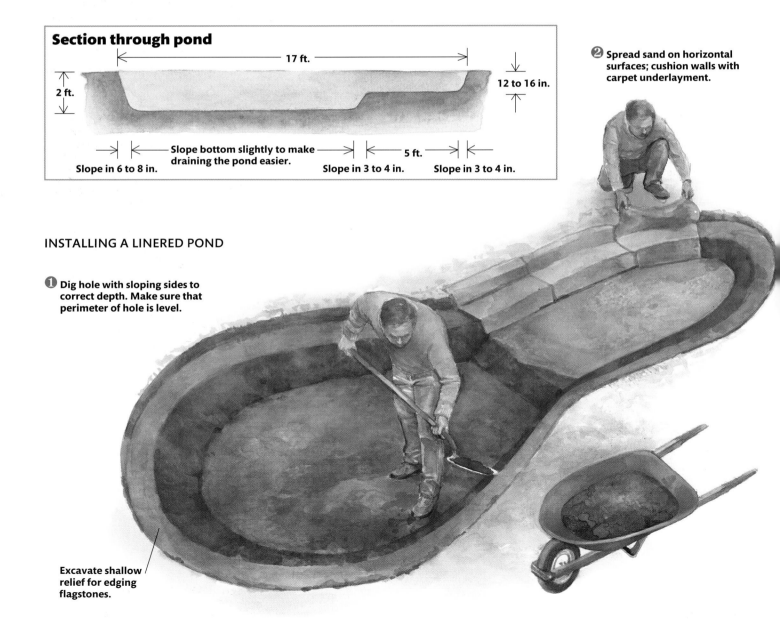

Section through pond

17 ft.

2 ft.

12 to 16 in.

Slope bottom slightly to make draining the pond easier.

5 ft.

Slope in 6 to 8 in.

Slope in 3 to 4 in.

Slope in 3 to 4 in.

❷ Spread sand on horizontal surfaces; cushion walls with carpet underlayment.

INSTALLING A LINERED POND

❶ Dig hole with sloping sides to correct depth. Make sure that perimeter of hole is level.

Excavate shallow relief for edging flagstones.

tom surfaces and carpet underlayment on the sloping walls. Fiberglass batting insulation also works well, as do old blankets or even heavy landscaping fabric.

Stretch the liner across the hole, letting it sag naturally to touch the walls and bottom but keeping it taut enough so it does not bunch up. Weight its edges with bricks or stones; then fill it with water ❸. The water's weight will push the liner against the walls; the stones will prevent it from blowing around. As it fills, tuck and smooth out as many creases as you can; the weight of the water makes this difficult to do after the pond is full. If you

stand in the pond to do so, take care not to damage the liner. Don't be alarmed if you can't smooth all the creases. Stop filling when the water is 2 in. below the rim of the pond, and cut the liner to fit into the overlap relief ❹. Hold it in place with a few long nails or large "staples" made from coat hangers while you install the edging.

Edging the pond

Finding and fitting flagstones so there aren't wide gaps between them is the most time-consuming part of this task. Cantilevering the stones an inch or two over the water will hide the liner somewhat.

The stones can be laid directly on the liner, as shown ❺. Add sand under the liner to level the surface where necessary so that the stones don't rock. Such treatment will withstand the occasional gingerly traffic of pond and plant maintenance but not the wear and tear of young children or large dogs regularly running across the edging. (The liner won't go long without damage if used as a wading pool.) If you anticipate heavier traffic, you can bed the stones in 2 to 3 in. of mortar. It's prudent to consult with a landscape contractor about whether your intended use and soil require some sort of footing for mortared stones.

Elevation detail of pond overflow

Flagstone edging, 12 in. or more wide

Cover pipe with flagstone.

Pond liner

To overflow area

PVC pipe, 1- or 2-in.-dia., about 12 in. long

Garden bed or lawn

1-in. layer of sand (horizontal surfaces)

Carpet underlayment (walls)

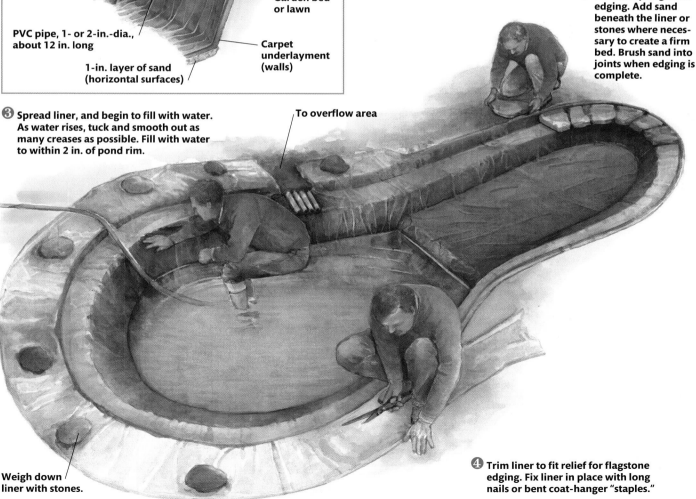

❸ Spread liner, and begin to fill with water. As water rises, tuck and smooth out as many creases as possible. Fill with water to within 2 in. of pond rim.

To overflow area

❺ Fit and lay flagstone edging. Add sand beneath the liner or stones where necessary to create a firm bed. Brush sand into joints when edging is complete.

Weigh down liner with stones.

❹ Trim liner to fit relief for flagstone edging. Fix liner in place with long nails or bent coat-hanger "staples."

Building a Retaining Wall

Contours and sloping terrain can add considerable interest to a home landscape. But you can have too much of a good thing. Two designs in this book employ retaining walls to alter problem slopes. The wall shown on p. 84 eliminates a small but abrupt grade change, producing two almost level surfaces and the opportunity to install attractive plantings on them. On p. 36 a curving retaining wall helps turn a steep slope into a showpiece.

Retaining walls can be handsome landscape features in their own right. Made of cut stone, fieldstone, brick, landscape timbers, or concrete, they can complement the materials and style of your house or nearby structures. However, making a stable, long-lasting retaining wall of these materials can require tools and skills many homeowners do not possess.

For these reasons we've chosen retaining-wall systems made of precast concrete for designs in this book. Readily available in a range of sizes, surface finishes, and colors, these systems require few tools and no special skills to install. They have been engineered to resist the forces that soil, water, freezing, and thawing bring to bear on a retaining wall. Install these walls according to the manufacturer's specifications, and you can be confident that they will do their job for many years.

A number of systems are available through nurseries, garden centers, and local contracting suppliers (search the Web or get a referrals from neighbors). But they all share basic design principles. Like traditional dry-stone walls, these systems rely largely on weight and friction to contain the weight of the soil. In many systems, interlocking blocks or pegs help align the courses and increase the wall's strength. In all systems, blocks must rest on a solid, level base. A freely draining backfill of crushed stone is essential to avoid buildup of water pressure (both liquid and frozen) in the retained soil, which can buckle even a heavy wall.

The steps shown here are typical of those recommended by most manufacturers for retaining walls up to 3 to 4 ft. tall; be sure to follow the instructions for the system you choose. (Some installation guides are excellent; others are less helpful. Weigh the quality of instructions when selecting a system.) For higher walls, walls on loose or heavy clay soils, and walls retaining very steep slopes, consult with a landscape architect or contractor.

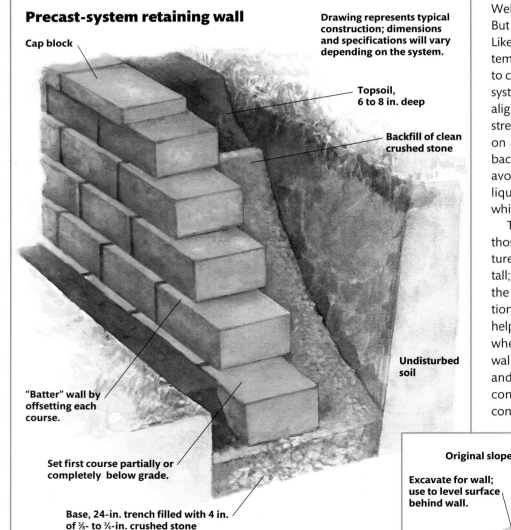

Precast-system retaining wall

Drawing represents typical construction; dimensions and specifications will vary depending on the system.

Cap block

Topsoil, 6 to 8 in. deep

Backfill of clean crushed stone

Undisturbed soil

"Batter" wall by offsetting each course.

Set first course partially or completely below grade.

Base, 24-in. trench filled with 4 in. of ⅜- to ¾-in. crushed stone

Original slope

New grade level

Excavate for wall; use to level surface behind wall.

30–45° from plumb

New grade

Building a wall

Installing a wall system is just about as simple as stacking up children's building blocks. The most important part of the job is establishing a firm, level base. Start by laying out the wall with string and hose (for curves) and excavating a base trench.

As the boxed drawing opposite bottom shows, the position of the wall in relation to the base of the slope determines the height of the wall, how much soil you move, and the leveling effect on the slope. Unless the wall is very long, it is a good idea to excavate along the entire length and fine-tune the line of the wall

before beginning the base trench. Remember to excavate back far enough to accommodate the stone backfill. Systems vary, but a foot of crushed-stone backfill behind the blocks is typical.

Systems vary in the width and depth of trench and type of base material, but in all of them, the trench must be level across its width and along its length. We've shown a 4 in. layer of ⅜-to- ¾-in. crushed stone (blocks can slip sideways on rounded aggregate or pea gravel, which also don't compact as well). Depending on the system and the circumstances, a portion or the entire first course lies below grade, so the soil helps hold the blocks in place.

Add crushed stone to the trench; level it with a rake; and compact it with a hand tamper or mechanical compactor. Lay the first course of blocks carefully ❶. Check frequently to make sure the blocks are level across their width and along their length. Stagger vertical joints

as you stack subsequent courses. Offset the faces of the blocks so the wall leans back into the retained soil. Some systems design this "batter" into their blocks; others allow you to choose from several possible setbacks.

As the wall rises, shovel backfill behind the blocks ❷. Clean crushed rock drains well; some systems suggest placing a barrier of landscaping fabric between the rock and the retained soil to keep soil from migrating into the fill and impeding drainage.

Thinner cap blocks finish the top of the wall ❸. Some wall systems recommend cementing these blocks in place with a weatherproof adhesive. The last 6 to 8 in. of the backfill should be topsoil, firmed into place and ready for planting.

BUILDING A WALL

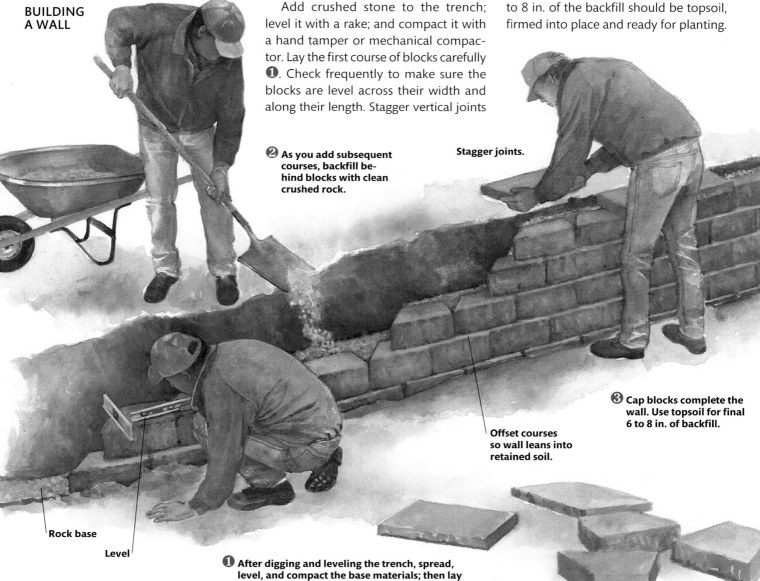

❷ As you add subsequent courses, backfill behind blocks with clean crushed rock.

Stagger joints.

❸ Cap blocks complete the wall. Use topsoil for final 6 to 8 in. of backfill.

Offset courses so wall leans into retained soil.

Rock base

Level

❶ After digging and leveling the trench, spread, level, and compact the base materials; then lay the blocks. Check frequently to see that they are level across their width and length.

Wall parallel with a slope: Stepped base

Construct walls running parallel with a slope in "steps," each with a level base.

Backfill so grade behind finishes level with top of wall.

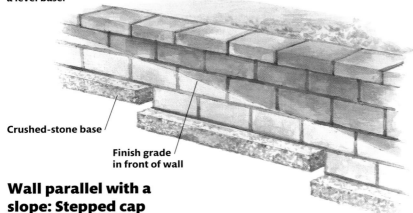

Crushed-stone base

Finish grade in front of wall

Wall parallel with a slope: Stepped cap

Sometimes the top of a wall needs to step up or down to accommodate grade changes in the slope behind.

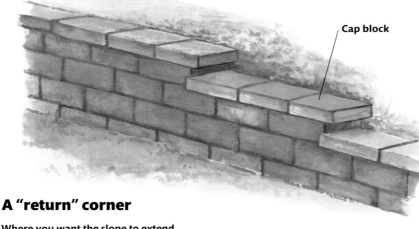

Cap block

A "return" corner

Where you want the slope to extend beyond the end of the wall, make a corner that cuts into the slope.

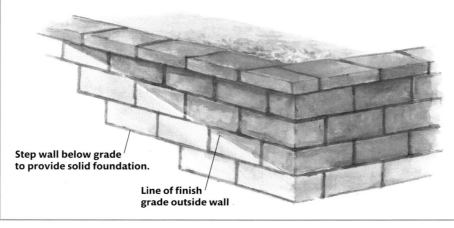

Step wall below grade to provide solid foundation.

Line of finish grade outside wall

Sloped sites

If your site slopes along the wall's length, you'll need to "step" the bottom of the wall, as shown at top left. Create a length of level trench along the lowest portion of the site; then work up the slope, creating steps as necessary.

The top of the wall can also step if the slope dissipates at one end. Such slopes are common on sites such as the one shown on p. 36, which slopes away from the house and toward the driveway. Here the base of the wall will rest on level ground, but the slope behind the wall decreases along the wall's length. The design on p. 36 shows one solution to this dilemma—a wall of uniform height with a "return" corner at one end (see bottom left), backfilled to raise the grade behind to the top of the wall. Another solution, shown at center left, is to step the wall down as the slope decreases, which saves material, produces a different look, but still works with the planting design.

Curves and corners

Wall-system blocks are designed so that curves are no more difficult to lay than straight sections. Corners may require that you cut a few blocks or use specially designed blocks, but they are otherwise uncomplicated. If your wall must fit a prescribed length between corners, consider working from the corners toward the middle (after laying a base course). Masons use this technique, which to avoids cut blocks at the corners.

You can cut blocks with a mason's chisel and mallet or rent a mason's saw. Chiseling works well where the faces of the blocks are rough textured, so the cut faces blend right in. A saw is best for smooth-faced blocks and projects requiring lots of cutting.

Where the wall doesn't run the full length of the slope, the best-looking and most structurally sound termination is a return corner shown at bottom left.

Steps

Steps in a low retaining wall are not difficult to build, but they require forethought and careful layout. Systems differ on construction details. The drawing below shows a typical design where the blocks and stone base rest on "steps" cut into firm subsoil. If your soil is less stable or is recent fill, you should excavate the entire area beneath the steps to the same depth as the wall base and build a foundation of blocks, as shown in the boxed drawing.

These steps are independent of the adjacent "return" walls, which are vertical, not battered (stepped back). In some systems, steps and return walls are interlocked. To match a path, you can face the treads with the same stone, brick, or pavers, or you can use the system's cap blocks or special treads.

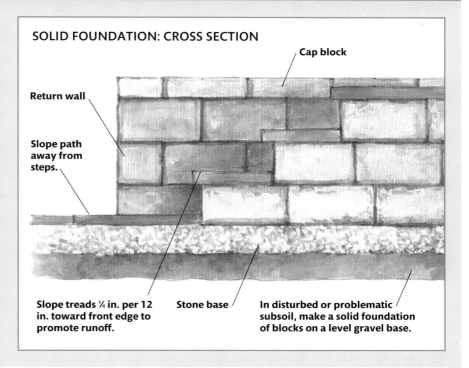

SOLID FOUNDATION: CROSS SECTION

Cap block

Return wall

Slope path away from steps.

Slope treads ¼ in. per 12 in. toward front edge to promote runoff.

Stone base

In disturbed or problematic subsoil, make a solid foundation of blocks on a level gravel base.

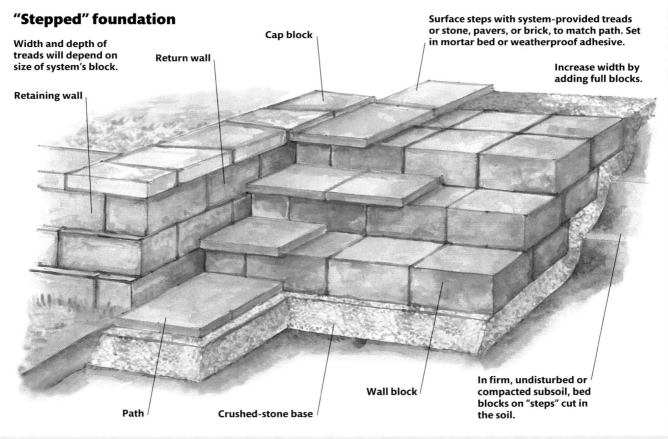

"Stepped" foundation

Width and depth of treads will depend on size of system's block.

Cap block

Return wall

Surface steps with system-provided treads or stone, pavers, or brick, to match path. Set in mortar bed or weatherproof adhesive.

Increase width by adding full blocks.

Retaining wall

Path

Crushed-stone base

Wall block

In firm, undisturbed or compacted subsoil, bed blocks on "steps" cut in the soil.

Fences, Pergolas, Arbors, and Trellises

Novices who have no trouble tackling a simple flagstone path often get nervous when it comes time to erect a fence, an arbor, or even a trellis. While such projects can require more skill and resources than others in the landscape, the ones in this book have been designed with less-than-confident do-it-yourself builders in mind. The designs are simple, the materials are read-ily available, and the tools and skills will be familiar to anyone accustomed to ordinary home maintenance.

First we'll introduce you to the materials and tools needed for the projects. Then we'll present the small number of basic opera-tions you'll employ when building them. Finally, we'll provide drawings and comments on each of the projects.

Tools and materials

Even the least-handy homeowner is likely to have most of the tools needed for these projects: claw hammer, crosscut handsaw, circular saw, cordless drill, adjustable wrench, com-bination square, tape measure, carpenter's level, and saw-horses. You may even have Grandpa's old posthole digger. If you have more than a few holes to dig, consider renting a gas-powered posthole digger.

Materials

Of the materials offering strength, durability, and attractive-ness in outdoor settings, wood is the easiest to work and affords the quickest results. While almost all commercially available lumber is strong enough for landscape structures, most decay quickly when in prolonged contact with soil and water. Cedar, cypress, and redwood, however, contain natural preservatives and are excellent for landscape use. Alternatively, a range of softwoods (such as pine, fir, and hemlock) are pressure-treated with preservatives and will last for many years. Parts of structures that do not come in contact with soil or are not continually wet can be made of ordinary construction-grade lumber, but unless they're regularly painted, they will not last as long as treated or naturally decay-resistant material.

In addition to dimension lumber, several of the designs incorporate lattice, which is thin wooden strips crisscrossed to form patterns of diamonds or squares. Premade lattice is widely available in sheets 4 ft. by 8 ft. and smaller. Lattice comes in decay-resistant woods as well as in treated and untreated softwoods. Local supplies vary, and you may find lattice made of thicker or narrower material.

Fasteners

For millennia, even basic structures such as these would have been assembled with complicated joints, the cutting and fitting of which required long training to master. Today, with simple nailed, bolted, or screwed joints, a few hours' practice swinging a hammer or wielding a cordless drill is all the training necessary.

All these structures can be assembled entirely with nails. But screws are stronger and, if you have a cordless screw-driver, make assembly easier. Buy common or box nails (both have flat heads) hot-dipped galvanized to prevent rust. Self-tapping screws ("deck" screws) require no pilot holes. For rust resistance, buy galvanized screws or screws treated with zinc dichromate.

Galvanized metal connectors are available to reinforce the joints used in these projects. (See the joinery drawings on pp. 152–153.) For novice builders, connectors are a great help in aligning parts and making assembly easier.

Finishes

Cedar, cypress, and redwood are handsome when left unfinished to weather, when treated with clear or colored stains, or when painted. Pressure-treated lumber is best painted or stained to mask the cast of the preservatives. .

Outdoor stains are becoming increasingly popular. Clear or lightly tinted stains can preserve or enhance the rich reddish browns of cedar, cypress, and redwood. Stains also come in a range of colors that can be used like paint. Be-cause they penetrate the wood rather than forming a film, stains don't form an opaque surface—you'll still need paint to make a picket fence white. On the other hand, stains won't peel or chip like paint and are therefore easier to touch up and refinish.

When choosing a finish, take account of what plants are growing on or near the structure. It's a lot of work to remove yards of vines from a trellis or squeeze between a large shrub and a fence to repaint; consider an unfinished decay-resistant wood or an initial stain that you allow to weather.

Setting posts

All the projects are anchored by firmly set, vertical posts. In general, the taller the structure, the deeper the post should be set. For the pergola, arbors, and the tallest fences, posts should be at least 3 ft. deep. Posts for fences up to 4 ft. tall can be set 2 ft. deep. To avoid post movement caused in cold-winter areas by expansion and contraction of the soil during freeze-thaw cycles, set all arbor posts below the frost line. Check with local building authorities.

The length of the posts you buy depends, of course, on the depth at which they are set and their finished heights. When calculating lengths of pergola and arbor posts, remember that the tops of the posts must be level. The easiest method of achieving this is to cut the posts to length after installation. For example, buy 12-ft. posts for an arbor finishing at 8 ft. above grade and set 3 ft. in the ground. The convenience is worth the expense of the foot or so you cut off. The site and personal preference can determine whether you cut fence posts to length after installation or buy them cut to length and add or remove fill from the bottom of the hole to position them at the correct heights.

Pergola and arbor posts

When laying out pergola and arbor posts, take extra care when positioning them. The corners of the structure must be right angles, and the sides must be parallel. Locating the corners with batter boards and string is fussy but accurate. Make the batter boards by nailing 1x2 stakes to scraps of 1x3 or 1x4, and position them about 1 ft. from the approximate location of each post as shown in the boxed drawing at right. Locate the exact post positions with string; adjust the string so the diagonal measurements are equal, which ensures that the corners of the structure will be at right angles.

At the intersections of the strings, locate the postholes by eye or with a plumb bob ❶. Remove the strings and dig the holes; then reattach the strings to position the posts exactly ❷. Plumb and brace the posts. Check positions with the level and by measuring between adjacent posts and across diagonals. Diagonal braces between adjacent posts will stiffen them and help align their faces ❸. Then add concrete ❹ and let it cure for a day.

To establish the height of the posts, measure up from grade on one post; then use a level and straightedge to mark the heights of the other posts from the first one. Where joists will be bolted to the faces of the posts, you can install the joists and use their top edges as a handsaw guide for cutting the posts to length.

SETTING ARBOR POSTS

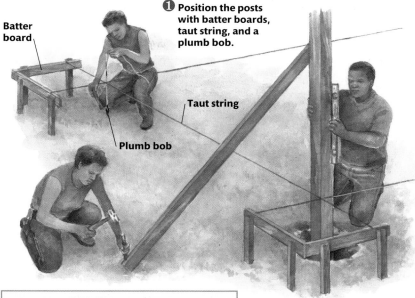

Batter board

❶ Position the posts with batter boards, taut string, and a plumb bob.

Taut string

Plumb bob

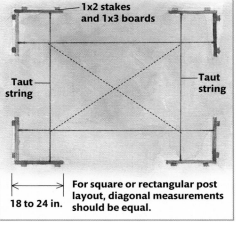

BATTER BOARDS
Set L-shaped batter boards at each corner and stretch string to position the posts exactly.

1x2 stakes and 1x3 boards

Taut string

Taut string

18 to 24 in.

For square or rectangular post layout, diagonal measurements should be equal.

❷ Remove the string to dig the holes; then reattach it and align the outer faces of the posts with the string while you plumb and brace them.

❸ Check distances between posts at top. Add diagonal bracing between posts to fix positions.

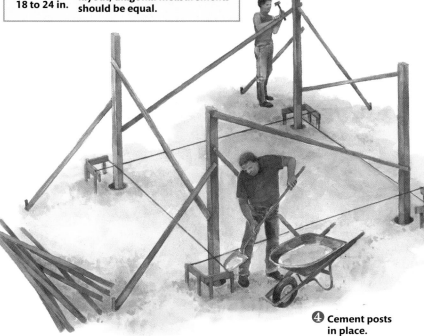

❹ Cement posts in place.

Fence posts

Lay out and set the end or corner posts of a fence first; then add the intermediate posts. Dig the holes by hand or with a power digger ❶. To promote drainage, place several inches of gravel at the bottom of the hole for the post to rest on. Checking with a carpenter's level, plumb the post vertically and brace it with scrap lumber nailed to stakes ❷. Then add a few more inches of gravel around the post's base.

If your native soil compacts well, you can fix posts in place with tamped earth. Add the soil gradually, tamping it continu- ously with a heavy iron bar or 2x4. Check regularly with a level to see that the post doesn't get knocked out of plumb. This technique suits rustic or informal fences, where misalignments caused by shifting posts aren't noticeable or damaging.

For more formal fences, or where soils are loose or fence panels are buffeted by winds in coastal areas, it's prudent to fix posts in concrete ❸. Mix enough concrete to set the two end posts; as a rule of thumb, figure one 80 lb. bag of premixed concrete per post. As you shovel it in, prod the concrete with a stick to settle it, particularly if you've added rubble to extend

SETTING A FENCE POST

❷ Plumb the post, checking on adjacent faces with a level. Hold it in position with stakes and braces.

❶ Position the end or corner posts; then dig holes for them.

❸ Fill the hole with concrete and rubble.

Post

Slope top surface for drainage.

3 ft. (typical)

Concrete and rubble (shown), or tamped earth

Coarse gravel

1 ft. (typical)

the mix. Build the concrete slightly above grade and slope it away from the post to aid drainage.

Once the end posts are set, stretch a string between the posts. (The concrete should cure for 24 hours before you nail or screw rails and panels in place, but you can safely stretch string while the concrete is still wet.) Measure along the string to position the intermediate posts; drop a plumb bob from the string at each intermediate post position to gauge the center of the hole below ❹. Once all the holes have been dug, again stretch a string between the end posts, near the top. Set the intermediate posts as described previously; align one face with the string and plumb adjacent faces with the carpenter's level ❺. Check positions of intermediate posts a final time with a tape measure.

If the fence is placed along a slope, the top of the slats or panels can step down the slope or mirror it (as shown in the drawings below). Either way, make sure that the posts are plumb, rather than leaning with the slope.

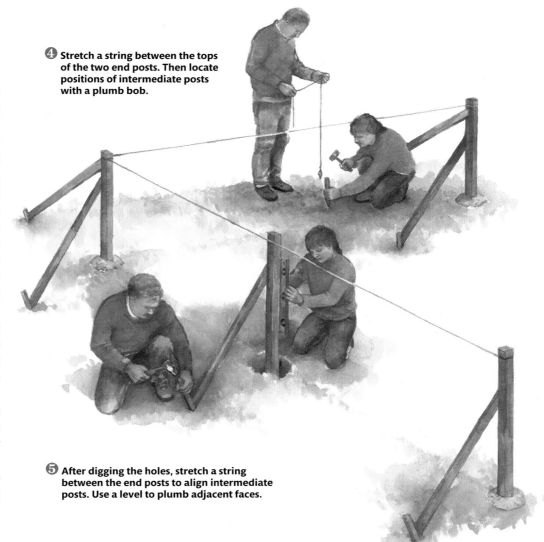

❹ **Stretch a string between the tops of the two end posts. Then locate positions of intermediate posts with a plumb bob.**

❺ **After digging the holes, stretch a string between the end posts to align intermediate posts. Use a level to plumb adjacent faces.**

Fencing a slope

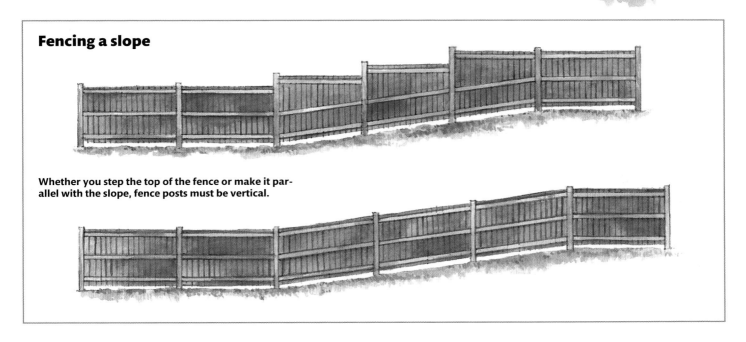

Whether you step the top of the fence or make it parallel with the slope, fence posts must be vertical.

Joints

The components of the fences, pergolas, arbors, and trellises used in this book are attached to the posts and to each other with the simple joints shown below. Because all the parts are made of dimensioned lumber, the only cuts you'll need to make are to length. For strong joints, cut ends as square as you can so the mating pieces make contact across their entire surfaces. If you have no confidence in your sawing, many lumberyards will cut pieces to length for a modest fee.

Beginners often find it difficult to keep two pieces correctly positioned while trying to drive a nail into them, particularly when the nail must be driven at an angle, called "toenailing". If you have this problem, predrill for nails, or use screws, which draw the pieces together, or metal connectors, which can be nailed or screwed in place on one piece and then attached to the mating piece.

For several designs, you need to attach lattice panels to posts. The panels are made by sandwiching store-bought lattice be-

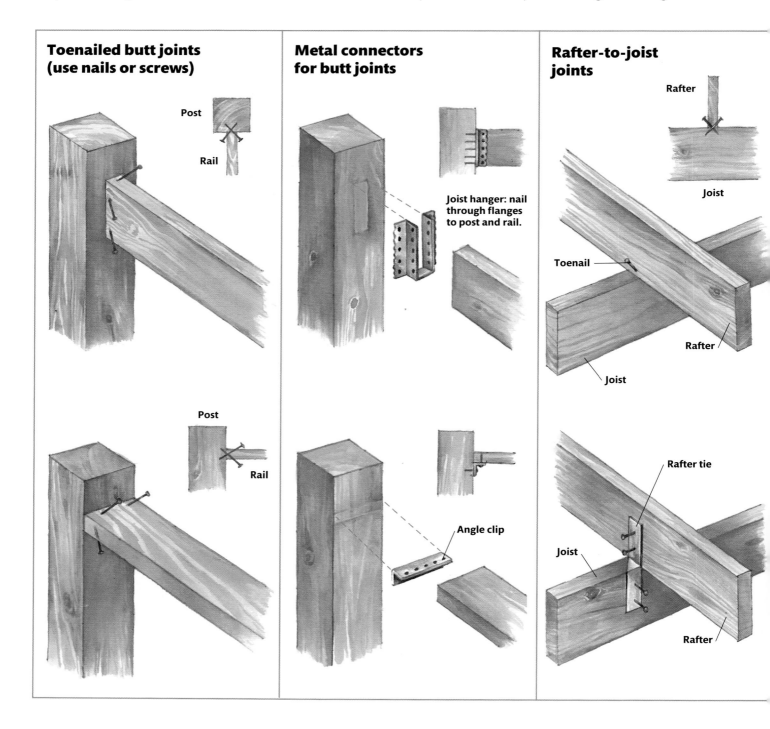

**Toenailed butt joints
(use nails or screws)**

Post

Rail

Post

Rail

**Metal connectors
for butt joints**

Joist hanger: nail through flanges to post and rail.

Angle clip

Rafter-to-joist joints

Rafter

Joist

Toenail

Rafter

Joist

Rafter tie

Joist

Rafter

tween frames of dimension lumber (construction details are given on the following pages). While the assembled panels can be toenailed to the posts, novices may find that the job goes easier using one or more types of metal connector, as shown in the drawing at below right. Attach the angle clips or angle brackets to the post; then position the lattice panel and fix it to the connectors. For greatest strength and ease of assembly, attach connectors with self-tapping screws driven by an electric screwdriver.

In the following pages, we'll show and comment on construction details of the fences, pergolas, arbors, and trellises presented in the Portfolio of Designs. (The page number indicates the design.) Where the basic joints discussed here can be used, we have shown the parts but left choice of fasteners to you. Typical fastenings are indicated for other joints. We have kept the constructions shown here simple and straightforward. They are not the only possibilities, and we encourage experienced builders to adapt designs to suit personal preferences.

Frame corner with metal connector

Nailing plate

Angled plate

Attaching framed lattice panels to posts

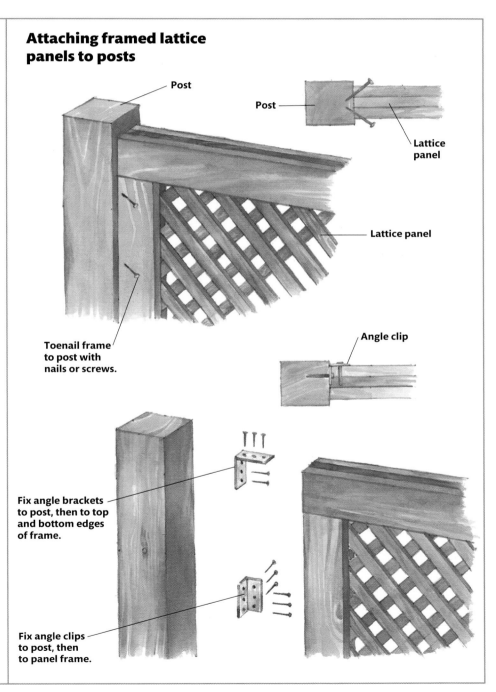

Post

Post

Lattice panel

Lattice panel

Toenail frame to post with nails or screws.

Angle clip

Fix angle brackets to post, then to top and bottom edges of frame.

Fix angle clips to post, then to panel frame.

Homemade lattice trellis
(pp. 16–20, 62–63, and 80–83)

The trellis shown here supports climbing plants to make a vertical garden of a blank wall. The design can be altered to fit walls of different sizes. The three 32-in.-wide modules are simpler to make than a single large trellis. Hung on L-hangers, they're easy to remove when you need to paint the wall behind. (You can also just attach store-bought lattice to 2x2 frameworks of the same dimensions as shown here.)

Start by cutting all the pieces to length. (Here we'll call the horizontal members "rails" and the vertical members "stiles.") Working on a flat surface, nail or screw the two outer stiles to the top and bottom rails, checking the corners with a framing square. The 2x2 rails provide ample material to house the L-hangers.

Carefully attach the three intermediate stiles, then the 1x2 rails. Cut a piece of scrap 6 in. long to use as a spacer. Fix the L-shaped hangers to 2x4 studs inside the wall. Buy hangers long enough to hold the trellis several inches away from the wall.

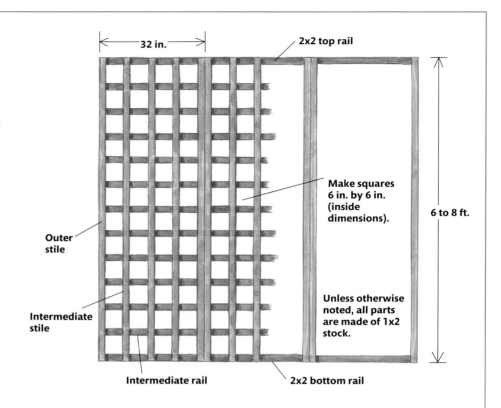

32 in.

2x2 top rail

Make squares 6 in. by 6 in. (inside dimensions).

6 to 8 ft.

Outer stile

Intermediate stile

Unless otherwise noted, all parts are made of 1x2 stock.

Intermediate rail

2x2 bottom rail

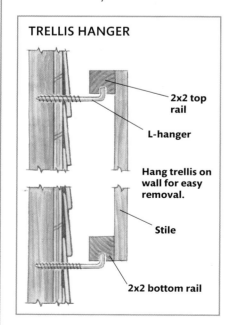

TRELLIS HANGER

2x2 top rail

L-hanger

Hang trellis on wall for easy removal.

Stile

2x2 bottom rail

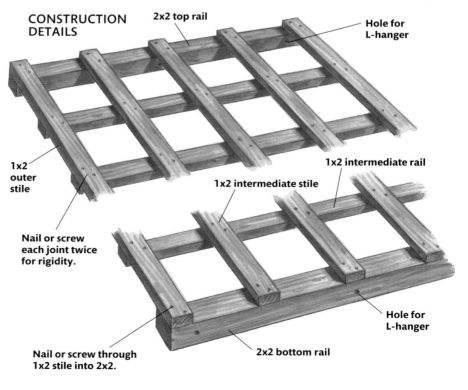

CONSTRUCTION DETAILS

2x2 top rail

Hole for L-hanger

1x2 outer stile

Nail or screw each joint twice for rigidity.

1x2 intermediate stile

1x2 intermediate rail

Hole for L-hanger

Nail or screw through 1x2 stile into 2x2.

2x2 bottom rail

Arbor (with or without trellis panels)
(pp. 44–45, 56–57, and 88–89)

This cozy enclosure is either a gateway over a walkway or can shelter a bench while it supports vines to shade the occupants. Once the posts are set in place, this project can be finished in a weekend.

Build the arbor before laying paving under it. After setting the posts (see p. 149), attach the 2x10 joists with carriage bolts. (The sizes of posts and joists have been chosen for visual effect; 4x4 posts and 2x6 or 2x8 joists will work, too.) Tack the joists in place with nails; then bore holes for the bolts through post and both joists with a long electrician's auger bit. Fix the rafters by toenailing or using rust-protected metal rafter ties. Nail or screw the rafters at each end to the posts for added stability.

Sandwich store-bought lattice between 1x3s to make the trellis panels for the vines, and fix them to the posts with metal connectors. Offset the corner joints, as shown in the drawing, or reinforce them with metal brackets, or both.

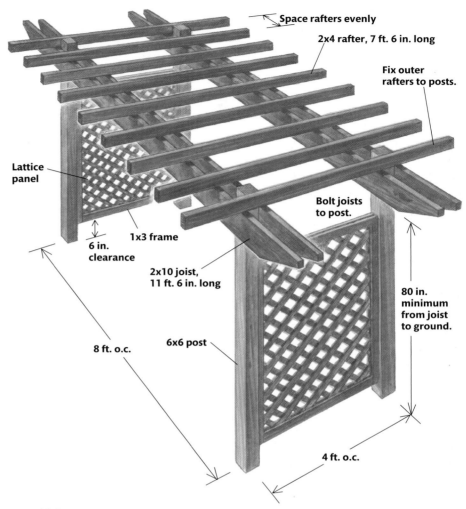

Space rafters evenly
2x4 rafter, 7 ft. 6 in. long
Fix outer rafters to posts.
Lattice panel
Bolt joists to post.
6 in. clearance
1x3 frame
2x10 joist, 11 ft. 6 in. long
80 in. minimum from joist to ground.
8 ft. o.c.
6x6 post
4 ft. o.c.

TRELLIS-PANEL CONSTRUCTION

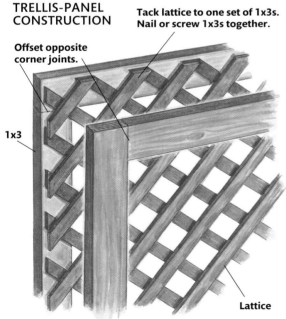

Tack lattice to one set of 1x3s. Nail or screw 1x3s together.
Offset opposite corner joints.
1x3
Lattice

POST-TO-JOIST DETAIL

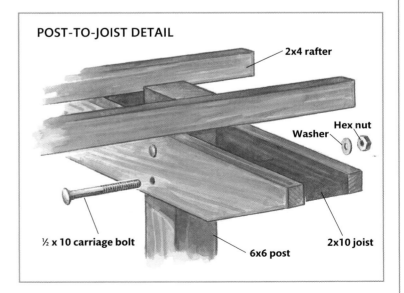

2x4 rafter
Hex nut
Washer
½ x 10 carriage bolt
6x6 post
2x10 joist

Screen
(pp. 44–45)

Made of vertical slats spaced a small distance apart, these 6-ft.-tall screens allow air circulation to plants and people near the screen while providing privacy. Be sure to check local codes about height and setback from property lines.

The slats are supported by three rails. The top and middle rails are 2x4s; a 2x6 bottom rail adds visual weight to the design. Set the posts (see pp. 149–151). Then cut and fix the rails to their back faces. Position the 1x6 slats with a spacer block 1½ in. wide. (To ensure uniform spacing, position all the slats before assembly.) Alternatively, assemble the slats and rails on a flat surface first, and then set the posts at a distance determined by the assembly. Add the 1x6 cap piece to complete the screen.

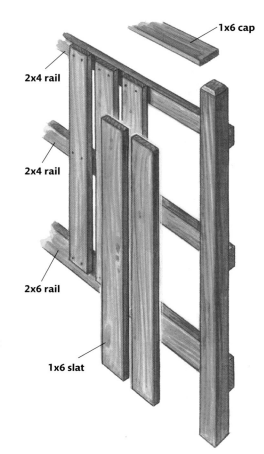

1x6 cap
2x4 rail
2x4 rail
2x6 rail
1x6 slat

Scene-setting fence
(pp. 44–45 and 88–89)

This design provides privacy and an attractive backdrop for any plantings. If the fence is used on a property line, be sure to check local codes for restrictions on placement and height.

This is a simple fence to construct. Assemble the panels on a flat surface, nailing or screwing the slats to the three 2x4 rails. You can lay out the arc at the top of each panel by "springing" a thin strip of wood, as shown on the facing page. Place the strip against a nail driven into a slat at the highest point of the arc in the center of the panel ❶. Enlist a couple of assistants to bend each end of the strip down to nails near each edge of the panel indicating the lowest points of the arc ❷. Pencil in the arc against the strip ❸; then cut to the line. (A handheld electric jigsaw does the job quickly, but the curve is gentle enough to cut with a handsaw.)

VIEW FROM BACK OF FENCE

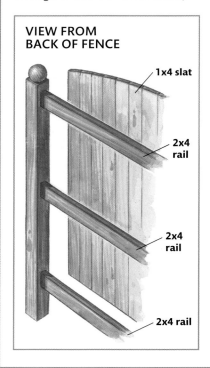

1x4 slat
2x4 rail
2x4 rail
2x4 rail

FRONT ELEVATION

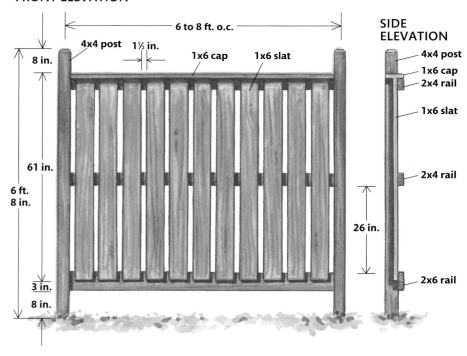

6 to 8 ft. o.c.
4x4 post   1½ in.
8 in.
1x6 cap   1x6 slat
61 in.
6 ft. 8 in.
3 in.
8 in.

SIDE ELEVATION

4x4 post
1x6 cap
2x4 rail
1x6 slat
2x4 rail
26 in.
2x6 rail

Set the posts (see pp. 150–151) according to the widths of the finished panels. The 6x6 posts shown here add an eye-pleasing heft to the fence, an effect emphasized by setting the face of the panel 1 in. back from the faces of the posts. (Posts made of 4x4s will work just as well.) Metal fasteners are the easiest means of attaching the completed panels to the posts. To allow yourself access to the rails when mounting the metal fasteners, leave the last slats at each end off when you assemble the panels. We've shown a spherical finial attached to the end of each post; you can buy finials of various types at home centers.

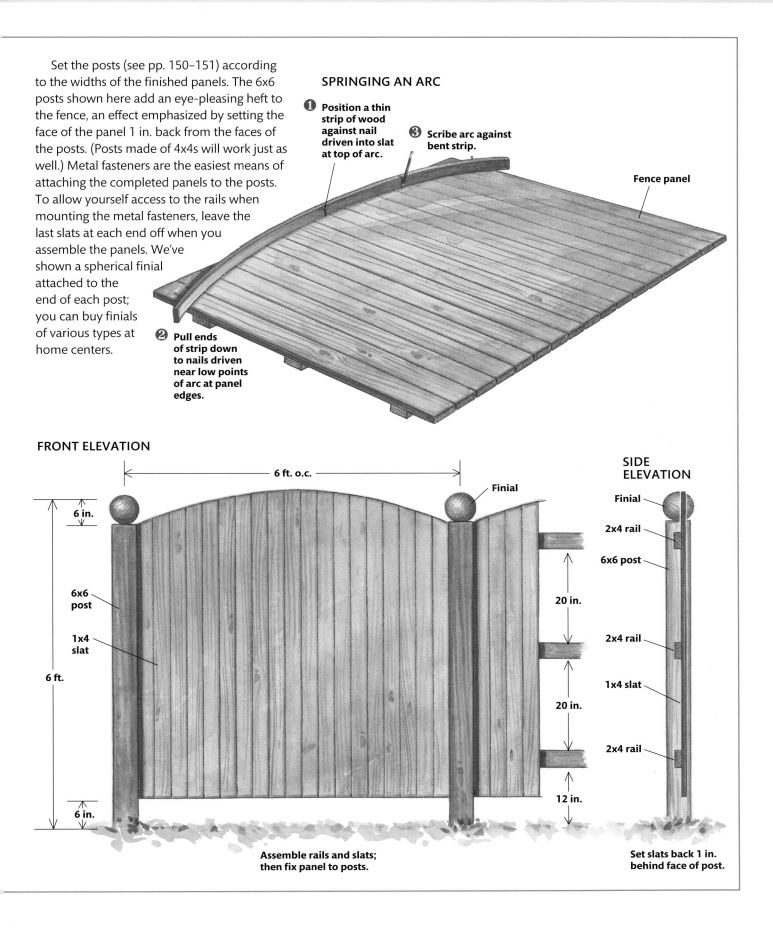

SPRINGING AN ARC

❶ Position a thin strip of wood against nail driven into slat at top of arc.

❸ Scribe arc against bent strip.

Fence panel

❷ Pull ends of strip down to nails driven near low points of arc at panel edges.

FRONT ELEVATION

6 ft. o.c.

Finial

6 in.

6x6 post

1x4 slat

6 ft.

6 in.

20 in.

20 in.

12 in.

Assemble rails and slats; then fix panel to posts.

SIDE ELEVATION

Finial

2x4 rail

6x6 post

2x4 rail

1x4 slat

2x4 rail

Set slats back 1 in. behind face of post.

Bench swing
(pp. 40–41 and 58–59)

A bench swing adds breezy animation to the simple pleasure of sitting in a garden. A swing is used in two Portfolio designs and could replace a bench in many others.

Once posts are set in concrete (see pp. 149–151), it is a simple task to complete the frame and add the optional decorative molding and hang the swing. Set the beam onto the notched posts, and tack it in place before attaching it with the lag bolts and brackets cut from a 2x6. Anchor the three joists; install the eyebolts with washers for the swing; and attach the rafters and decorative molding. Then hang the heavy duty swing springs and chain. Finally use a level when hanging the swing, and adjust the chair accordingly. Finish up by planting vines at the base of the posts, and take a swing in the shade.

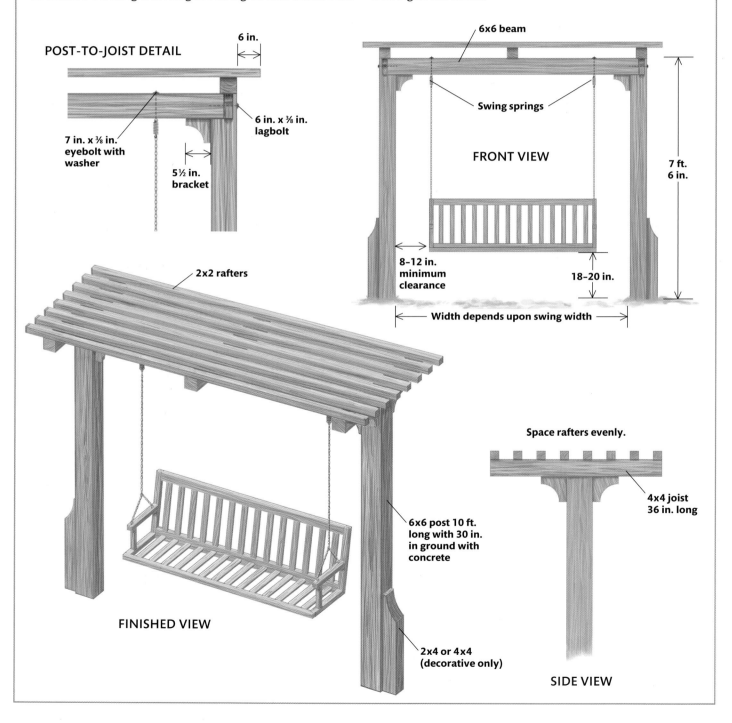

POST-TO-JOIST DETAIL

6 in.

7 in. x ⅜ in. eyebolt with washer

6 in. x ⅜ in. lagbolt

5½ in. bracket

6x6 beam

Swing springs

FRONT VIEW

7 ft. 6 in.

8–12 in. minimum clearance

18–20 in.

Width depends upon swing width

2x2 rafters

FINISHED VIEW

6x6 post 10 ft. long with 30 in. in ground with concrete

2x4 or 4x4 (decorative only)

Space rafters evenly.

4x4 joist 36 in. long

SIDE VIEW

Patio pergola and sun screen
(pp. 34–35 and 72–75)

This simple structure offers relief from the sun on a portion of a backyard patio. The closely spaced 2x4 rafters form a sun screen, while allowing air circulation. Adapt rafter spacing and orientation to accommodate your site. In the design on pp. 72–75, the pergola supports a cross vine, which provides additional cooling shade as well as a pleasant leafy ambiance.

If you're building the patio and pergola at the same time, set the 6x6 posts (see pp. 149–151) before you lay the patio surface. If you're adding the pergola to an existing patio, you'll need to break through the paving to set the posts or pour footings to support surface attachments. Consult local building officials or a landscape contractor for advice on how best to proceed.

Once the posts are set, fix the 2x8 beams to pairs of posts with carriage bolts. Nail the 2x8s in place; then make the bolt holes by boring through the 2x8s and the post with a long electrician's bit. Fix the long 2x6 joists and the 2x4 rafters in place with metal connectors. Metal connectors fixed with screws will stand up best to the vigorous growth of the vine.

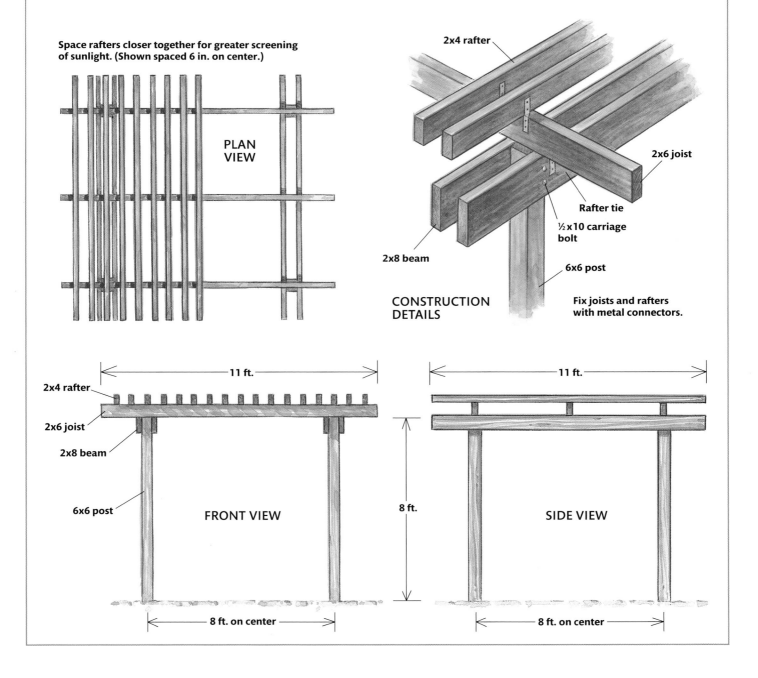

Space rafters closer together for greater screening of sunlight. (Shown spaced 6 in. on center.)

PLAN VIEW

2x4 rafter

2x6 joist

Rafter tie

½ x 10 carriage bolt

2x8 beam

6x6 post

CONSTRUCTION DETAILS

Fix joists and rafters with metal connectors.

2x4 rafter
2x6 joist
2x8 beam
6x6 post

11 ft.

FRONT VIEW

8 ft. on center

11 ft.

8 ft.

SIDE VIEW

8 ft. on center

Preparing the Soil for Planting

The better the soil, the better the plants. Soil quality affects how fast plants grow, how big they get, how good they look, and how long they live. But on many residential lots, the soil is shallow and infertile. Unless you're lucky enough to have a better-than-average site where the soil has been cared for and amended over the years, perhaps for use as a vegetable garden or flower bed, you should plan to improve your soil before planting in it. However, if you have existing plants that are growing well, you may not need to amend the soil.

If you were planting just a few trees or widely spaced shrubs, you could pre-pare individual planting holes for them and leave the surrounding soil undisturbed. However, for plants with close spacing—18 to 24 in. apart—it's much better for the plants if you prepare the soil throughout the entire area that will be planted. (The major exception is when you're planting under or near a tree, which we'll discuss on p. 169.)

For most of the situations shown in this book, you could prepare the soil with hand tools—a spade, digging fork, and rake. The job goes faster, though, if you use a rototiller, and a rototiller is better than hand tools for mixing amendments into the soil. Unless you grow vegetables, you probably won't use a rototiller often enough to justify buying one yourself, but you can easily borrow or rent a rototiller or hire someone with a tiller to come and prepare your site.

Loosen the soil

After you've removed any sod or other vegetation from the designated area (see pp. 128–129), the first step is digging or tilling to loosen the soil ❶. Do this on a day when the soil is moist—not so wet that it sticks to your tools or so dry that it makes dust. Start at one end of the bed and work back and forth until you reach the other end. Try to dig down at least 8 in. or deeper if possible. If the ground is very compacted, you'll have to make repeated passes with a tiller to reach 8 in. deep. Toss aside any large rocks, roots, or debris that you encounter. When you're working near a house or other buildings, be sure to locate buried wires, cables, and pipes. This is required by law in some towns; fortunately, most municipalities will assist you in locating buried utilities.

After this initial digging, the ground will probably be very rough and lumpy. Whack the clods with the back of a digging fork or make another pass with the tiller. Continue until you've reduced all the clumps to the size of apples.

After loosening the existing soil and digging it as deeply as possible, you may need to add topsoil and fill in low spots, refine the grade, or raise the planting area above the surrounding grade for better drainage. If your soil drains well, leave the grade low so that storm water can collect and not flow onto surrounding pavement. Remember when you add new plantings, you will have additional soil because new root balls add to the soil volume. Unless you need just a few bags of it, order screened topsoil by the cubic yard from a landscape contractor.

Common fertilizers and soil amendments

The following materials serve different purposes. Follow soil-test recommendations or the advice of an experienced gardener in choosing which amendments would be best for your soil. If so recommended, you can apply two or three of these amendments at the same time, using the stated rate for each one.

Material	Description	Amount for 100 sq. ft.
Bagged steer manure	A weak all-purpose fertilizer.	6–8 lb.
Dried poultry manure	A high-nitrogen fertilizer.	2 lb.
5-5-5 all-purpose fertilizer	An inexpensive and popular synthetic fertilizer.	2 lb.
Superphosphate or rock phosphate	Supplies phosphorus. Work into the soil as deep as possible.	2–4 lb.
Greensand	Supplies potassium and many trace elements.	2–4 lb.
Regular or dolomitic limestone	Used primarily to sweeten acid soil.	5 lb.
Gypsum	Helps loosen clay soil. Also helps reduce salt buildup in roadside soil.	2 lb.
Wood ashes	Supply potassium, phosphorus, and lime.	2–4 lb.

Add organic matter

Common dirt (and purchased topsoil, too) consists mainly of rock and mineral fragments of various sizes—which are mostly coarse and gritty in sandy soil, and dust-fine in clay soil. To solve these problems, add some organic matter. Organic materials include all kinds of composted plant parts and animal manures. Be sure that the material you select has been composted for several months. Fresh, raw manure can "burn" plant roots. Fresh sawdust or chipped bark can take nitrogen from the soil; fresh hay may contain weed seeds.

How much organic matter should you use? Spread a layer 2 to 3 in. thick across the entire area you're working on ❷. At this thickness, a cubic yard (about one heaping pickup-truck load) of bulk material, or six bales of peat moss, will cover 100 to 150 sq. ft. If you're working on a large area and need several cubic yards of organic matter, have it delivered. Ask the driver to dump the pile as close to your project area as possible, even if he has to drive across your lawn.

Add fertilizers and mineral amendments

Organic matter improves the soil's texture and helps it retain water and nutrients, but it doesn't actually supply many nutrients. To provide the nutrients that plants need, you need to use organic or synthetic fertilizers and powdered minerals. It's most helpful if you mix these materials into the soil before you do any planting, putting them down into the root zone as shown in the drawing ❸, but you can also sprinkle them on top of the soil in subsequent years to maintain a planting.

Getting a sample of soil tested (a service that's usually available free or at low cost through your County Extension Service) is the most accurate way to determine how much of which nutrients is needed. Less precise, but often adequate, is asking the advice of an experienced gardener in your neighborhood. Test results or a gardener's advice will point out any significant deficiencies in your soil, but these are uncommon. Most soil just needs a moderate, balanced dose of nutrients.

Most important is to avoid using too much of any fertilizer or mineral. Don't guess at this; measure and weigh carefully. Calculate your plot's area. Follow your soil-test results, instructions on a commercial product's package, or the general guidelines given in the chart opposite, and weigh out the appropriate amount, using a kitchen or bathroom scale. Apply the material evenly across the plot with a spreader or by hand.

PREPARING THE SOIL FOR PLANTING

❶ Use a spade, digging fork, or tiller to dig at least 8 in. deep and break the soil into rough clods. Discard rocks, roots, and debris. Watch out for underground utilities.

❷ Spread a 2- to 3-in. layer of organic matter on top of the soil.

❸ Sprinkle measured amounts of fertilizer and mineral amendments evenly across the entire area, and mix thoroughly into the soil.

Mix and smooth the soil

Finally, use a digging fork or tiller and go back and forth across the bed again until the added materials are mixed thoroughly into the soil and everything is broken into nut-size or smaller lumps ❹. Then use a rake to smooth the surface ❺.

The soil level may look too high compared with adjacent pavement or lawn. It will settle a few inches over the next several weeks and end up close to its original level. Take into account that extra soil is added to the site with every root ball you plant.

Working near trees

Plantings under the shade of old trees can be cool lovely oases, like the ones shown on pp. 40–43. But to establish the plants, you'll need to contend with the tree's roots. Contrary to popular belief, most tree roots are in the top 12 in. of the soil, and they extend at least as far away from the trunk as the limbs do. If you dig any place in that area, you'll probably cut or bruise some of the tree's roots. When preparing for planting beneath a tree, therefore, it is important to disturb as few roots as possible and not cut roots larger than 2 in. in diameter. Do not rototill or amend soils in beds within this zone. Planting plants with smaller root balls makes it easier to fit plants between roots.

It is natural for a tree's trunk to flare out at the bottom and for the roots near the trunk to be partly above ground. Don't bury them. However, if the soil has eroded away from roots farther out from the trunk, add a layer of soil up to several inches deep and top the new soil with a thinner layer of mulch. Adding soil like this makes it easier to start plants underneath a tree. (See p. 169 for planting instructions.) Just don't overdo it—covering roots with more than a few inches of soil can starve them of oxygen, damaging or killing them, and piling soil close to the trunk can rot the bark.

❹ Use a tiller or digging fork to mix everything together, again working as deep as possible.

❺ Finish by smoothing the surface with a rake.

Making neat edges

All but the most informal landscapes look best if you define and maintain neat edges between the lawn and any adjacent plantings. There are several ways to do this, varying in appearance, effectiveness, cost, and convenience. For the South, the best methods are trench, brick or stone, and plastic strip edges. In any case, the time to install an edging is after you prepare the soil but before you plant the bed.

Trench edge

Lay a hose or rope on the ground to mark the line where you want to cut. Then cut along the line using a sharp spade or edging tool. Lift away any grass that was growing into the bed (or any plants that were running out into the lawn). Use a rake or hoe to smooth out a shallow trench on the bed side of the cut. Keep the trench empty; don't let it fill with mulch.

Pros and cons: Free. Good for straight or curved edges, level or sloped sites. You have to recut the edge every four to eight weeks during the growing season, but you can cut 50 to 100 ft. in an hour or so. Don't cut the trench too deep; if a mower wheel slips down into it, you will scalp the lawn. Crabgrass and other weeds may sprout in the exposed soil; if this happens, hoe or pull them out.

Brick mowing strip

Dig a trench about 8 in. wide and 4 in. deep around the edge of the bed. Fill it halfway with sand; then lay bricks on top, setting them level with the soil on the lawn side. You'll need three bricks per foot of edging. Sweep extra sand into any cracks between the bricks. In cold-winter areas, you'll probably need to reset a few frost-heaved bricks each spring. You can substitute cut stone blocks or concrete pavers for bricks.

Pros and cons: Good for straight or curved edges on level or gently sloped sites. Looks good in combination with brick walkways or brick house. Fairly easy to install and maintain. Some kinds of grass and plants will grow under, between, or over the bricks.

Plastic strip edging

Garden centers and home-improvement stores sell heavy-duty plastic edging in strips 5 or 6 in. wide and 20 or 50 ft. long. To install it, use a sharp tool to cut straight down through the sod around the edge of the bed. Hold the edging so the round lip sits right at soil level, and drive the stakes through the bottom of the edging and into the undisturbed soil under the lawn. Stakes, which are supplied with the edging, should be at least 8 in. long and set about 3 ft. apart. Select edging with a small diameter lip to minimize its visibility.

Pros and cons: Good for straight or curved edges, but it works best only on relatively level sites. Neat and carefree when well-installed, but installation is a two- or three-person job. If the lip isn't set right on the ground, you're likely to hit it with the mower blade. Liable to shift or heave unless it's very securely staked. Hard to drive stakes in rocky soil. Some kinds of grass and ground covers can grow across the top of the edging.

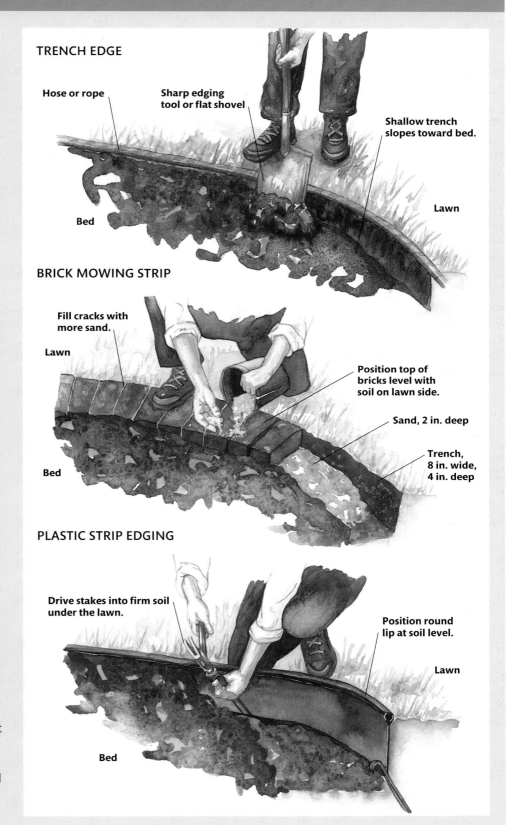

TRENCH EDGE

Hose or rope

Sharp edging tool or flat shovel

Shallow trench slopes toward bed.

Lawn

Bed

BRICK MOWING STRIP

Fill cracks with more sand.

Lawn

Position top of bricks level with soil on lawn side.

Sand, 2 in. deep

Trench, 8 in. wide, 4 in. deep

Bed

PLASTIC STRIP EDGING

Drive stakes into firm soil under the lawn.

Position round lip at soil level.

Lawn

Bed

Buying Plants

Once you have chosen and planned a landscape project, make a list of the plants you want and start thinking about where to get them. You'll need to locate the kinds of plants you're looking for, choose good-quality plants, and get enough of the plants to fill your design area.

Where and how to shop

You may already have a favorite place to shop for plants. If not, look in the Yellow Pages and search the Web under Nursery Stock, Nurserymen, Garden Centers, and Landscape Contractors, and choose a few places to visit. Take your shopping list; find a salesperson; and ask for help. The plants in this book are commonly available in the South, but you may not find everything you want at one place. The salesperson may refer you to another nursery, offer to special-order plants, or recommend similar plants as substitutes.

If you're buying too many plants to carry in your car or truck, ask about delivery—it's usually available and sometimes free. Some nurseries offer to replace plants that fail within a limited guarantee period, so ask about that, too.

The staff at a good nursery or garden center will usually be able to answer most of the questions you have about which plants to buy and how to care for them. If you can, go shopping on a rainy weekday when business is slow so staff will have time to answer your questions.

Don't be lured by the low prices of plants for sale at supermarkets or discount stores unless you're sure you know exactly what you're looking for and what you're looking at. The salespeople at these stores rarely have the time or knowledge to offer you much help, and the plants are often disorganized, unlabeled, and stressed by poor care.

If you can't find a plant locally or have a retailer order it for you, you can always order it yourself from a mail-order nursery. Most mail-order nurseries produce good plants and pack them well, but if you haven't dealt with a business before, be smart and place a minimum order first. Judge the quality of the plants that arrive; then decide whether or not to order larger quantities from that firm.

Timing

It's a good idea to plan ahead and start shopping for plants before you're ready to put them in the ground. That way, if you can't find everything on your list, you'll have time to keep shopping around, place special orders, or choose substitutes. Most nurseries will let you "flag" an order for later pickup or delivery, and they'll take care of the plants in the meantime. Or you can bring the plants home; just remember to check the soil in the containers every day and water if needed.

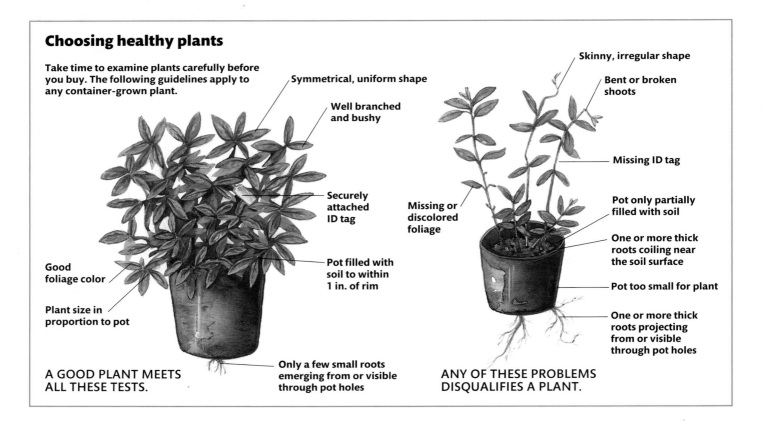

Choosing healthy plants

Take time to examine plants carefully before you buy. The following guidelines apply to any container-grown plant.

Symmetrical, uniform shape

Well branched and bushy

Securely attached ID tag

Pot filled with soil to within 1 in. of rim

Good foliage color

Plant size in proportion to pot

Only a few small roots emerging from or visible through pot holes

A GOOD PLANT MEETS ALL THESE TESTS.

Skinny, irregular shape

Bent or broken shoots

Missing ID tag

Missing or discolored foliage

Pot only partially filled with soil

One or more thick roots coiling near the soil surface

Pot too small for plant

One or more thick roots projecting from or visible through pot holes

ANY OF THESE PROBLEMS DISQUALIFIES A PLANT.

Choosing particular plants

If you need, for example, five azaleas and the nursery or garden center has a whole block of them, how do you choose which five to buy? The sales staff may be too busy to help you decide; you often have to choose by yourself.

Most plants nowadays are grown in containers, so it's possible to lift them one at a time and examine them from all sides. Following the guidelines shown in the drawings opposite, evaluate each plant's shape, size, health and vigor, and root system.

Trees and shrubs are frequently sold "balled-and-burlapped," that is, with a ball of soil and roots wrapped tightly in burlap. For these plants, look for strong limbs with no broken shoots, an attractive profile, and healthy foliage. Then press your hands against the burlap-covered root-ball to make sure that it feels firm, solid, and damp, not loose or dry. (If the ball is buried within a bed of wood chips, carefully pull the chips aside; then push them back after inspecting the plant.)

To make the final cut when you're choosing a group of plants, line them up side by side and select the ones that are most closely matched in height, bushiness, and foliage color. If your design includes a hedge or mass planting where uniformity is very important, it's a good idea to buy a few extra plants as potential replacements in case of damage or loss. It's easier to plan ahead than to find a match later. Plant the extras in a spare corner and you'll have them if you need them.

Sometimes a plant will be available in two or more sizes. Which is better? That depends on how patient you are. The main reason for buying bigger plants is to make a landscape look impressive right away. If you buy smaller plants and set them out at the same spacing, the planting will look sparse at first, but it will soon catch up. A year after planting, you can't tell if a perennial came from a quart- or gallon-size pot: they look the same. For shrubs, the difference between one size pot and the next usually represents one year's growth.

The Planting Process

Throughout the South, summer is not the best season for starting a garden, because new plantings are very vulnerable to heat waves and droughts. It's better to plant during the cooler, moister weather of early spring or fall. Most nurseries have a wider selection of perennials and grasses in spring; shrubs and trees are available in spring and again in fall.

Although it's handy to plant a whole bed at once, you can divide the job, setting out some plants in fall and adding the rest in spring, or vice versa. If possible, do the actual planting on a cloudy day or evening when rain is forecast. Compared with preparing the soil, putting plants in the ground goes quite quickly. On the following pages, we'll give an overview of the process, and discuss how to handle individual plants.

Try to stay off the soil

Throughout the planting process, do all you can by reaching in from outside the bed—don't step on the newly prepared soil if you can help it. Stepping or walking in the bed compacts the soil and makes it harder to dig planting holes. Use short boards or scraps of plywood as temporary stepping-stones if you do need to walk around on the soil. As soon as you can decide where to put them, you might want to lay permanent stepping-stones for access to plants that need regular maintenance.

Check placement and spacing

The first step in planting is to mark the position of each plant. The simplest way to do this is to arrange the plants on the bed. Use an empty pot or a stake for plants too heavy to move easily. Follow the site plan for the design; use a yardstick to check the spacing; and set the plants in place.

Then step back and take a look. Walk around and look from all sides. Go into the house and look out the window. What do you think? Should any of the plants be adjusted a little? Don't worry if the planting looks a little sparse now—it should. Plants almost always grow faster and get bigger than you can imagine when you're first setting them out, and it's almost always better to allow space and wait a few years for them to fill in than to crowd them too close together at first and have to keep pruning and thinning them later.

PLANTING POINTERS

When working on top of prepared soil, kneel on a piece of plywood to distribute your weight.

Use empty pots or stakes to mark positions of plants not yet purchased or too heavy to move frequently.

Moving through the job

When you're satisfied with the arrangement, mark the position of each plant with a stake or stone, and set the plants aside out of the way, so you won't knock them over or step on them as you proceed. Start planting in order of size. Do the biggest plants first, then move on to the medium-size and smaller plants. If all the plants are about the same size, start at the back of the bed and work toward the front, or start in the center and work to the edges.

Position trees and shrubs to show their best side

Most trees and shrubs are slightly asymmetric. There's usually enough irregularity in their branching or shape that one side looks a little fuller or more attractive than the other sides do. After you've set a tree or shrub into its hole, step back and take a look. Then turn it partway, or try tilting or tipping it a little to one side or the other. Once you've decided which side and position looks best, start filling in the hole with soil. Stop and check again before you firm the soil into place.

The fine points of spacing

When you're planting a group of the same kind of plants, such as perennials or ferns, it normally looks best if you space them informally, in slightly curved or zigzag rows, with the plants in one row offset from those of the next row. Don't arrange plants in a straight row unless you want to emphasize a line, such as the edge of a bed. In that case, make the row perfectly straight. Use a string stretched between stakes for long rows. After planting, step back and evaluate the effect. If you want to adjust the placement or position of any plant, now is the time to do so.

Water, rake, and mulch

As you plant, eliminate air pockets at the roots by watering in the plants using a hose. Use a garden rake to level out any high and low spots. Mulch the area with 2 to 3 in. of composted bark, wood chips, or other organic matter. Mulch is indispensable for controlling weeds and regulating the moisture and temperature of the soil. If pressed for time, you don't have to spread the mulch right away, but try to get it done within the next few days..

Coastal conditions

Living close to the ocean provides some unique challenges for the home landscape. Offshore winds pick up salt and distribute it onto plants. If you live within about one-eighth of a mile of the coast, use plants with some salt tolerance, but select plants with high salt tolerance if you live near the beach. Add windbreaks, such as fences or walls, to improve plant performance of even highly salt-tolerant plants.

Sandy soils found near the shore have poor water-holding capacity, may be high in soluble salts—which interferes with how plants take in nutrients—and alkaline (pH above 6-6.5). Add organic matter to increase the soil's nutrient- and water-holding ability. Avoid plants that require low pH soils, or try lowering the pH by adding gypsum (calcium sulfate) or fertilizing with sulfur-coated urea. It takes time to obtain results; additional applications will be required.

If you use well water to irrigate your landscape, check the salt level before selecting plants. Salt-water intrusion from underground sources or surface flooding can elevate salinity levels. A salt level over 2,000 parts-per-million is unsuitable for all but highly salt-tolerant plants. Municipal drinking water has a salt level of about 10 parts-per-million.

One way to decrease the effects of salt on your plantings is to irrigate thoroughly every third time with water from a low-salt municipal source or collected rainwater. This will wash salt off of leaf surfaces and flush it from the soil.

The more frequent and stronger coastal winds dry out plants quickly, abrade the leaves with sand, and disperse droplets of irrigation water, decreasing its efficiency. Using low-volume irrigation that applies water at the soil surface alleviates this dispersal problem and conserves water.

See pp. 32, 36, 54, 76, 78, 80, 82, 86, and 88 for moderate- and high-salt-tolerant designs. The other designs in this book can be made more salt tolerant by changing out a few plants. See the Plant Profiles section (pp. 92–123) for the salt tolerance for each plant listed.

Hurricane-type conditions may extend many miles inland. High winds can uproot and damage trees and other plantings. During hurricane season—June 1 to November 30—keep trees and shrubs properly pruned, and dispose of the debris promptly because high winds can turn branches into damaging missiles. Leave the majority of green fronds on palms. Removing too many fronds exposes the bud to wind damage. Store or anchor garden ornaments and outdoor furniture; move containers inside.

Plant trees far enough away from structures so that they have room to sway in the wind without causing damage. A good rule-of-thumb for the distance is one-half the ultimate mature height of the tree.

After a storm, use caution when surveying damage. Consult a certified arborist on whether damaged trees should be removed or restored. It takes palms at least six months to develop new growth, up to two years for a full canopy.

Planting Basics

Most of the plants that you buy for a landscaping project today are grown and sold in individual plastic containers, but large shrubs and trees may be balled-and-burlapped. Mail-order plants may come bare-root. And ground covers are sometimes sold in flats. In any case, the basic concern is the same: be careful what you do to a plant's roots. Spread them out; don't fold or coil them or cram them into a tight hole. Keep them covered; don't let the sun or air dry them out. And don't bury them too deep; set the top of the root ball an inch above the surrounding soil.

Planting container-grown plants

The steps are the same for any plant, no matter what size its container. Dig a hole that's a little wider than the container but not quite as deep ❶. Check by setting the container into the hole—the top of the soil in the container should be slightly higher than the surrounding soil. Dig several holes at a time, at the positions that you've already marked out.

Remove the container ❷. With one hand, grip the plant at the base of its stems or leaves, like pulling a ponytail, while you tug on the pot with the other hand. If the pot doesn't slide off eas-ily, don't pull harder on the stems. Try whacking the pot with your trowel; if it still doesn't slide off, use a strong knife to cut or pry it off.

Examine the plant's roots ❸. If there are any thick, coiled roots, unwind them and cut them off close to the root-ball, leaving short stubs. If the root-ball is a mass of fine, hairlike roots, use the knife to cut three or four slits from top to bottom, about 1 in. deep. Pry the slits apart, and tease the cut roots to loosen them. This cutting or slitting may seem drastic, but it's actually good for the plant because it forces new roots to grow out into the surrounding soil. Work quickly. Once you've taken a plant out of its container, get it in the ground as soon as possible. If you want to prepare several plants at a time, cover them with an old sheet or tarp to keep the roots from drying out.

Set the root-ball into the hole ❹. Make sure that the plant is positioned right, with its best side facing out, and that the top of the root-ball is slightly higher than the surface of the bed. Slowly add enough soil to fill the hole, watering with a slow stream from a hose to eliminate air pockets.

PLANTING CONTAINER-GROWN PLANTS

❶ Dig a hole a little wider than the container but not as deep.

❷ Remove the plant from the container.

❸ Unwind any large, coiled roots, and cut them off short. Cut vertical slits through masses of fine roots.

❹ Position the plant in the hole, and fill in around it with soil.

Planting a balled-and-burlapped shrub or tree

Local nurseries often grow shrubs and trees in fields; then wrap the root-ball in a layer of burlap. The drawback with this system is that even a small ball of soil is very heavy. If the ball is more than 1 foot wide, moving the plant is a two-person job. If you're buying a tree with a ball bigger than that, ask the nursery to deliver and plant it.

For plants that you can handle, find the top main root on the trunk. Dig a hole several inches wider than the root-ball but not quite as deep as the root-ball is high. Firm the soil so the plant won't sink. Remove soil from the top of the root-ball to expose the top root. Set the plant into the hole, and lay a stick across the top of the root-ball to make sure it's a little higher than grade level. Rotate the plant until its best side faces out. Cut or untie any twine around the trunk. Fold the burlap down around the sides of the ball; roots can grow through it, and it will decompose. Remove it if it is synthetic (will melt with a flame). Fill soil all around the ball watering it in as you go.

The top of the ball should be 1 in. above the soil. Cut twine from the trunk. Fold down the burlap, but don't remove it unless it is synthetic.

Planting bare-root plants

Mail-order nurseries sometimes dig perennials, roses, and other plants when the plants are dormant, cut back the tops, and wash all the soil off the roots to save space and weight when storing and shipping them. If you receive a plant in bare-root condition, unwrap it, trim away any roots that are broken or damaged, and soak the roots in a pail of water for several hours.

To plant, dig a hole large enough that you can spread the roots across the bottom without folding them. Start covering the roots with soil, then lay a stick across the top of the hole, and hold the plant against it to check the planting depth, as shown in the drawing. Raise or lower the plant if needed in order to bury just the roots, not the buds. Add more soil, firming it down around the roots, and watering to eliminate air pockets.

Dig a hole wide enough that you can spread out the roots. A stick helps position the plant at the correct depth as you fill the hole with soil.

Planting ground covers from flats

Sometimes ground covers are sold in flats of 25 or more rooted cuttings. Start at one corner, reach underneath the soil, and lift out a portion of the flat's contents. Working quickly, because the roots are exposed, tease the cuttings apart, trying not to break off any roots, and plant them individually. Then lift out the next portion and continue planting.

Remove a clump of little plants; tease their roots apart; and plant them quickly.

Planting bulbs

Plant spring- or summer-blooming bulbs in late winter or early spring after the last threat of frost. Fall bloomers, such as hurricane lily, are best planted in late summer or early fall. Sometimes bulbs can be purchased already potted and grown, allowing you to add instant foliage and possibly color to your garden. If the soil in the bed was well prepared, you can plant individual bulbs; where you have room, you can dig a wider hole or trench for planting a group of bulbs. Check with your garden center or see "Recommended Bulbs" on page 100 for spacing and planting depths.

Plant bulbs with the pointed end up, at a depth and spacing determined by the size of the bulb.

Basic Landscape Care

Planting under a tree

When planting beneath a mature tree, as for the design on pp. 40–43, remember that most tree roots are in the top 12 inches of the soil, and they extend at least as far away from the trunk as the limbs do. For areas of ground cover and most container-grown perennials, you can add topsoil and organic amendments up to about 2 in. deep over the entire area while staying away from the trunk. Dig carefully, disturbing as few tree roots as possible. Larger plants require deeper holes. If you encounter a large root, move the planting hole rather than sever the root. Installing plants with smaller root balls makes it easier to fit plants between tree roots.

Confining perennials

Yarrow, bee balm, artemisia, and various other perennials, grasses, and ferns are described as invasive because they spread by underground runners. To confine these plants to a limited area, install a barrier when you plant them. Cut the bottom off a 5-gal. or larger plastic pot; bury the pot so its rim is above the soil; and plant the perennial inside. You'll need to lift, divide, and replant part of the perennial every second or third year.

Position rim above soil surface.

Remove bottom of pot.

The landscape plantings in this book will grow increasingly carefree from year to year as the plants mature, but of course you'll always need to do some regular maintenance. Depending on the design you choose, this ongoing care may require as much as a few hours a week during the season or as little as a few hours a month. No matter what you plant, you'll have to control weeds, use mulch, water as needed, and do spring and fall cleanups. Trees, shrubs, and vines may need staking or training at first and occasional pruning or shearing afterward. Perennials, ground covers, and grasses may need to be cut back, staked, deadheaded, or divided. Performing these tasks, which are explained on the following pages, is sometimes hard work, but for many gardeners it is enjoyable labor, a chance to get outside in the fresh air. Also, spending time each week with your plants helps you identify and address problems before they become serious.

Mulches and fertilizers

Covering the soil in all planted areas with a layer of organic mulch does several jobs at once: it improves the appearance of your garden while you're waiting for the plants to grow, reduces the number of weeds that emerge, reduces water loss from the soil during dry spells, moderates soil temperatures, and adds nutrients to the soil as it decomposes. Inorganic mulches, such as landscape fabric and gravel, also provide some of these benefits, but their conspicuous appearance and the difficulty of removing them if you ever want to change the landscape are serious drawbacks, and they are not recommended.

Many materials are used as mulches; the box on p. 170 presents the most common, with comments on their advantages and disadvantages. Consider appearance, availability, cost, and convenience when you're comparing different products. Most garden centers have a few kinds of bagged mulch materials, but for mulching large areas, it's easier and cheaper to have a landscape contractor or other supplier deliver a truckload of bulk mulch. A landscape looks best if you see the same mulch throughout the entire planting area, rather than a patchwork of different mulches. You can achieve a uniform look by spreading a base layer of homemade compost, rotten hay, or other inexpensive material and topping that with a neater-looking material such as bark chips or shredded bark.

It takes at least a 2- to 3-in. layer of mulch to suppress weeds, but there's no need to spread it more than 3 in. deep. As you're spreading it, don't put mulch against the stems of any plants, because that can lead to disease or insect problems. Put most of the mulch between plants, not right around them. Check the mulch each spring and more often in the warmer zones. Be sure it's pulled back away from the plant stems. Rake the surface of the mulch lightly to loosen it, and top it off with a fresh layer if the old material has decomposed. If you see bare soil, it is time to reapply mulch.

Fertilizer

Decomposing mulch frequently supplies enough nutrients to grow healthy plants, but using fertilizer helps if you want to boost the plants—to make them grow faster, get larger, or produce more flowers. There are dozens of fertilizer products on the market— liquid and granular, fast-acting and slow-release, organic and synthetic. All give good results if applied as directed. And observe the following precautions: don't overfertilize, don't fertilize when the soil is dry, and don't fertilize after midsummer in Zones 8 and 9, because plants need to slow down and finish the season's growth before cold weather comes.

Mulch materials

Bark products

Bark nuggets, chipped bark, shredded bark, and compos-ted bark, usually from conifers, are available in bags or in bulk from garden centers. All are attractive, long-lasting, medium-price mulches.

Chipped tree trimmings

The chips from utility companies and tree services are a mixture of wood, bark, twigs, and leaves. These chips cost less than pure bark products (you may be able to get a load for free), but they don't look as good and you have to replace them more often, because they decompose faster than pure bark mulches.

Sawdust and shavings

These are cheap or free at sawmills and woodshops. They make good path coverings, but they aren't ideal mulches, because they tend to pack down into a dense, water-resistant surface.

Hulls and shells

Cottonseed hulls, peanut shells, and nut shells are available for pickup at food-processing plants and are sometimes sold in bags or bulk at garden centers. They're all attractive, long-lasting mulches. Price varies from free to quite expen-sive, depending on where you get them.

Tree leaves and needles

A few big trees on your property, or near your property, may supply all the mulch you need. And the supply replen-ishes itself, providing material year after year. You can just rake the leaves onto a bed in fall, but they'll probably blow off it again. It's better to chop up large leaves with the lawn mower, store them, and spread them when needed. Pine needles make good mulch, too, especially for rhododen-drons, azaleas, and other acid-loving shrubs. You can spread pine needles in fall because they cling together and don't blow around.

Grass clippings

A 1- to 2-in. layer of dried grass clippings makes an accept-able mulch that decomposes within a single growing sea-son. Don't pile clippings too thick, though. If you do, the top surface dries and packs into a water-resistant crust, and the bottom layer turns into nasty slime. Don't use clippings for a few weeks after applying chemicals to the lawn.

Hay and straw

Farmers sell hay that's moldy, old, or otherwise unsuitable for fodder as "mulch" hay. This hay is cheap, but it's likely to include weed seeds, particularly seeds of weedy grasses such as barnyard grass. Straw—the stems of grain crops such as wheat—is usually seed-free but more expensive. Both hay and straw are more suitable for mulching vegetable gardens than landscape plantings because they have to be renewed each year. They are bulky at first but decompose quickly. They also tend to attract rodents.

Gravel

A mulch of pea gravel or crushed rock, spread 1 to 2 in. thick, helps keep the soil cool and moist, but reflects heat onto plants. Compared with organic materials, such as bark or leaves, it's much more tiring to apply a gravel mulch in the first place; it's harder to remove leaves and litter that accumulate on the gravel or weeds that sprout up through it; it's annoying to dig through the gravel if you want to replace or add plants later; and it's extremely tedious to remove the gravel itself, should you ever change your mind about having it there.

Landscape fabrics

Various types of synthetic fabrics, usually sold in rolls 3 to 4 ft. wide and 20, 50, or 100 ft. long, can be spread over the ground as a weed barrier and topped with a layer of gravel, bark chips, or other mulch. Unlike plastic, these fabrics allow water and air to penetrate into the soil. It's useful to lay fabric under paths, but not in planted areas. In a bed, it's a two-person job to install the fabric in the first place, it's inconvenient trying to install plants through holes cut in the fabric, and it's hard to secure the fabric neatly and invis-ibly at the edges of the bed. Weeds eventually root in the mulch on top and then root into the fabric. The fabric lasts indefinitely, and removing it—if you change your mind—is a messy job.

Clear or black plastic

Don't even think about using any kind of plastic sheeting as a landscape mulch. The soil underneath a sheet of plastic gets bone-dry, while water accumulates on top. Any loose mulch you spread on plastic slips or floats around and won't stay in an even layer. No matter how you try to secure them, the edges of plastic sheeting always pull loose, appear at the surface, degrade in the sun, and shred into tatters.

Watering

Watering, as discussed previously (see pp. 130–131) is a necessity for all residential landscapes. To use water efficiently and effectively, it is helpful to know how to gauge when your plants need water, how much water they need, and how to ensure that your system supplies the desired amounts.

Deciding if water is needed

The best way to determine whether you need to water is to examine the soil. If the top 3 to 4 in. is dry, most annuals, perennials, and shallow-rooted shrubs, such as azaleas, will need to be watered. Most trees and larger shrubs need water if the top 6 to 8 in. is dry.

An easy method to gauge soil moisture is to use a paint stirrer as a dipstick. Push it down through the mulch and 6 to 8 in. into the soil; leave it there for an hour or so; and pull it out to see if moisture has discolored the wood. If it has, the soil is moist enough for plants. If not, it's time to water.

It is also helpful to make a habit of monitoring rainfall by having your own rain gauge and marking a calendar to keep track of rainfall amounts. Pay attention to soil moisture or rainfall amounts year-round because plants can suffer from dryness in any season, not just in the heat of summer. As for time of day, its best to water early in the morning when the wind is calm, evaporation is low, and plant foliage will have plenty of time to dry out before nightfall (wet leaves at night can promote some foliar diseases). Early morning (before 5 A.M.) is also when most urban and suburban neighborhoods have plenty of water pressure.

How much to water

Determining how much water to apply and how often to apply it is one of gardening's greatest challenges. Water too often and plants drown. Water too little and they dry out and die. The key to watering just right is to be a good observer. Examine your soil often; keep an eye on the plants; and make adjustments with the weather.

New plantings, even those of drought-tolerant plants, require frequent watering during the first year until the plants are established. In the heat of summer, new plantings may require water every day, then every other day, then twice a week. Trees require extra water for many months until they are well established.

Established landscape plants vary in their water needs. (The descriptions for the plants in the Plant Profiles include water requirements.) When you do water, it is always best to water deeply, wetting a large portion of the plant's root zone. Shallow watering encourages shallow rooting, and shallow-rooted plants dry out fast and need watering more frequently. Furthermore, a water-stressed plant is also more susceptible to disease and insect damage. As a rule of thumb, water most perennials to a depth of 12 to 18 in., most shrubs to 2 to 3 ft. deep, and most trees to 3 to 4 ft. deep. (Lawns, in contrast, should be watered 6 to 8 in. deep, but they require frequent watering.)

Determining how much water will be required to penetrate to these depths depends on your soil. Water moves through different soils at different speeds. In general, 1 in. of water will soak about 4 to 5 in. deep in clay soil, 6 to 7 in. deep in loam, and 10 to 12 in. in sandy soil.

Different watering systems deliver water at different rates. Manufacturers often provide these rates in the product descriptions. You can determine the delivery rate for a sprinkler by setting tuna-fish cans in the area it covers and timing how long it takes to deposit an inch of water in one or more cans.

Whatever your system, you will need to know how long it runs for water to penetrate to the desired depths in your soil. To gauge penetration to a foot or so deep, you can use wooden "dip sticks" as described below. (Insert the sticks after you water.) To gauge deeper watering, dig down, and sample the soil to check penetration depths.

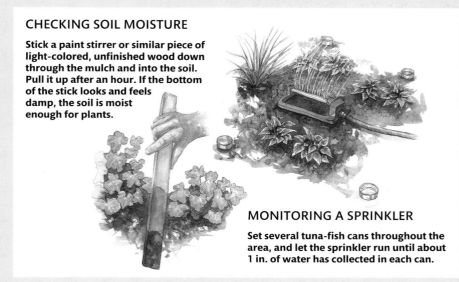

CHECKING SOIL MOISTURE

Stick a paint stirrer or similar piece of light-colored, unfinished wood down through the mulch and into the soil. Pull it up after an hour. If the bottom of the stick looks and feels damp, the soil is moist enough for plants.

MONITORING A SPRINKLER

Set several tuna-fish cans throughout the area, and let the sprinkler run until about 1 in. of water has collected in each can.

Controlling weeds

Weeds are not much of a problem in established landscapes. Once the "good" plants have grown big enough to merge together, they tend to crowd or shade out all but the most persistent weeds. But weeds can be troublesome in a new landscape unless you take steps to prevent and control them.

There are two main types of weeds: those that mostly sprout up as seedlings and those that keep coming back from perennial roots or runners. Try to identify and eliminate any perennial weeds before you start a landscaping project. (See p. 128.) Then you'll only have to deal with new seedlings later, which is an easier job.

Annual and perennial weeds that commonly grow from seeds include crabgrass, chickweed, dandelions, plantain, purslane, and sorrel. Trees and shrubs such as cherry, laurel, Chinese tallow tree, camphor, Chinaberry, chokeberry, privet mimosa, cottonwood, and honeysuckle produce weedy seedlings, too. For any of these weeds, the strategy is twofold: try to keep the weed seeds from sprouting, and eliminate any seedlings that do sprout as soon as you see them, while they are still small.

Almost any patch of soil includes weed seeds that are ready to sprout whenever that soil is disturbed. You have to disturb the soil to prepare it before planting, and that will probably cause an initial flush of weeds, but you'll never see that many weeds again if you leave the soil undisturbed in subsequent years. You don't have to hoe, rake, or cultivate around perennial plantings. Leave the soil alone, and fewer weeds will appear. Using mulch helps even more; by shading the soil, it prevents weed seeds from sprouting. And if weed seeds blow in and land on top of the mulch, they'll be less likely to germinate there than they would on bare soil.

Pull or cut off any weeds that appear while they're young and small. Don't let them mature and go to seed. Most weed seedlings emerge in late spring and early summer.

Using herbicides

Two kinds of herbicides can be very useful and effective in maintaining home landscapes, but only if used correctly. You have to choose the right product for the job and follow the directions on the label regarding dosage and timing of application exactly.

Preemergent herbicides. Usually sold in granular form, these herbicides are designed to prevent weed seeds, particularly crabgrass and other annual weeds, from sprouting. Make the first application in early spring. Depending on your climate, you'll probably need to make a second or third application later in the growing season. Follow package directions to determine how long to wait between applications.

WEEDS THAT SPROUT FROM SEEDS

Simple root systems can be easily pulled while still small.

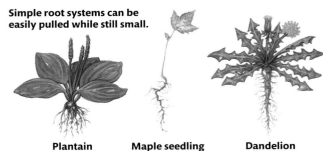

Plantain   Maple seedling   Dandelion

WEEDS THAT SPROUT BACK FROM PERENNIAL ROOTS OR RUNNERS

Connected by underground runners, the shoots of these weeds need to be pulled repeatedly, smothered with a thick mulch, or killed with an herbicide.

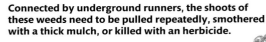

Mother plant

Ground ivy

Runner

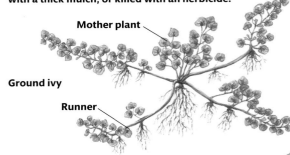

Use a disposable, sponge-type paintbrush to apply the herbicide selectively, painting only the weeds. Prepare the solution as directed for spray application. Use only enough to wet the leaves, so none drips off.

USING HERBICIDES ON PERENNIAL WEEDS

Ready-to-use spot-weeder sprays are convenient, but you must aim carefully. Try using a sheet of cardboard as a backdrop to protect desirable plants from herbicide drift.

Caring for Woody Plants

Read the label carefully, and make sure the herbicide you buy is registered for use around the plants you have. Measure the area of your bed; weigh out the appropriate amount of granules; and sprinkle them as evenly as possible across the soil. Wear heavy rubber gloves that are rated for use with farm chemicals, not common household rubber gloves, and follow the safety precautions on the product label.

Postemergent herbicides. These chemicals are used to kill plants. Some kinds kill only the aboveground parts of a plant; other kinds are absorbed into the plant and kill it, roots and all. Postemergent herbicides are typically applied as sprays, which you can buy ready-to-use or prepare by mixing a concentrate with water. Look for those that break down quickly, and read the label carefully for registered applications, specific directions, and safety instructions.

Postemergent herbicides work best if applied when the weeds are growing vigorously. You usually have to apply enough to thoroughly wet the plant's leaves, and do it during a spell of dry weather. Applying an herbicide is an effective way to get rid of a perennial weed that you can't dig or pull up, but it's really better to do this before you plant a bed, as it's hard to spray herbicides in an established planting without getting some on your good plants. Aim carefully; shield plants as shown opposite; and don't spray on windy days. Brushing or sponging the herbicide on the leaves is slower, but it avoids damaging other plants.

Using postemergent herbicides in an established planting is a painstaking job, but it may be the only way to get rid of a persistent perennial weed. For young seedlings, it's usually easier and faster to pull them by hand than to spray them.

A well-chosen garden tree, such as the ones recommended in this book, grows naturally into a neat, pleasing shape; won't get too large for its site; is resistant to pests and diseases; and doesn't drop messy pods or other litter. Once established, these trees need very little care from year to year.

Regular watering is the most important concern in getting a tree off to a good start. Don't let it suffer from drought for the first few years. To reduce competition, don't plant ground covers or other plants within 2 ft. of the tree's trunk. Just spread a thin layer of mulch there.

Arborists now dismiss other care ideas that once were common practice. According to current thinking, you don't need to fertilize a tree when you plant it (in fact, most landscape trees never need fertilizing). Keep pruning to a minimum at planting time; remove only dead or damaged twigs, not healthy shoots. Finally, if a tree is small enough that one or two people can carry and plant it, it doesn't need staking and the trunk will grow stronger if unstaked. Larger trees that are planted by a nursery may need staking, especially on windy sites, but the stakes should be removed within a year.

Pruning to direct growth

Pruning shapes plants not only by removing stems, branches, and leaves but also by inducing and directing new growth. All plants have a bud at the base of every leaf. New shoots grow from these buds. Cutting off the end of a stem encourages the lower buds to shoot out and produces a bushier plant. This type of pruning makes a hedge fill out and gives an otherwise lanky perennial or shrub a better rounded shape.

The same response to pruning also allows you to steer the growth of a plant. The bud immediately below the cut will produce a shoot that extends in the direction the bud was pointing. To direct a branch or stem, cut it back to a bud pointing in the direction you want to encourage growth. This technique is useful for shaping young trees and shrubs and for keeping their centers open to light and air.

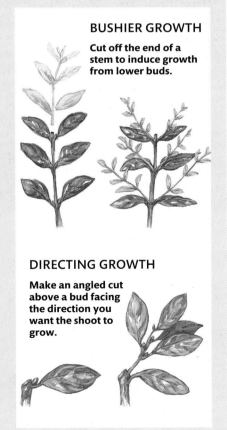

BUSHIER GROWTH

Cut off the end of a stem to induce growth from lower buds.

DIRECTING GROWTH

Make an angled cut above a bud facing the direction you want the shoot to grow.

Pruning roses

Roses are vigorous, fast-growing shrubs that need regular pruning to keep them shapely and attractive. Most of this pruning is done in early spring, just as the buds start to swell but before the new leaves start to unfold. Always use sharp pruning shears and cut back to a healthy bud, leaving no stub. Right after pruning is a good time to add fresh mulch around the plant.

Prune hybrid tea roses to keep them neat, compact, and shapely. Remove any extremely skinny or weak stems plus a few of the oldest stems (you can tell by looking at their bark, which is tan or gray instead of green) by cutting them off at the ground. Prune off any shoots that got frozen or broken during the winter, remove old or weak shoots and crossing or crowded stems, and trim back any asymmetric or unbalanced shoots. Don't be afraid of cutting back too hard; it's better to leave just a few strong shoots than a lot of weak ones. If you cut old stems off at ground level, new ones will grow to replace them. Cut damaged or asymmetric stems back partway and they will branch out.

Hybrid tea roses bloom on new growth, so if you prune in spring you aren't cutting off any flower buds. During the growing season, make a habit of removing the flowers as soon as they fade. This keeps the plant neat and makes it bloom more abundantly and over a longer season. At least once a week, locate each faded flower, follow down its stem to the first or second five-leaflet leaf, and prune just above one of those leaves. (Follow the same steps to cut roses for a bouquet.)

Climbing roses don't need as much spring pruning as hybrid tea roses do. Remove any weak, dead, or damaged shoots by cutting them back to the ground or to healthy wood. You may need to untie and untangle the canes in order to do this spring pruning.

Climbing roses need regular attention throughout the summer, because their stems or canes can grow a foot or more in a month. Check regularly and tie this new growth to the trellis while it's still supple and manageable. When the canes grow long enough to reach the top of the trellis or arbor, cut off their tips and they will send out side shoots, which are where the flowers form. Remove the individual roses or clusters of roses as the petals fade by cutting the stems back to the nearest healthy five-leaflet leaf.

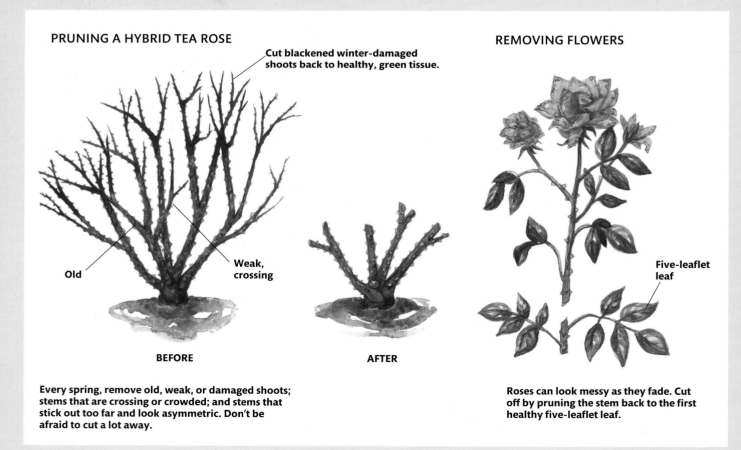

PRUNING A HYBRID TEA ROSE

Cut blackened winter-damaged shoots back to healthy, green tissue.

Old

Weak, crossing

BEFORE

AFTER

Every spring, remove old, weak, or damaged shoots; stems that are crossing or crowded; and stems that stick out too far and look asymmetric. Don't be afraid to cut a lot away.

REMOVING FLOWERS

Five-leaflet leaf

Roses can look messy as they fade. Cut off by pruning the stem back to the first healthy five-leaflet leaf.

Shaping young trees

As a tree grows, you can direct its shape by pruning once a year, in winter or summer. (See the box at right.) Take it easy, though. Don't prune just for the sake of pruning; that does more harm than good. If you don't have a good reason for making a cut, don't do it. Follow these guidelines:

▌ **Use sharp pruning shears, loppers, or saws,** which make clean cuts without tearing the wood or bark.

▌ **Cut branches back** to a healthy shoot, leaf, or bud, or cut back to the branch collar at the base of the branch, as shown at right. The collar tissue is rich in energy reserves and chemicals that hinder the spread of decay. Don't leave any stubs; they're ugly and prone to decay.

▌ **Remove any dead or damaged** branches and any twigs or limbs that are very spindly or weak.

▌ **Where two limbs cross over or rub** against each other, save one limb—usually the thicker, stronger one—and prune off the other one.

▌ **Prune or widen narrow crotches.** Places where a branch and trunk or two branches form a narrow V are weak spots, liable to split apart as the tree grows. Where the trunk of a young tree exhibits such a crotch or where either of two shoots could continue the growth of a branch, prune off the weaker of the two. Where you wish to keep the branch, insert a piece of wood as a spacer for about a year to widen the angle, as shown in the drawings below.

One trunk or several?

If you want a young tree to have a single trunk, identify the leader or central shoot and let it grow straight up, unpruned. The trunk will grow thicker faster if you leave the lower limbs in place for the first few years, but if they're in the way, you

WHERE TO CUT

When removing the end of a branch, cut back to a healthy leaf, bud, or side shoot. Don't leave a stub. Use sharp pruning shears to make a neat cut that slices the stem rather than tears it.

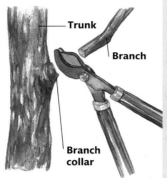

Trunk

Branch

Branch collar

When removing an entire branch, cut just outside the slightly thickened area, called the branch collar, where the branch grows into the trunk.

can remove them. At whatever height you choose—usually about 8 ft. off the ground if you want to walk or see under the tree—select the shoots that will become the main limbs of the tree. Be sure they are at different heights evenly spaced around the trunk, pointing outward at wide angles. Remove any lower or weaker shoots. As the tree matures, the only further pruning required will be an annual checkup to remove dead, damaged, or crossing shoots.

Several of the trees in this book, including crape myrtle, fringe tree, redbud, and river birch are often grown with multiple trunks, for a graceful, clumpike appearance. When buying a multiple-trunk tree, choose one with trunks that diverge at the base. The more space between them, the better. Prune multiple-trunk trees as previously described for single-trunk trees. Remove some of the branches that are growing toward the center of the clump.

AVOIDING NARROW CROTCHES

A tree's limbs should spread wide. If limbs angle too close to the trunk or to each other, there isn't room for them to grow properly. Those weak crotches may split apart after a few years, ruining the tree.

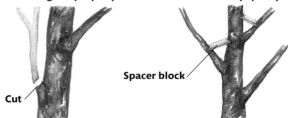

Cut

Spacer block

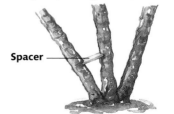

Spacer

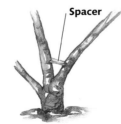

Spacer

SINGLE-TRUNK TREES: Correct narrow crotches on a young tree by removing the less desirable limb or by widening the angle with a wooden spacer block. Choose well-spaced shoots to become the main limbs of a shade tree.

MULTIPLE-TRUNK TREES: Whether the stems of a multiple-trunk tree emerge from the ground or from a single trunk near the ground, widen angles if necessary to keep the trunks from touching.

Pruning shrubs

Shrubs are generally carefree plants, but they almost always look better if you do some pruning at least once or twice a year. Finish pruning well before the threat of frost so emerging buds stimulated by pruning aren't damaged. As a minimum, remove dead twigs from time to time, and if any branches are broken by storms or accidents, remove them as soon as convenient, cutting back to a healthy bud or to the plant's crown.

Beyond this routine pruning, some shrubs require more attention. (The entries in Plant Profiles, pp. 92–123, give more information on when and how to prune particular shrubs.) Basically, shrub pruning falls into three categories: selective pruning, severe pruning, and shearing.

Selective pruning means using pruning shears to remove or cut back individual shoots in order to refine the shape of the bush and maintain its vigor, as well as limit its size. (See the drawing right.) This job takes time but produces a very graceful and natural-looking bush. Cut away weak or spindly twigs and any limbs that cross or rub against each other, and cut all the longest shoots back to a healthy, outward-facing bud or to a pair of buds. You can do selective pruning on any shrub, deciduous or evergreen, at any time of year.

Severe pruning means using pruning shears or loppers to cut away most of a shrub's top growth, leaving just short stubs or a gnarly trunk. This kind of cutting back is usually done once a year in late winter or early spring. Although it seems drastic, severe pruning is appropriate in several growing situations.

It makes certain fast-growing shrubs, such as plumbago and lantana, flower more profusely. It keeps others, such as 'Powis Castle' artemisia, compact and bushy.

One or two severe prunings done when a shrub is young can make it branch out at the base, producing a bushier specimen or a fuller hedge plant. Nurseries often do this pruning as part of producing a good plant, and if you buy a shrub that's already bushy, you don't need to cut it back yourself.

Older shrubs that have gotten tall and straggly sometimes respond to a severe pruning by sprouting out with renewed vigor, sending up lots of new shoots that bear plenty of foliage and flowers. This strategy doesn't work for all shrubs, though—sometimes severe pruning kills a plant. Don't try it unless you know it will work (check with a knowledgeable person at a nursery) or are willing to take a chance.

Shearing means using hedge shears or an electric hedge trimmer to trim the surface of a shrub, hedge, or tree to a neat, uniform profile, producing a solid mass of greenery. Both deciduous and evergreen shrubs and trees can be sheared; those with small, closely spaced leaves and a naturally compact growth habit usually look best. Avoid shearing large-leaved plants. A good time for shearing most shrubs is early summer, after the new shoots have elongated but before the wood has hardened, but you can shear at other times, and shearing may be necessary more than once a year.

Start shearing a plant when it is young to establish the shape—cone, pyramid, flat-topped hedge, or whatever. Always make the shrub wider at the bottom, or the lower limbs will be shaded and won't be as leafy. Shear off as little as needed to maintain the shrub's shape. Once it gets as big as you want it, shear as much as necessary to keep it that size.

SELECTIVE PRUNING. Remove weak, spindly, bent, or broken shoots (red). Where two branches rub on each other, remove the weakest or the one that's pointing inward (orange). Cut back long shoots to a healthy, outward-facing bud (blue).

SEVERE PRUNING. In late winter or early spring, before new growth starts, cut all the stems back close to the ground.

SHEARING. Trim with hedge clippers to a neat profile.

Making a hedge

To make a hedge that's dense enough that you can't see through it, choose shrubs that have many shoots at the base. If you can only find skinny shrubs, prune them severely the first spring after planting to stimulate bushier growth.

Set hedge plants as described on pp. 165–168, but space them closer together than they would be if planted as individual specimens. We took that into account in creating the designs and plant lists for this book; just follow the recommended spacings. If you're impatient for the hedge to fill in, you can space the plants closer together, but don't put them farther apart.

A hedge can be sheared, pruned selectively, or left alone, depending on how you want it to look. Slow-growing, small-leaved plants such as boxwood and Japanese holly make rounded but natural-looking hedges with no pruning at all, or you can shear them into any profile you choose and make them perfectly neat and uniform. (Be sure to keep them narrower at the top.) Choose one style and stick with it. Once a hedge is established, you can neither start nor stop shearing it without an awkward transition that may last a few years before the hedge looks good again.

Getting a vine off to a good start

Nurseries often sell Carolina jasmine, cross vine, bougainvillea, and other vines as young plants with just one or two stems fastened to a bamboo stake. To plant them, remove the stake, and cut off the stem right above the lowest pair of healthy leaves, usually about 4 to 6 in. above the soil ❶. This forces the vine to send out new shoots low to the ground. As soon as those new shoots have begun to develop (normally a month or so after planting), cut them back to their first pairs of leaves ❷. After this second pruning, the plant will become bushy at the base. Now, as new shoots form, use sticks or strings to direct them toward the base of the support they are to climb ❸.

Once they're started, twining vines can scramble up a lattice trellis, although it helps if you tuck in any stray ends. The plants can't climb a smooth surface, however. To help them cover a fence with wide vertical slats or a porch post, you have to provide something the vine can wrap around.

Screw a few eyebolts to the top and bottom of such a support, and stretch wire, nylon cord, or polypropylene rope between them. (The wires or cords should be a few inches out from the fence, not flush against it.)

Clinging vines, such as Confederate jasmine, are slow starters, but once under way, they can climb any surface by means of their adhesive rootlets and need no further assistance or care. So-called climbing roses don't really climb at all by themselves—you have to fasten them to a support. Twist-ties are handy for this job. Roses grow fast, so you'll have to tie in the new shoots every few weeks from spring to fall.

After the first year, the vines in this book are trouble-free and don't require pruning on a regular basis, but you can cut them back whenever they get too big, and you should remove any dead or straggly stems from time to time for a neat appearance.

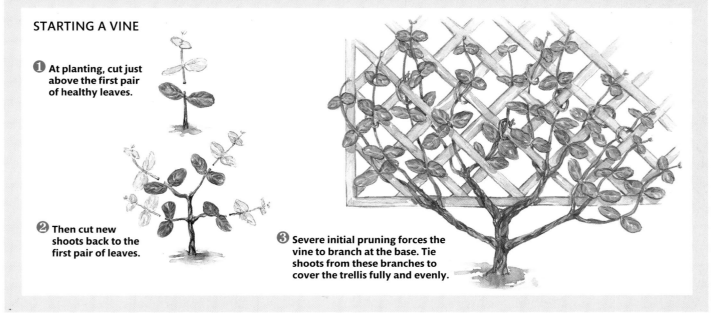

STARTING A VINE

❶ At planting, cut just above the first pair of healthy leaves.

❷ Then cut new shoots back to the first pair of leaves.

❸ Severe initial pruning forces the vine to branch at the base. Tie shoots from these branches to cover the trellis fully and evenly.

Caring for Perennials

Perennials are simply plants that send up new growth year after year. A large group, perennials include flowering plants, such as daylilies and coreopsis, as well as grasses, ferns, and hardy bulbs. Although some perennials need special conditions and care, most of the ones in this book are adaptable and easygoing. Get them off to a good start by planting them in well-prepared soil, adding a layer of mulch, watering as often as needed throughout the first year, and keeping weeds away. After that, keeping perennials attractive and healthy typically requires just a few minutes per plant each year.

Routine annual care

Some of the perennials that are used as ground covers, such as cast-iron plant, lilyturf, and mondo grass, need virtually no care. On a suitable site, they'll thrive for decades even if you pay them no attention at all.

Most garden perennials, though, look and grow better if you clean away the old leaves and stems at least once a year. When to do this depends on the plant.

Perennials such as daylily, hosta, cinnamon fern, and purple cone flower have leaves and stalks that turn tan or brown after they are frosted in fall. Cut these down to the ground in late fall or early spring; either time is okay and will provide good results.

Perennials such as autumn fern, holly fern, yarrow, and African iris have foliage that is more or less evergreen, depending on the severity of the winter. For those plants, wait until early spring; then cut back any leaves or stems that are discolored or shabby-looking. Do not compost diseased stems or leaves, because the disease can be transferred to the compost.

Right after you've cleared away the dead material is a good time to renew the mulch on the bed. Use a fork, rake, or cultivator to loosen the existing mulch, and add some fresh mulch if needed. Also, if you want to sprinkle some granular fertilizer on the bed, do that now, when it's easy to avoid getting any on the plants' leaves or stems. Fertilizing perennials is optional, but it does make them grow bigger and bloom more than they would otherwise.

Remove faded flowers

Removing flowers as they fade (called "deadheading") makes the garden look neater, prevents unwanted self-sown seedlings, and often stimulates a plant to continue blooming longer than it would if you left it alone, or to bloom a second time later in the season. (This is true for shrubs and annuals as well as for perennials.)

Pick large flowers such as daylilies and African iris one at a time, snapping them off by hand. Use pruning shears on perennials such as hosta, pentas, and yarrow that produce tall stalks crowded with lots of small flowers, cutting the stalks back to the height of the foliage. Use hedge shears on bushy plants that are covered with lots of small flowers on short stalks, such as autumn sage, Moonbeam coreopsis, and lantana. For plants such as these, cut the stems back by about one-half.

Instead of removing them, you may want to let the flowers remain on such plants as coneflower, purple coneflower, yarrow, and the various grasses. These plants all bear conspicuous seedpods or seed heads on stiff stalks that remain standing and look interesting throughout the fall and winter.

Pruning and shearing perennials

Some perennials that grow vigorously respond well to being lightly pruned during the growing season. Tall stems are liable to flop over in stormy weather, and even if they don't, too-tall clumps can look leggy or top-heavy.

Prune back one-third of the weakest stems from each clump by cutting them off one-third of the way off of the ground. Pruning in this way keeps these plants shorter, stronger, and bushier, so you don't have to bother with stakes to keep them upright.

'Powis Castle' artemisia is grown more for their foliage than for their flowers. You can use hedge shears to keep them neat, compact, and bushy, shearing off the tops of the stems once or twice in spring and summer.

PRUNING A PERENNIAL

Prune to create neater, bushier clumps of some summer- and fall-blooming perennials such as autumn sage. When the stalks are about 1 ft. tall, cut them all back by one-third. Remove the weakest stalks at ground level.

Dividing perennials

Most perennials send up more stems each year, forming denser clumps or wider patches. Dividing is the process of cutting or breaking apart these clumps or patches. This is an easy way to make more plants to expand your garden, to control a plant that might otherwise spread out of bounds, or to renew an old specimen that doesn't look good or bloom well anymore.

Most perennials can be divided as often as every year or two if you're in a hurry to make more plants, or they can go for several years if you don't have any reason to disturb them. You can divide them in early spring, just as new growth is starting, or in late summer and fall, up until a month before hard frost. In frost-free zones even winter is an option.

There are two main approaches to dividing perennials, as shown in the drawings at right. You can leave the plant in the ground and use a sharp shovel to cut it apart, like slicing a pie, then lift out one chunk at a time. Or you can dig around and underneath the plant and lift it out all at once, shake off the extra soil, and lay the plant on the ground or a tarp where you can work with it.

Some plants, such as yarrow and most ferns, are easy to divide. They almost fall apart when you dig them up. Others, such as daylily, African iris, and most grasses, have very tough or tangled roots and you'll have to wrestle with them, chop them with a sharp butcher knife, pry them apart with a strong screwdriver or garden fork, or even cut through the roots with a hatchet or pruning saw. However you approach the job, before you insert any tool, take a close look at the plant right at ground level, and be careful to divide between, not through, the biggest and healthiest buds or shoots. Using a hose to wash loose mulch and soil away makes it easier to see what you're doing.

Don't make the divisions too small; they should be the size of a plant that you'd want to buy. If you have more divisions than you need or want, choose just the best-looking ones to replant, and discard or give away the others. Replant new divisions as soon as possible in freshly prepared soil. Water them right away, and water again whenever the soil dries out over the next few weeks or months, until the plants are growing again.

Divide hardy bulbs, such as lily of the Nile, every few years by digging up the clumps after they have finished blooming but before the foliage turns yellow. Shake the soil off the roots; pull the bulbs apart; and replant them promptly.

DIVIDING PERENNIALS

You can divide a clump or patch of perennials by cutting down into the patch with a sharp spade, like slicing a pie or a pan of brownies, then lifting out the separate chunks.

Or you can dig up the whole clump; shake the extra soil off the roots; then pull or pry it apart into separate plantlets.

Problem Solving

Some plants are much more susceptible than others to damage by severe weather, pests, or diseases. In this book, we've recommended plants that are generally trouble-free, especially after they have had a few years to get established in your garden. But even these plants are subject to various mishaps and problems. The challenge is learning how to distinguish which problems are really serious and which are just cosmetic, and deciding how to solve—or, better yet, prevent—those problems that are serious.

Pests, large and small

Deer, rabbits, and woodchucks are liable to be a problem if your property is surrounded by or near fields or woods. You may not see them, but you can't miss the damage they do—they bite the tops off or eat whole plants of hostas, daylilies, and many other perennials. Deer also eat the leaves and stems of maples, azaleas, and many other trees and shrubs. Commercial repellents may be helpful if the animals aren't too hungry. (See the box at right for the types of plants that deer may avoid.) But in the long run, the only solution is to fence out deer and to trap and remove smaller animals.

Chipmunks and squirrels normally don't eat much foliage, but they do eat some kinds of flowers and several kinds of bulbs. They also dig up new transplants, and they plant nuts in your flower beds and lawns. Meadow voles and mice can kill trees and shrubs by stripping the bark off the trunk, usually near the ground. Pine voles eat the roots of shrubs and perennials, too. Moles don't eat plants, but their digging makes a mess of a lawn or flower bed and may disturb roots. Persistent trapping is the most effective way to control all of these little critters.

There are countless insects and other pests that can cause damage in a home landscape. Most plants can afford to lose part of their foliage or sap without suffering much of a setback, so don't panic if you see a few holes chewed in a leaf. However, if you suspect that insects are attacking one of your plants, try to catch one of them in a glass jar and get it identified, so you can decide what to do.

Identify, then treat

Don't jump to conclusions and start spraying chemicals on a supposedly sick plant before you know what (if anything) is actually wrong with it. That's wasteful and irresponsible, and you're likely to do the plant as much harm as good. Pinpointing the exact cause of a problem is difficult for even experienced gardeners, so save yourself frustration and seek out expert help from the beginning.

If it seems that there's something wrong with one of your plants—for example, if the leaves are discolored, have holes in them, or have spots or marks on them—cut off a sample branch, wrap it in damp paper towels, and put it in a plastic bag (so it won't wilt). Take the sample to the nursery or garden center where you bought the plant, and ask for help. If the nursery can't help, contact the nearest office of your state's Cooperative Extension Service or a public garden in your area, and ask if they have a staff member who can diagnose plant problems.

Meanwhile, look around your property and around the neighborhood, too, to see whether any other plants (of the same or different kinds) show similar symptoms. If a problem is widespread, you shouldn't have much trouble finding someone who can identify it and tell you what, if anything, to do. If only one plant is affected, it's often harder to diagnose the problem, and you may just have to wait and see what happens to it. Keep an eye on the plant; continue with watering and other regular maintenance; and see if the problem gets worse or goes away. If nothing more has happened after a few weeks, stop worrying. If the problem continues, intensify your search for expert advice.

Plant problems stem from a number of causes: insect and animal pests, diseases, too little or too much water, and poor care, particularly in winter. Remember that plant problems are often caused by a combination of these; all the more reason to consult with experts about their diagnosis and treatment.

Deer-resistant plants

Although it may seem as though deer will eat anything, they definitely have favorite plants. However, they generally dislike plants with highly aromatic or tough or highly textured foliage. Unfortunately their tastes vary from neighborhood to neighborhood and depend upon the season and the availability of other food sources. Look around your neighborhood to see what is left untouched. To determine whether they will eat a new plant, place just a few around the garden to see whether they are nibbled on or gobbled up. If you leave them in the container, stake them to the ground so that they don't disappear.

DEER-CONTROL FENCING Deer have been known to jump very tall fences, so use at least an 8-ft.-high fence. For a larger property, a wide fence is one of the best ways to protect your landscape plants from deer. It is about 6 ft. wide and 5 ft. high, and consists of angled poles fixed to posts spaced about 10 ft. apart. You may attach electric wires at 12-in. intervals to the poles. For advice on deer fences that work best in your area, consult your Cooperative Extension agent.

There are several new kinds of insecticides that are quite effective but much safer to use than the older products. For example, insecticidal soap, a special kind of detergent, quickly kills aphids and other soft-bodied insects, but it's nontoxic to mammals and birds and breaks down quickly, leaving no harmful residue. Horticultural oil, a highly refined mineral oil, is a good control for scale insects, which frequently infest gardenias, camellias, and other broad-leaved evergreens. Most garden centers stock these and other relatively safe insecticides.

Before using any insecticide, make sure the product is registered to control your particular pest. Carefully follow the directions for how to apply the product. Only treat when there is a problem to minimize killing the beneficial insects.

Diseases

Several types of fungal, bacterial, and viral diseases can attack garden plants, causing a wide range of symptoms such as disfigured or discolored leaves or petals, powdery or moldy-looking films or spots, mushy stems or roots, and overall wilting. As with insect problems, if you suspect that a plant is infected with a disease, gather a sample of the plant and show it to someone who can identify the problem before you do any spraying.

In general, plant diseases are hard to treat, so it's important to take steps to prevent problems. These steps include choosing plants adapted to your area, choosing disease-resistant plants, spacing plants far enough apart so that air can circulate between them, not over-watering, and removing dead stems and litter from the garden.

Perennials that would otherwise be healthy are prone to fungal infections during spells of hot humid weather, especially if the plants are crowded together or if they have flopped over and are lying on top of each other or on the ground. If your garden has turned into a jungle, look closely for moldy foliage, and if you find any, prune it off and discard (don't compost) it. It's better to cut the plants back severely than to let the disease spread. Avoid repeated problems by dividing the perennials, replanting them farther apart, and pruning them early in the season so they don't grow so tall and floppy again. Crowded shrubs are also subject to fungal problems in the summer and should be pruned so that air can flow around them.

Winter damage

More plants are damaged or killed during a cold winter than in any other season. Severe cold spells, a sudden change from mild to freezing weather, or a frost can damage cold-tender plants. In this case, wait until early spring to assess the severity of the damage. Scratch the stem with a fingernail to search for green, living tissue under the bark. Then prune off the branches or stems that are definitely brown and dead. In most cases, new growth will sprout out from the surviving stems; if buds do not appear by late spring, replace the plant.

Even in midwinter, evergreen trees, shrubs, vines, and perennials lose moisture through their leaves on warm, sunny, breezy days. Normally, rain wets the soil enough to meet these plants' water needs during the winter months, but you should give them a deep watering if there's a long dry spell. In the cooler zones, deciduous plants rarely need watering in winter.

Glossary

Amendments. Organic or mineral materials such as peat moss, perlite, or compost that are used to improve the soil.

Annual. A plant that germinates, grows, flowers, produces seeds, and dies in the course of a single growing season; a plant that is treated like an annual and grown for a single season's display.

Antitranspirant. A substance sprayed on the stems and leaves of evergreen plants to protect them from water loss caused by winter winds.

Balled-and-burlapped. Describes a tree or shrub dug out of the ground with a ball of soil intact around the roots; the ball is then wrapped in burlap and tied for transport.

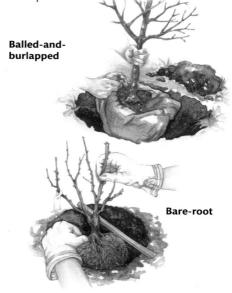

Balled-and-burlapped

Bare-root

Bare-root. Describes a plant dug out of the ground and then shaken or washed to remove the soil from the roots.

Compound leaf. A leaf with two or more leaflets branching off a single stalk.

Container-grown. Describes a plant raised in a pot that is removed before planting.

Crown. That part of a plant where the roots and stem meet, usually at soil level.

Cultivar. A cultivated variety of a plant, often bred or selected for some special trait such as double flowers, compact growth, cold hardiness, or disease and pest resistance.

Deadheading. Removing old flowers during the growing season to prevent seed formation and to encourage the development of new flowers.

Deciduous. Describes a tree, shrub, or vine that drops all its leaves in winter.

Division. Propagation of a plant by separating it into two or more pieces, each of which has at least one bud and some roots. Used mostly for perennials, grasses, ferns, and bulbs.

Drainage. The movement of water down through the soil. With good drainage, water disappears from a planting hole in just a few hours. If water remains standing overnight, the drainage is poor.

Drip line. An imaginary line on the soil around a tree that mirrors the circumference of the canopy above. Many of the tree's roots are found in this area.

Dry-laid. Describes a masonry path or wall that is installed without mortar.

Edging. A shallow trench or physical barrier of steel, plastic, brick, or boards used to define the border between a flower bed and adjacent turf.

Exposure. The intensity, duration, and variation in sun, wind, and temperature that characterize any particular site.

Feeder roots. Slender branching roots that spread close to the soil surface and absorb most of the nutrients for a tree or shrub.

Formal. Describes a style of landscaping that features symmetrical layouts, with beds and walks related to adjacent buildings, and often with plants sheared to geometric or other shapes.

Foundation planting. Traditionally, a narrow border of evergreen shrubs planted around the foundation of a house. Contemporary foundation plantings often include deciduous shrubs, grasses, perennials, and other plants as well.

Frost heaving. A disturbance or uplifting of soil, pavement, or plants caused when moisture in the soil freezes and expands.

Full shade. Describes a site that receives no direct sun during the growing season.

Full sun. Describes a site that receives at least eight hours of direct sun each day during the growing season.

Garden soil. Soil specially prepared for planting to make it loose enough for roots and water to penetrate easily. Usually requires digging or tilling and the addition of some organic matter.

Grade. The degree and direction of slope on a piece of ground.

Ground cover. A plant such as ivy, liriope, or juniper used to cover the soil and form a continuous low mass of foliage. Often used as a durable substitute for turfgrass.

Habit. The characteristic shape or form of a plant, such as upright, spreading, or rounded.

Hardiness. A plant's ability to survive the winter without protection from the cold.

Hardiness zone. A geographic region where the coldest temperature in an average winter falls within a certain range, such as between 0° and –10°F.

Hardscape. Parts of a landscape constructed from materials other than plants, such as walks, walls, and trellises made of wood, stone, or other materials.

Herbicide. A chemical used to kill plants. Preemergent herbicides are used to kill weed seeds as they sprout, and thus to prevent weed growth. Postemergent herbicides kill plants that are already growing.

Hybrid. A plant resulting from a cross between two parents that belong to different varieties, species, or genera.

Interplant. To combine plants with different bloom times or growth habits, making it possible to fit more plants in a bed, thus prolonging the bed's appeal.

Invasive. Describes a plant that spreads quickly, usually by runners, and mixes with or dominates adjacent plantings.

Landscape fabric. A synthetic fabric, sometimes water-permeable, spread under paths or mulch to serve as a weed barrier.

Lime, limestone. White mineral compounds used to combat soil acidity and to supply calcium for plant growth.

Loam. An ideal soil for gardening, containing plenty of organic matter and a balanced range of small to large mineral particles.

Microclimate. Local conditions of shade, exposure, wind, drainage, and other factors that affect plant growth at any particular site.

Mowing strip. A row of bricks or paving stones set flush with the soil around the edge of a bed, and wide enough to support one wheel of the lawn mower.

Mulch. A layer of bark, peat moss, compost, shredded leaves, hay or straw, lawn clippings, gravel, paper, or other material, spread over the soil around the base of plants. During the growing season, a mulch can help retard evaporation, inhibit weeds, and moderate soil temperature. In the winter, a mulch of evergreen boughs, coarse hay, or leaves is used to protect plants from freezing.

Native. Describes a plant that occurs naturally in a particular region and was not introduced from some other area.

Nutrients. Nitrogen, phosphorus, potassium, calcium, magnesium, and other elements needed by plants. Nutrients are supplied by the minerals and organic matter in the soil and by fertilizers.

Organic matter. Plant and animal residues such as leaves, trimmings, and manure in various stages of decomposition.

Peat moss. Partially decomposed mosses and sedges, mined from boggy areas and used to improve garden soil or to prepare potting soil.

Perennial. A plant that lives for a number of years, generally flowering each year. By "perennial," gardeners usually mean "herbaceous perennial," although woody plants, such as vines, shrubs, and trees, are also perennial.

Pressure-treated lumber. Softwood lumber treated with chemicals that protect it from decay.

Propagate. To produce new plants by sowing seeds, rooting cuttings, dividing plant parts, layering, grafting, or other means.

Retaining wall. A wall built to stabilize a slope and keep soil from sliding or eroding downhill.

Rhizome. A horizontal underground stem, often swollen into a storage organ. Both roots and shoots emerge from rhizomes. Rhizomes generally branch as they creep along and can be divided to make new plants.

Root-ball. The mass of soil and roots dug with a plant when it is removed from the ground; the soil and roots of a plant grown in a container.

Rosette. A low, flat cluster of leaves arranged like the petals of a rose.

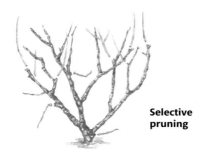

Selective pruning

Severe pruning

Selective pruning. Using pruning shears to remove or cut back individual shoots, in order to refine the shape of a shrub, maintain its vigor, or limit its size.

Severe pruning. Using pruning shears or loppers to cut away most of a shrub's top growth, leaving just short stubs or a gnarly trunk.

Shearing. Using hedge shears or an electric hedge trimmer to shape the surface of a shrub, hedge, or tree and produce a smooth, solid mass of greenery.

Specimen plant. A plant placed alone in a prominent position, to show it off.

Spike. An elongated flower cluster, with individual flowers borne on very short stalks or attached directly to the main stem.

Tender. Describes a plant that is damaged by cold weather.

Underplanting. Growing short plants, such as ground covers, under a taller plant, such as a shrub.

Variegated. Describes foliage that is marked, striped, or blotched with color other than green.

Index

NOTE: Page numbers in **bold italic** refer to illustrations.

Photo Credits

Front Cover: *(main image)* Colleen Coombe/Dreamstime.com; *top all* Stephen Pategas

Back Cover: *left* Jerry Pavia; *right* Stephen Pategas, Designer: Bruce Templin

page 1: Stephen G. Pategas

page 5: Stephen G. Pategas

page 7: Stephen G. Pategas

page 8: *left* Neil Soderstrom/Michael Cady; *center* Neil Soderstrom; *right* Derek Fell

page 9: Rita Buchanan

pages 14-15: Robert Elias/Dreamstime.com

page 18: *top* Stephen G. Pategas; *bottom right* Jerry Pavia; *bottom left* Saxon Holt

page 23: *all* Jerry Pavia

page 27: *top* Jerry Pavia; *bottom* Stephen G. Pategas

page 30: *top* Stephen G. Pategas; *bottom right* Jerry Pavia; *bottom left* Charles Mann

page 34: *top* Stephen G. Pategas; *bottom both* Jerry Pavia

page 39: *top* Jerry Pavia; *bottom* Karen Bussolini

page 42: *top* Stephen G. Pategas; *bottom both* Jerry Pavia

page 46: *top* Jerry Pavia; *bottom* Stephen G. Pategas

page 51: *left & top right* Jerry Pavia; *bottom right* Stephen G. Pategas

page 55: *top* Stephen G. Pategas; *center & bottom* Jerry Pavia

page 58: *both* Stephen G. Pategas

page 63: *top* Karen Bussolini; *bottom* Saxon Holt

page 67: *all* Stephen G. Pategas

page 71: *top* Stephen G. Pategas, Designer: Design by the Yard, LLC, Orlando, FL; *bottom* Stephen G. Pategas, Designer: Bruce Templin; *center* Jerry Pavia

page 74: *top & center* Stephen G. Pategas; *bottom* Saxon Holt, Designer: Suzanne Arca

page 79: *top* Stephen G. Pategas; *bottom* Saxon Holt, Designer: Brandon Tyson

page 82: *top & bottom left* Stephen G. Pategas; *bottom right* Charles Mann, Designer: Tina Rousselot

page 86: *top* Jerry Pavia; *center* Saxon Holt; *bottom* Saxon Holt, courtesy of Gemes Garden

page 90: *top & bottom* Stephen G. Pategas; *center* Saxon Holt

page 92-93: Tazzymoto/Dreamstime.com

page 94: *top left* Stephen G. Pategas; *top right* Galen Gates

page 95: *top left* Rita Buchanan; *all others* Stephen G. Pategas

pages 96-97: *bottom left* Charles Mann; *center & right all* Stephen G. Pategas

page 98: *top left & bottom right* Stephen G. Pategas; *top right* Rita Buchanan; *center right* Galen Gates

page 99: *top* Jerry Pavia; *center* Stephen G. Pategas; *bottom* Richard Shiell

page 100: *left* Stephen G. Pategas; *right* Thomas Eltzroth

page 101: *all* Stephen G. Pategas

page 102: *top left* Stephen G. Pategas; *top right* Greg Grant; *bottom both* Thomas Eltzroth

page 103: *top center* Saxon Holt; *all others* Stephen G. Pategas

page 104: *third image down* Stephen G. Pategas; *all others* Jerry Pavia

page 105: *top left & top center* Jerry Pavia; *top right & middle right* Stephen G. Pategas; *bottom right* Charles Mann

page 106: *left* Rick Mastelli; *center & right* Stephen G. Pategas

page 107: *top* Stephen G. Pategas; *middle* Jerry Pavia; *bottom* Saxon Holt

page 108: *top* Jerry Pavia; *center & bottom* Stephen G. Pategas

page 109: *top left* Lauren Springer Ogden; *top center* Rita Buchanan; *top right* Richard Shiell; *middle right & bottom left* Michael Dirr; *bottom right* Stephen G. Pategas

page 110: *top left* Stephen G. Pategas; *middle left* Saxon Holtl *bottom left* Stephen G. Pategas; *bottom right* Jerry Pavia

page 111: *top left* Saxon Holt; *top center* Jerry Pavia; *top right* Richard Shiell; *middle right* Jerry Pavia; *bottom* Stephen G. Pategas

page 112: *bottom right* Karen Bussolini; *all others* Stephen G. Pategas

page 113: *bottom left* Charles Mann; *all others* Stephen G. Pategas

page 114: *left & top right* Charles Mann; *bottom right* Rita Buchanan

page 115: *top* Charles Mann; *bottom* Stephen G. Pategas

page 116: *all* Stephen G. Pategas

page 117: *top left* Rita Buchanan; *top right* Richard Shiell; *bottom* Stephen G. Pategas

page 118: *top left* Jerry Pavia; *top right* Stephen G. Pategas

page 119: *top left* Jerry Pavia; *top right* Stephen G. Pategas; *center* Karen Bussolini; *bottom* Galen Gates

page 120: *top left & bottom* Stephen G. Pategas; *top center & top right* Charles Mann; *middle left* Jerry Pavia

page 121: *top both* Stephen G. Pategas; *bottom right* Michael Dirr

page 122: *top left* Greg Grant; *top center & bottom* Jerry Pavia; *top right* Saxon Holt

page 123: *top left* Jerry Pavia; *all others* Stephen G. Pategas

pages 124-125: Beata Becla/Dreamstime.com

page 185: Stephen G. Pategas

page 186: Karen Bussolini

page 188: Jerry Pavia

page 190: Stephen G. Pategas

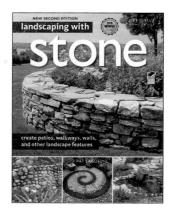
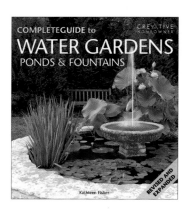